Charlie Two Shoes and
the Marines of Love Company

Charlie Two Shoes

and the

MARINES

of Love Company

～❦

Michael Peterson and David Perlmutt

Naval Institute Press
Annapolis, Maryland

Library of Congress Cataloging-in-Publication Data
Peterson, Michael, 1943–
    Charlie Two Shoes and the marines of Love Company /
    Michael Peterson and David Perlmutt.
        p. cm.
        Includes bibliographical references (p.   ).
        ISBN 1-55750-672-8
        1. Tsui, Chi Hsii, 1934–   . 2. Chinese Americans—Biography.
    3. United States. Marine Corps. Marines, 4th. 4. Children—
    China—Tsingtao—Biography. 5. Tsingtao (China)— Biography.
    I. Perlmutt, David, 1953–   . II. Title.
    E184.C5T8356   1998   98-30090

Printed in the United States of America on acid-free paper ∞
05 04 03 02 01 00 99 98   9 8 7 6 5 4 3 2
First printing

For Richard White Adams and his godsons, Clayton and Todd.

—*Michael Peterson*

For Christie and Ainslie, my best friends; and for my parents,
Joseph and Helen Perlmutt, who gave me the gift of curiosity.

—*David Perlmutt*

Preface

If you were reading this book as fiction, you might not finish it, certain that nothing like this could ever happen. But it did happen, to Tsui Chi Hsii, known as Charlie Two Shoes, and a group of men who once belonged to Love Company, 4th Marines, 1st Marine Division, United States Marine Corps, during and just after World War II.

Parts of the story were told in newspapers and on dozens of television programs and newscasts in the 1980s. Norman Vincent Peale, reading Charlie's story in *Reader's Digest,* wrote that his odyssey to freedom was one of the most inspirational he'd ever heard. But the complete story of Charlie Two Shoes has never been told, and it is even more remarkable than previously described.

Yet it's not just his story. It's a tale of the bravery, loyalty, and devotion of everyday young men from different parts of America who joined the Marines to fight for their country. They befriended a little Chinese boy, hungry and frightened. The men fed and clothed him and paid his tuition to school, where a nun converted him to Catholicism and a young missionary taught him to speak and write proper English. But against all they believed in, they were forced to abandon him. Then, decades later, they gathered to fulfill the promise they'd made— to bring him to America.

Little has been written about the Marines in China after World War II. They arrived as an awful civil war resumed, and they were caught in the midst of the strife that brought the world's most populated country to the brink of ruin. In 1949, the Marines left China as Mao Tse-tung emerged triumphant. (One of the many changes the Communists brought was the spelling of the Chinese language. For example, Mao Tse-tung became Mao Zedong, Peking became Beijing, and Tsui Chi Hsii became Cui Zhixi in the new pinyin romanization of the language introduced in 1958 and formalized in 1979.) The Marines were forced to leave the little boy behind, where he suffered terribly because of their friendship with him. Caught in the Great Leap Forward, the Cultural Revolution, the terror of the Gang of Four, he was imprisoned, humiliated, and degraded.

More than three decades after leaving Charlie, the Marines learned that he was still alive. No longer strapping youths, they came together again to bring him to America, overcoming incredible adversity. Then, in the United States, where so many positive experiences changed his and his family's life permanently for the better, Charlie became immersed in another trial—this one of a friendship gone bad.

This is the story we set out to write in 1995.

Auspiciously, Michael first met Charlie at a gathering of former Marines who were celebrating the USMC birthday, on 10 November 1991, in Durham, North Carolina. Former Marine and U.S. congressman Nick Galifianakis brought Charlie to the celebration.

Michael had spent most of the 1980s in Europe, yet when he talked with Charlie, the story sounded familiar. He decided that he must have read it in *Stars and Stripes,* the overseas newspaper for the U.S. military. Galifianakis and others suggested that he write a book about Charlie, but he was already under contract to finish his third novel and didn't have time. The following year, in Germany, he got a call from Galifianakis with an update on Charlie, including the news that a Charlotte reporter had written a story that had been picked up by *Reader's Digest* and *Parade* magazine. Galifianakis suggested that Michael contact the reporter and explore the possibilities of a book. He did, and the result is this book—the story of Charlie, the young Marines who went to war, and events of the past five decades that have intertwined to bring us to a new threshold in Chinese-American relations.

David learned of Charlie in 1992, when his editor at the *Charlotte Observer* handed him a press release from U.S. senator Terry Sanford's office and requested a story by first-edition deadline that afternoon.

"Keep it short, fifteen inches," were his instructions.

The release contained information about a private bill that Sanford had introduced in the Senate on behalf of a Chinese family who lived in Chapel Hill: Tsui Chi Hsii, his wife, Jin Mie, and their three children. The bill would make them permanent residents of the United States, eligible for green cards. Included in the release was a brief synopsis of their story.

It sounded vaguely familiar, and intriguing, but David didn't know how much until he interviewed Charlie at his restaurant and then contacted some of the Marines—Don Sexton and William Bullard, both from North Carolina, and Jack Hutchins in Kentucky. He knew that fifteen column inches wouldn't do the story justice, and he finagled more space (and time). He spent a week interviewing the parties, including the Marine captain who had formed Love Company, Charles Robertson. The following Sunday, 28 June 1992, the *Observer* published a seventy-inch front-page story, headlined "Charlie and the Marines."

Though long for a newspaper article, it was hardly comprehensive. David knew the story had book potential, but like every reporter who dreams of writing a book, he had little time to do so.

He gave the book possibility little thought until his article was printed in *Reader's Digest* and *Parade* magazines, after which he got a phone call from Nick Galifianakis. He suggested that David team up with Mike.

Some of the tales, dialogue, and quotations in this book are based on the participants' recollections of fifty to sixty years ago. It is a uniquely American story, one guided by fate. Had Charlie lived in another part of China, even a few miles farther away from the remote airstrip where the Marine planes landed just after the war, he might still be behind a plow tilling rocky black dirt for peanuts and sweet potatoes. Instead, the Marines took him in, and their devotion has survived the political cataclysms of two powerful nations for half a century.

This is a true story of the American Dream, an affirmation of love, loyalty, and dedication.

Charlie Two Shoes and
the Marines of Love Company

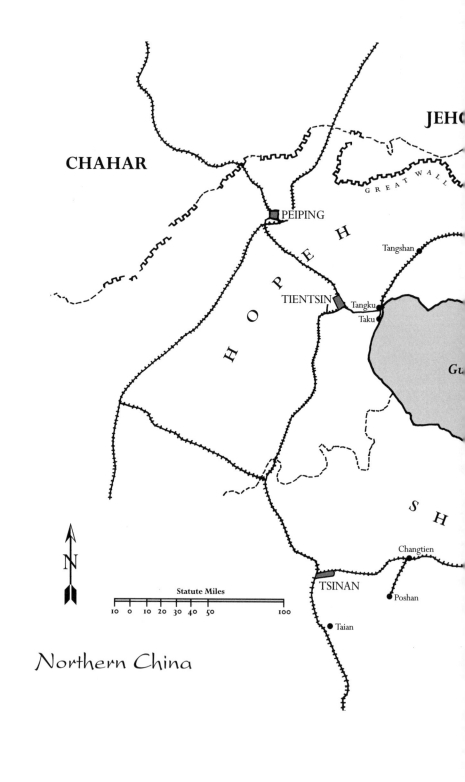

Northern China

Hulutao

LIAONING

Shanhaikua
angtao

li

Gulf of
Liaotung

LIAOTUNG
PENINSULA

Port
Arthur ● DAIREN

West Korea
Bay

hihli

Penglai

Chefoo Weihaiwei
Jungchen

Yehsien

T U N G

sien

TSINGTAO

Yellow Sea

City of Tsingtao

1 Marine compound
2 St. Michael's Cathedral
3 St. Joseph School
4 Tsingtao American School
5 Pagoda pier
6 YMCA
7 Edgewater Hotel

8 U.S. consulate
9 Chukechuang, Charlie's village
10 Tsangkou Air Base
11 Navy port facilities
12 Iltus Hook
13 Racetrack

1

They stared at one another across barbed wire. On one side, young men with rifles, far from home in a strange land, more lonely and afraid than they wanted to admit or have anyone know. On the other side, a little boy, also afraid, there out of hunger and desperation. To him it was not a strange land; it was Tsingtao, in northern China, his home.

The young men with rifles were U.S. Marines, in China because the last great battle of World War II, the invasion of Japan's main islands, had not been necessary. Japan had surrendered, and the Marines were sent to Tsingtao to repatriate remnants of the Japanese army.

The little boy was Tsui Chi Hsii. He was eleven and lived in a mud hut in the remote village of Chukechuang, only a hundred yards from the wire. He had never seen an American and knew nothing of the war that had just ended. All he knew was that the Japanese soldiers guarding his village had become very sad in the last months. Some had been crying. Then suddenly they were gone, and now there were new soldiers, Americans, at the wire.

They were tall, as conquering heroes should be, and, unlike the Japanese, they smiled at the children. They also always seemed to be eating, for they were constantly chewing.

The boy was so hungry; all the children were, dressed in rag cotton cloth pieced together by their mothers. They had a look of starvation, flesh stretched over their faces; their ribs were like bird cages. They held out their hands. The soldiers grinned, reached into their pockets, and tossed small packages of foil-wrapped strips to them. As the children gobbled them down, the soldiers laughed. The strips were green and sweet and tasted like nothing the boy had ever eaten. He didn't know what gum was.

It was mid-November 1945, and the young men were in the little boy's country, a harsh, bitterly cold environment of two landing strips, hangars, and Quonset huts surrounded by mountains. A long time had passed since they'd seen their own country.

One of the Marines at the wire was Jack Hutchins, called Big Hutch by his buddies. They called him Big Hutch because he played basketball and towered over most everybody else, and also to distinguish him from Little Hutch—James Hutchinson, his best buddy and teammate from Dalton, Georgia. Big Hutch was eighteen, a strapping six-foot-three, his blood a mix of Iroquois and Cherokee, his roots in the backwoods of Kentucky. In June 1944, the week after graduating from high school, he joined the Marines, partly out of patriotism drummed into his head by his father, Holt Lafayette, who had lost the use of his hands in World War I when his troop train was bombed in southern France. Another reason Big Hutch joined was to escape from that long-suffering, hard-drinking father.

Eight months later, in February 1945, he was on the black, volcanic-ash beach of Iwo Jima, 760 miles south of Tokyo, in one of the bloodiest battles of World War II, as the American flag was raised on Mount Suribachi. Physical training in boot camp at Parris Island, South Carolina, and advanced infantry training at New River, North Carolina, hadn't been hard, but Big Hutch hated being yelled at, so he worked out his frustrations playing basketball. He was good; like most Kentucky boys, basketball consumed him, and he preferred practicing his jump shot to studying.

After infantry training, he went home to Kentucky on ten days' liberty while Little Hutch returned to Georgia to get married. Then they shipped out for the Pacific. Three months later they landed on Iwo Jima, an island a third the size of Manhattan, with 71,000 other Marines. Iwo was vital to the Americans in their island-hopping campaign across the Pacific; it would provide an emergency landing strip for B-29s bombing Japan from bases in the more distant Marianas.

But the Japanese were ready, having bored a maze of tunnels and caves in the coral to conceal eight hundred guns. Though Lieutenant General Tadamichi Kuribayashi privately acknowledged that the end was near for Japan, he told his troops that Americans had no "desire for the glory of their ancestors, posterity, or for the glory of their family name. They go into battle with no spiritual incentive and rely on material superiority."[1]

Iwo was to be a battle between the way of the warrior, Bushido, where death was honorable and surrender no option, and modern warfare—planes, artillery, and ship-to-shore landings.

For weeks, American B-24s had relentlessly bombed the island. On 15 February, six battleships, five cruisers, and planes from twelve carriers joined them, and four days later the Marines began their assault. The Japanese let the first waves get ashore, waiting until they reached predetermined zones, then they hit hard and cut off the rest. Marines loaded down with weapons and supplies drowned in the surf, while those who made it ashore found awkward footing in the volcanic ash.

A thousand Marines landed on the right wing that first day. By nightfall, only 150 hadn't been killed or wounded. Corpses washed ashore and bodies lay everywhere. It looked like hell had burned over. Hutchins's unit couldn't get on the beach the first day because of heavy fire, but the next morning, they got orders to make a break for it.

"The fan's been hit," Hutchins yelled in the landing craft at his friend Herbert Huwatacheck from Milwaukee, then they stormed the beach.

As they dug in, laying down fire for those clawing up the volcano, Big Hutch saw a small, tattered American flag rise triumphantly on Iwo's 556-foot summit. "My God," he thought, a wave of patriotic emotion washing over him, "We've taken Suribachi!" But then a burst of wind kicked up blinding black dust, and he lost sight of the flag.

By the end of the second day, they'd advanced only two hundred yards, taking horrific losses. At week's end, Kuribayashi reported half his 22,000 troops dead or wounded. By the time the Japanese surrendered a month later, 5,931 Marines had been killed and 17,000 wounded—Hutchins had been hit three times. Counting replacements, his unit suffered 135 percent casualties. Big Hutch was one of only eight in his original company to walk off the island.

Little Hutch took a bullet at the hairline, dying instantly; he had just celebrated his nineteenth birthday. Another friend, Big Hicks, carried a metal-tipped Bible under his shirt to protect his heart, but it didn't save him—they shot him in the head. A third buddy, Little Hix, a judo expert who could toss men twice his size, was killed, too: a mine got him.

If the Japanese had fought so hard for Iwo Jima and other islands, like Okinawa and Saipan, surely they would fight with even greater ferocity to save their homeland. That fear was on everybody's minds as they trained for the greatest battle of all, Operation Olympic: the invasion of Japan, X-Day, code-named Downfall, scheduled for 1 November 1945. It was to be the largest amphibious operation of the war, bigger, even, than Normandy.

Hutchins and his unit trained for the invasion on Guam. Staring out across the ocean he'd have to cross, he knew it was going to be awful: 540,000 Japanese troops were poised to defend the homeland. Five thousand kamikaze planes stood ready; the Japanese would use poison gas; and civilians were prepared to fight to the last man, woman, and child.

One hundred thousand Purple Hearts were rumored to have been ordered; killed-in-action estimates were fifty thousand. But then a miracle occurred.[2]

As Hutchins returned from a training detail one day, Henry Sykowski ran up to him, wild with news. "The war's over!" Ski shouted, grabbing Hutchins's shoulders, trying to lead him in a crazy, joyful dance.

"Yeah sure," he said.

"No, Johnny, it's true," Sykowski said. "They just dropped a metallic bomb on Japan!"

"A what kind of bomb?" Hutchins asked, incredulous.

"They say it's a metallic bomb. The Japs are going to surrender. We're going home!"

When Hutchins later learned that the bomb was atomic, it still didn't make any sense. Physics hadn't been a strong subject at Hazel Green Academy back in Kentucky, but he didn't care what kind of bomb it was, only that it had worked. It saved a lot of lives—probably his own, he believed.

As they walked along the beach on Guam the day after the surrender, the news blared over speakers that were hung in coconut trees. Ski turned to Hutchins. "Johnny, the world's changed. Everything's different now. We'll be home soon."

But Jack Hutchins didn't go home. He was sent to a place even more mysterious and unknown to him—northern China—and found himself at a perimeter wire of a remote airstrip. Chewing gum at the wire, wishing he were home with his nine brothers and sisters, he saw hungry children across from him holding out their hands. He reached into his pocket and tossed what he had.

To the little boy, the Americans were so big, and they all looked alike, with their big noses. But they were friendly, and that made them different from the Japanese.

The Japanese had arrived in 1937, when he was three years old. Six years earlier, Japan had invaded Manchuria. Afterward, a tenuous peace lingered between Japan and China, as Chiang Kai-shek fought a civil war against the Communist peasant forces of Mao Tse-tung, but Tsingtao was spared until overt hostilities with Japan broke out in July 1937.

Within months, Japan overran Chiang's forces, attacking with barbarous brutality. Shanghai fell in November, and the capital, Nanking, in December. The Japanese held Tsingtao because of its natural harbor, and because it was the terminus of the critically important railroad that ran to Tsinan, where it joined the trunk that linked Peking to Shanghai.

Soon the Japanese came to Tsui Chi Hsii's village. He was playing in a field with friends when suddenly there was chaos. The children saw villagers scattering into the mountains as old men screamed for everyone to run. The children cried. In the distance, the little boy saw terrible fires, the whole horizon in flames. His father took him in his arms. "The Japanese are coming," he told his son. "The government is burning the textile factories so the invaders can't use them."

For the next eight years, the Japanese occupied his village of 150 families with a squad-size garrison, thirteen troops who kept mostly to themselves behind a fortress. No one in the village approached the garrison, except for two girls who were allowed in—comfort girls, they were called later.

Squads of Japanese guarded all the villages that lined the train tracks, to make sure there was no sabotage. If there was, the soldiers took it out on the villagers. Otherwise, the soldiers weren't bad to the villagers. They didn't hurt them or take things from them.

It was the soldiers at the airfield who frightened them. They guarded the air base just beyond the village and built an electric fence to keep everyone out. Even worse were the Chinese who were recruited as their puppet troops; their grip was felt everywhere. They took meat, anything of value, and forced the children to learn Japanese in school.

One day in the dead of winter, when Tsui Chi Hsii was four, puppet soldiers arrested a young man who lived two huts away. They accused him of stealing food and tied him to a stake just inside the wire, where everyone in the village could see. The soldiers stripped him to his underwear, threw water on him until he froze like an icicle, then turned dogs loose on him. Standing at the fence, the little boy turned away. How could anyone be treated so cruelly?

Another time, when Tsui Chi Hsii was five, he was in the fields and heard horses' hooves. He hid in a grove of trees and saw a troop of soldiers stampede over an old man tottering down the road.

Those times were hard. There was little food, except for whatever peanuts and sweet potatoes they could grow that were not plundered by the Japanese. So they ate anything they could find, even bark and leaves off trees. Then there was a terrible drought and the trees died. The boy spent hours each day with his grandmother, who comforted him in her lap. But one day, standing at the wok in the middle of the hut, she fell ill and died. Later the boy's father told him she had poisoned herself because she couldn't bear the struggle and poverty any longer.

The following year, when Tsui Chi Hsii was six, he began school in the village. His grandfather, Tsui Gin Chung, whom the boy adored, often lectured that proper schooling was the only way to escape oppression. "The reason we are so poor is because we have no education, and the reason people are in high positions is because they do," the old man said. No one in the Tsui family had ever gone to school, and the old man beamed on the day his grandson headed off for the four-classroom building.

But the Japanese puppets forced the children to learn their language. If they learned it well, they said, there was potential for a good job. Tsui Chi Hsii didn't want to work for the Japanese, who treated his people poorly. So he learned only enough to make passing grades.

During his fourth year in school, when he was ten, another devastating drought gripped China. It did not rain for forty-nine days, and crops rotted in the fields. Famine struck everywhere. In Chukechuang, the school closed. Villagers ate bark or grass, soaking them in big pots to wash out the bitterness. Every two weeks, young men were lowered by thick ropes to the bottom of wells, with shovels to dig deeper for water. The soldiers didn't help. They took the water and the villagers' food when their own supplies were delivered late.

Each day the villagers walked in a solemn procession to burn incense and brown paper at a temple of brick and stone, built a century earlier. They prayed on their knees for rain. The paper symbolized money and the incense gold, and the villagers offered them in return for rain.

The boy had only a vague concept of God. Though no one in his family formally practiced religion, his grandfather passed on the notion of a great, supreme being who possessed the power of miracles. Still, as the drought continued, as people died from starvation, while the ashes from incense and paper piled high enough to fill a truck, he wondered how a powerful, good being could allow such suffering.

On the fiftieth day it rained, a soaking downpour that lasted day and night. Villagers danced in the street and mud in wild celebration. Tsui Chi Hsii began to believe in God that day, but it would be a few more years before he developed any understanding of that God.

Few in the village knew how to read or write. There was no radio and no news of the world beyond the wire, so in early autumn 1945, when Tsui Chi Hsii was eleven and the Japanese soldiers grew sad and suddenly disappeared, no one knew why. They had never heard of Hiroshima or Nagasaki.

Charles Robertson, a twenty-six-year-old Marine captain, didn't hear about the Hiroshima bomb either; in combat you didn't get much

7

news. He was on Guam when it fell, poring over his battalion's invasion plans for the landing on Kyushu, in southern Japan.

Robertson joined the Marines after graduating from high school in Rome, Georgia, passing a two-year college equivalency exam to become an officer in 1942. He'd been sent to Guam after Okinawa, the bloodiest battle in the Pacific. He had barely made it and did not believe he would survive the invasion of Japan. Intelligence reports indicated that the Japanese were poised to use children with explosives strapped to their bodies to prevent the landing.

From pilots on Tinian, the Mariana island next to Guam where the new B-29 Superfortresses were based, Robertson heard rumors of a bomb that would end the war. But he didn't believe it. He even bet the battalion doctor fifty dollars that there was no such weapon.

But at 8:15 A.M. on 6 August 1945, the sky over Hiroshima cracked open, and light screamed out in a primeval flash of energy. In that cataclysmic moment, eighty thousand people died from a uranium-235 bomb. Three days later, forty thousand instantly died after another atomic bomb, this one plutonium, was dropped on Nagasaki, propelling the world into a new and frightening age.

On payday, Robertson paid the doc his fifty dollars. The bombs were his salvation, he firmly believed.

The bombings of Hiroshima and Nagasaki were the final rounds in World War II, but also the first fired in the Cold War. After those first shots, the first skirmish in this new war was in China, where 630,000 Japanese troops were stranded. Adm. Chester Nimitz, commander in chief of Pacific Ocean Areas, ordered the 1st and 6th Marine Divisions, once scheduled for the invasion, to China to accept the enemy's surrender, oversee their repatriation, and help America's ally, Chiang Kai-shek, in his civil war against Mao Tse-tung.

Chiang's Nationalists had been no match for the Japanese, largely because Chiang had held his forces in reserve for the struggle against the Communists. But Mao had waged aggressive guerrilla warfare against the Japanese, winning the peasants' support and respect. With Japan's surrender, the two Chinese factions turned on each other. Russia, which had declared war on Japan the day before Nagasaki, rushed troops to the Manchurian border.

On 2 October, a month after the formal Japanese surrender, the 6th Marine Division on Guam joined an armada of ships bound for Tsingtao, on the Shantung Peninsula. Their mission was to help the Nationalists and to serve as a show of force against the Russians.

Aboard the ships were veterans of many beach landings, including gung-ho Fred McGowan from Michigan, and J. C. Lacey from Birmingham, Alabama. Never during the war had their prospects seemed so promising, for not long after Tsingtao was home.

The convoy steamed out of Apra Harbor past the barren cliffs of the Orote Peninsula, which the Marines had taken from the Japanese just a few months earlier. Cruising the East China Sea aboard the command ship, Gen. Lemuel Shepherd, 6th Marine Division commander, issued his orders: "Our mission is to land and occupy Tsingtao and adjacent Tsangkou Air Field, to assist local authorities in maintaining order . . . and accept when necessary, local surrender of Japanese force, . . . and to assist the Chinese in effecting the disarming and confining of these forces."[3]

The Marines were supposed to land on 10 October, Chinese Nationalist Anniversary Day, but the ships were tossed wildly by a giant typhoon, with forty-foot swells in the Yellow Sea. Ships' cooks couldn't keep pots on the stoves, and the men got little to eat. When the storm subsided the men saw land, the German-built observatory and St. Michael's Cathedral rising magnificently from the Laoshan Mountains.

On 11 October, the ships docked at Pagoda Pier in Tsingtao. Called the Riviera of the Far East, once a summer resort for the fashionable of Shanghai, it was a modern city of red tile roofs and stucco buildings. In the 1880s, the Germans had built the cathedral, a university, even a brewery. Later they provided electricity and a modern sewage system.

But the city rotted under the Japanese, who encouraged corruption and crime to keep the people demoralized and incapable of mounting resistance. By war's end, Tsingtao was a festering sore of humanity and instability—Japanese administrators and troops, Communist agents, Nationalist agents, puppets, Nazis, White Russians, Koreans, thieves. Outside the city lurked the Eighth Communist Route Army.

But the landing at Tsingtao—Green Island, in Chinese—was glorious for the Marines. Among them was Charles Robertson, operations officer of the 2d Battalion, 22d Regiment.

When the Americans came ashore, the Chinese lined the streets with American flags and greeted them as liberators. Another generation of Marines would be greeted the same way twenty years later at Da Nang, South Vietnam, where Robertson would become a general. The landing at Tsingtao marked entry into the first of three civil wars on the Asian continent in which Americans became embroiled, wars that would dominate U.S. foreign policy for the next thirty years and in which more than two hundred thousand Americans would be killed or wounded.

The Marines' arrival began auspiciously. Sixth Reconnaissance Company secured Tsangkou Air Base, ten miles north of the city, for planes from the carrier USS *Bougainville*. Meanwhile, Fox Company, 2d Battalion, 22d Marines—with McGowan, Lacey, Hutchins, and others— loaded onto trucks and drove through the crowd, with Chinese vendors running alongside selling peanuts, pears, and fifty-cent bottles of liquor with Johnny Walker labels hastily pasted on. By the time they got to Shantung University, where they were to be billeted, many of the Marines were half-drunk on liquor that wasn't Scotch, wasn't aged, and wasn't very good.

On the first night, 2d Lt. Kenneth Creswick ordered his platoon to draw .45-caliber pistols to stand guard duty. McGowan and Pfc. Richard Wood from Portland, Maine, drew first watch. "What are we guarding, Lieutenant?" McGowan asked. After all, the war was over.

Creswick said to make sure "bandits" didn't carry any of the military equipment out of the compound.

A month later, McGowan's company was sent to the air base to reinforce units guarding the strip shelled the night before by bandits. They went in charcoal-burning trucks, converted Japanese school buses. Because there was no petroleum, the Japanese had reconfigured the engines to burn charcoal, using released methane gas. As the Americans bounced along the dirt road, frequently one of them had to jump out and drop charcoal into the engines.

It was a bumpy ride up Shilu Road to a forlorn place that had become very important, for just beyond the air base was a new enemy in this new Cold War: the bandits, Chinese Communists.

ᴥ

Jack Hutchins had never heard the term "Cold War"; no one had, and he didn't know much more about China than the Chinese children across the wire from him knew about America.

Big Hutch had come to disarm the Japanese. But all who had been able to make it to safety were already at the harbor in Tsingtao, having fled as soon as the surrender was announced, some walking all the way from Manchuria to surrender to the Americans. Those in the interior of Shantung Province couldn't make it to the Marines' position, for most of Shantung was in the hands of the Communists.

Just beyond the airstrip, Mao Tse-tung's Communists were in control, and it was through this territory that the Japanese, holding the vital rail route, had to pass to reach safe haven in Tsingtao. But the Japanese wouldn't leave until Nationalist troops arrived to take control of the rail lines, a takeover that the Communists were determined to prevent. The Communists wanted the rail lines. They viewed the Americans as just another foreign invader there to help their enemy, Chiang's Nationalists, against whom they had fought for the last decade.

Control of the rail routes was critical. Shanghai needed one hundred thousand tons of coal monthly. Without the shipments, thousands would starve and freeze during the winter. But Nationalist troops couldn't safeguard the rails, so the Marines assumed responsibility. In November the Communists grew bolder in their attacks on the rails, blowing up track and ambushing and derailing trains. General Shepherd, determined to keep the rails open, ordered planes of the 32d Marine Aviation Group at Tsangkou to conduct reconnaissance patrols of the rail lines. The airstrip suddenly became strategically critical in the rapidly escalating Chinese civil war.

A huge battle raged around Tsinan, less than two hundred miles away. Within weeks Communist forces advanced through the province to probe the wire at the air base where Jack Hutchins, Fred McGowan, and other Marines stood guard. It was terribly cold that November, "cold as blue blazes," Pfc. J. C. Lacey was fond of saying. His feet were always cold in northern China. Years later, whenever his feet got cold in the fields of his Alabama farm, he would think of China.

They lived in pup tents, "buddy tents," the men called them, because each man carried half a tent in his pack and at night put it together with

11

his buddy, sleeping huddled next to him to keep from freezing. They had no sleeping bags, winter coats, or gear, because they had just been sent from the tropics. The wind howled, carrying dust and sand all the way from the Gobi Desert and covering the men sleeping on the ground who had only each other and small fires to keep them warm.

The only relief from the grimness was the village children. A few had begun to bring things: sweet potatoes, peanuts—a welcome change from K-rations—and one clever little boy brought kindling for their fires.

There was nothing remarkable about the little boy. He was small for his age, obviously malnourished after years of deprivation, but there was a glint in his eyes and a smile that cheered the dreary winter landscape. Clearly he was smart, too, and knew opportunity when he saw it.

Fox Company dug in on a hillside overlooking the base, just beyond one of the two runways nearest the boy's village. Adults were not allowed onto the base, but children were, and the first two days after the Marines arrived, Tsui Chi Hsii came with others to hunt for scraps of food and Coca Colas the men hadn't finished. Many of the boys ran behind trucks from the mess hall, and when the Marines on KP dumped cans of table scraps, they scavenged for anything edible. But Chi Hsii decided the men might like something from his family's farm, so he asked his mother to fix a basket. The next day he went off with boiled eggs and ten pounds of peanuts, still crisp and warm from his mother's wok. The Marines were quick to buy, despite orders not to eat food from the Chinese.

The first time they gave him a quarter each. The next day he returned with another basket of peanuts and boiled eggs, and sweet potatoes too, which his mother had been saving for a special occasion. The big-nosed men bought everything. In the following days, Tsui Chi Hsii brought even more peanuts, sometimes earning as much as ten dollars a day. His family traded the money for goods at a nearby flea market.

Most children begged or tried to steal, but the few who brought food and firewood were rewarded not just with money, but sometimes with a leftover Coke or a bite of rations.

Tsui Chi Hsii spent all day with the men; he sat on his haunches by the fire and kept it going. He sensed that they appreciated his work. No language was involved, but he understood that they liked him. He reasoned that since they seemed to like the food he brought, they might barter their own food to feed his family. So one day he waved away the money they offered for his peanuts and kindling and pointed to their K-rations. They cheerfully gave him cans and showed him how to open them with the key that wound off a thin strip of metal at the top.

He bundled them up and took them home. His family could not believe their good fortune. The boy's grandfather most of all was surprised. As a young man laboring for the Germans in the city, he had developed a healthy disrespect for anyone with "big noses," as he called all foreigners.

The situation in Tsingtao changed quickly. Two days after the Marines landed, the Communists offered to help them "destroy the remaining Japanese military forces and the rest of the traitor army."

In a message to General Shepherd, the Communist commander expressed fear that more of Chiang's forces were on their way to Tsingtao. He wrote that in the conflict sure to ensue between his forces and Chiang's, he hoped that Communists and Marines could "maintain friendly relations."

Shepherd rejected Communist assistance, stating that his combat veterans were capable of coping with whatever was thrown at them, and in any case, their mission was peaceful. He did, however, assure the Communists: "It is my determination that the 6th Marine Division in no way will assist any Chinese group in conflict with another."[4]

Nevertheless, on 25 October, a bright autumn day with a chill in the air and a cool wind scaling off Kiaochow Bay, the 6th Marine Division assembled at Tsingtao racetrack to accept Japan's formal surrender on behalf of the United States and Chiang's Nationalist government. The terms stated that all forces of the Japanese Imperial Army in the Tsingtao region were to surrender unconditionally to Chiang, all equipment and records were to be turned over to the Americans, and any prisoners of war were to be released immediately.

After signing, the Japanese representatives quietly climbed into cars.

When one wouldn't start, the crowd of Chinese erupted in cheers, jeering and laughing.

But the signing triggered conflict only two weeks later. When the 1st Battalion of the 29th Marines was sent to reinforce the 7th Marines, keeping the rail lines open and securing the harbor at Chinwangtao for Chiang's debarking troops, they met resistance from the Communist Eighth Route Army and suffered casualties.

Yet the stage had been set for tension earlier, in the first official U.S. contact with Mao. Months before, in a secret operation called the Dixie Mission, Washington had sent a delegation of officers and diplomats to Yenan, the cave city from which Mao ran his revolution, to assess the Communists as fighters and their future role in China.

On a freezing morning in December 1944, Mao handed Herbert Hitch, a young assistant naval attaché, a letter for the Joint Chiefs in Washington. He asked for support and arms, in return for a commitment of one million soldiers to clear a staging area along the North China coast for the planned Allied invasion of Japan. The Dixie Mission, firmly believing that the Communists would win the civil war, recommended that the United States nurture relations with Mao and lend him support. Gen. Joseph "Vinegar Joe" Stilwell, commander of the China-Burma-India theater, was also wary of Chiang, complaining that he was stockpiling U.S. supplies and arms for civil war after World War II ended.

Chiang adamantly opposed the recommendation, and under his strong urging, the Joint Chiefs refused Mao's offer, instructing Hitch to tell him that America would not assist the Communists against Chiang, whom the United States had supported for years. The response infuriated Mao and set the stage for bitter relations that lasted for decades.[5]

Lt. Gen. Albert Wedemeyer, U.S. military adviser to Chiang, warned the Nationalist leader that he had to consolidate his grip in North China before trying to regain the rich northeastern provinces of Manchuria. But Chiang would not listen, and he used the Marine-secured port in Chinwangtao to send troops into Manchuria.

From the Great Wall of China just beyond Chinwangtao up four hundred miles to Mukden and Changchun, every mile of track and every bridge was a Communist target. Wedemeyer told Chiang that before defending that territory, he must suppress the Communist guerrillas in North China. Instead, Chiang drained his forces in North China to send to Manchuria, putting the Marines at increasingly greater risk from the Communists and sowing the seeds of his own future destruction. By late 1945, Chiang's position had slipped precipitously.

Fred McGowan, on liberty with four other Marines in Tsingtao, found that out personally. Seated next to them in a downtown restaurant one night were two distinguished-looking Chinese businessmen. One rose to hoist his glass to the Marines: "I drink a toast to your president, Harry Truman."

McGowan and the other Marines stood and raised their glasses. "We drink a toast to your leader, Chiang Kai-shek."

The smiles on the two Chinese men disappeared; they sat down and turned over their glasses. McGowan knew then China was in serious trouble. Though the country had quickly fallen into civil war, Charles Robertson thought the people felt the same way the Vietnamese did twenty years later—they just wanted to be left alone.

The Marines at the air base wanted to be left alone, too. They'd seen enough battle. Their war was supposed to be over, but now another enemy was probing their wire and inflicting casualties. The conflict grew out of hand so quickly that on 27 November 1945, President Truman appointed General of the Army George C. Marshall to attempt mediation between the two warring factions. Representing the Nationalists was Gen. Chang Chun; Mao sent Chou En-lai.

Jack Hutchins knew nothing about the meetings in Nanking. The only thing he knew was that his feet were numb. He had filled his poncho with straw to use as a sleeping bag, and he was waiting for that little kid to show up with more firewood.

The little boy had become a regular feature of the landscape, arriving every sunup with food and firewood. He stayed until sundown, when he would slip back through the wire to his village, carrying whatever the big men with the big noses gave him for his family. "Charlie" was what McGowan and his squad began calling him, the same name they had given the Japanese plane that had buzzed them in an unnerving wake-up call early each morning on Okinawa. And he called them

15

"Joe"—all of them, because they all looked alike. They talked pidgin English to him and made exaggerated gestures to communicate, and he just grinned and laughed.

It was his smile that Ed Grady of Redding, Connecticut, would remember years later—bright and joyful, a contrast to his body, gaunt from years of hunger. Grady had joined the Marines to become a pilot. He'd gone to Dartmouth on the V-12 program, which had been designed to commission officers in the Navy and Marine Corps. But Grady had failed the eye test and ended up on Guam as a private first class, preparing to invade Japan. Then he got orders for China.

To Grady and the others, the boy was so cute and his smile infectious. For young Marines just out of combat, he provided human contact they desperately needed, a link to brothers and sisters at home.

One night as Charlie was about to leave for home, one of the Marines threw him a poncho and pointed to a place by the fire. He knew they wanted him to stay. "Go tell my parents I'm not coming home tonight, but I'm okay," he told a friend.

He sat with the Marines, ate rations, and stoked the fire. At dawn he went home, bringing his family food; then he returned. From then on he slept with the Marines around the fire. He was helpful, almost dutiful, polite, and always smiling. He became a little brother to the men.

"When we go back to the compound in Tsingtao, we'll take you with us," Pfc. Frank Zitnik told him, joking. He pointed at Charlie and then at the other Marines, motioning toward Tsingtao.

But Charlie took him seriously. Two weeks later, when Fox Company got orders to return to the compound in Tsingtao, Charlie gestured that he was ready to go, too.

Zitnik didn't know what to do. He went to Lieutenant Creswick. "All this time I've been joking with this kid to come with us when we went back to the compound, and now he's here and wants to go."

"Bring him," Creswick said. "But get his parents' permission."

"Mama, Papa; go get your Mama and Papa," Zitnik gestured to Charlie. "You're coming with us, but they have to say it's okay."

Charlie spoke no English except "Joe" and "hello," but he understood and ran home. The next day he returned with his father, who talked to the important man with the gold bar on his uniform. It was the first time Charlie had met Lieutenant Creswick. Using gestures and drawings, Creswick explained to Charlie's father that the Marines wanted to take him to Tsingtao. They would care for him, feed him, and send him to a Chinese school to learn to read and write.

Charlie's father understood. He was happy that the Marines were taking his son to the city. He would have a better chance with them, and an education. He wouldn't go hungry. And this would mean one less mouth to feed. Charlie was scared. He'd never been to the fabled city, never been beyond the air base, and he barely knew these big-nosed Marines. His father told him to go with them and assured him he would visit every chance he got. He thanked the lieutenant, told Charlie to be a good boy, then he said good-bye and left the boy with the Marines.

"Now what?" Zitnik asked.

"Well, at worst we can send him back," Creswick said.

So they packed their gear and boarded trucks. It was the very end of November 1945. For the little boy it was the beginning of an incredible adventure. Climbing into a truck, wedging in among the Marines, he had no way of knowing that the trip he was about to take would lead him to places and things unimagined.

Soon McGowan, Hutchins, and Lacey would leave Tsingtao, telling their replacements to look after him. Four years later, in 1949, the last of the Marines would leave him weeping at the harbor in Tsingtao, something they were loathe to do, for Marines never leave their own. And because of them, he would spend seven years in a Communist labor prison, then another ten under house arrest. But thirty-four years later the Marines would rescue him, the men no longer young Marines, Tsui Chi Hsii no longer a boy.

That adventure would be just as remarkable.

2

As they bumped along Shilu Road, narrow and rutted, to Tsingtao, the grizzled men of Fox Company already had been changed by the little Chinese boy beside them in the truck. The Marines were not much older than he, teenagers, most of them, youths who had lost their innocence on the beaches of Okinawa and Iwo Jima. So much blood had been spilled, so many fallen buddies left behind— but in the frail, rib-thin boy beside them, they saw the suffering endured from many years of living under Japanese control. To the men, the boy came to represent something beyond the war and their own loneliness: he was the sibling they'd left behind and ached to see again. He was the hope that their lives were returning to normal after all. He was their anchor in a strange and turbulent sea.

In grainy black-and-white photos that the men took during this early period, the boy stares ahead with no smile, dressed in an ill-fitting uniform cut to size and looking uncertain about his new life with these Americans. The Marines are clean-shaven, hair slicked back, with boyish grins that seem out of place in their harsh surroundings.

Squeezed into the truck were veterans like Fred McGowan, who grew up near Greenville, Michigan, thirty-five miles northeast of Grand Rapids. Months before enlisting, McGowan had married Mary Ellen Gladding; seeing her again was what had got him through Okinawa and the island-hopping campaign. Now, in China, he dreamed of her constantly, and he knew it wouldn't be long before they would be together.

Cramped in the truck was Jim Lacey, "J. C." to the men, from Birmingham, Alabama, where he'd grown up wanting to take his licks at the emperor after Pearl Harbor. It was J. C. and the other Okinawa veterans who'd suggested that the boy be called Charlie.

Ed Grady was perhaps the oldest among them, at twenty-two. He was a graduate of a Jesuit military school in New York City and a corporal, trained at Dartmouth College with six hundred other Marines and thirteen hundred sailors. At Dartmouth they'd lived in dormitories, and when taps was blown and the lights in rooms ordered off, Grady curled up in a hall to study under a 50-watt bulb—engineering, map drawing, everything an officer needed to know. He wanted to be a pilot, but poor eyesight dashed that dream, and after sixteen months at Dartmouth, he was sent to Parris Island for basic training.

In May 1945 he got orders for Guam, to train for the invasion of Japan. Then the bombs were dropped and the war ended. Grady was sent to Fox Company, 22d Marines, 6th Marine Division—Tsingtao, China. When he arrived at the Marine compound on Thanksgiving day, the barracks were empty, his unit ten miles north securing an airstrip from Communist attacks. So he drew his gear and hitched a ride in a mail truck.

At Tsangkou, it seemed to Grady there were a thousand kids at the wire, hands outreached, begging food. But one boy was different; he lived in the squad bay with the men in his new unit. As Grady would discover, fate has its own mysteries, and their meeting would change not just the boy's life, but Grady's as well.

Approaching Tsingtao for the first time, staring out the back of the truck, that boy couldn't believe what he saw. The buildings were so big, and there was glass. He could see through it, he marveled; he had never seen glass before. The harbor city of brick and mortar, a metropolis with a cathedral, railway station, university, beautiful beaches, and renowned racetrack, sparkled in the sunlight gleaming off the blue water.

Tsingtao, set in a landscape of hills at the base of the Laoshan Mountains, had been a German settlement and naval base from the end of the last century, given to Germany by China as recompense for the murder of a German missionary. It fell to Japanese troops in November 1914, and the occupation lasted eight years until Tsingtao was returned to China under the Washington Treaty.

The city prospered under progressive and efficient Chinese administration, but in 1937 war broke out again against Japan and this time the Japanese occupation lasted until 1945, when thousands of American troops came in a blur of ships and planes, two months after a mushroom cloud ended World War II. But by then the beleaguered city was a shambles, sacked and looted, a sore of fighting factions.

As Charlie rode over its paved streets, the city shimmered with glass, looking like something out of a fairy tale. He had never seen tall buildings, or the ocean, or even running water. Everything was a wonder; he'd heard only stories of the fabled city from his grandfather and father. The ten miles that separated his village from Tsingtao might as well have been ten thousand, for peasant life in Chukechuang seemed rooted in another century.

When the convoy pulled into the Marine compound, formerly Shantung University, its sprawling red brick buildings set on a hill overlooking the city and harbor, Charlie jumped out with the sack of clothes his father had brought him. His new home was a former girls' dormitory, now requisitioned as a barracks for several rifle companies. Each thirteen-man squad had a large room with double-deck bunks; set in the middle was a pot-bellied stove to warm them from the bitter North China winds.

Charlie slept beside Fred McGowan. Issued sheets and blanket, he was taught how to make his rack and given a footlocker in which to stow his gear. Then he went to the mess hall and had his first encounter with a knife and fork.

Immediately after the platoon arrived, Lieutenant Creswick went around to his men and established priorities. "All kids need a bike," he said without room for argument, holding out his hand for contributions. Everybody gave a buck or two, and the next day Creswick came back with the bike. It was black with a few scratches but otherwise fine—a quality Chinese bicycle with child-size wheels. Creswick paid fifty dollars; it was worth ten, but he didn't know. The men taught Charlie to ride it, guiding and encouraging him as he tottered through the barracks bouncing off walls—"bulkheads," he would learn to call them. When he fell to the "deck," they were quick to pick him up and hoist him back on the seat. Soon Charlie was tearing around the entire compound.

Then, damned if Creswick didn't come around again. "I promised Charlie's father we'd send him to school," the lieutenant said, hand out-reached again. "He needs a uniform and black cap." The men ponied up another couple of bucks. ·

School was two miles away, a twenty-minute bike ride, but Charlie hated it. He wanted to be a Marine, learn to march and drill and shoot a rifle. Even Marines have to go to school, they told him, though Charlie noticed they didn't. And he hated the school uniform they got him. He wanted a Marine uniform.

So in consolation—they hadn't particularly liked school either—they took him and their own discarded uniforms and old blankets to a tailor who'd been put out of business during the war, when the Japanese had confiscated his sewing machine. The tailor measured the boy and fashioned shirts and dungarees, and, from the blankets, a long overcoat. Over the right shirt pockets, he sewed the name Charlie TuShu: phonetically, that was how his name sounded to the Marines.

Pulling on his uniform and seeing that name, Charlie felt like a Marine. This was even better than playing: he got to live with real soldiers. He cleaned his gear and polished his brass and took his duties seriously, even standing in line to get his hair whacked into a crewcut. He learned to march and drill and make his bunk so a coin could bounce off it. He quickly picked up the language of Marines—chow, mess hall, head, gangway, deck. Other words too, but the men threatened to wash his mouth with soap for those.

And he got paid, just like they did. The men took up a collection, and every payday Charlie got seventy-five Chinese dollars—about fifty cents. He would draw it standing in line, like everybody else.

Life was good, except for school. It even caused the wreck of his beloved bike. On the way out of the compound one morning, he ran into a truck, bending the front wheel. Sobbing, he raced back to the barracks. "I no see truck; I late for school," he told his buddies. "He hit me. Bike busted." They went into town and got him a new wheel, then sent him back to school.

One day, peddling to school along the beach road, the lure of the ocean was just too great, and Charlie swerved toward the beach. Big Danny had just taught him to swim. Danny was a muscular, blond Irish kid who'd been a lifeguard before joining the Marines. On Sundays he now lifeguarded at the enlisted men's beach, seven miles from the compound. It was there, brought along by the men, that Charlie learned to swim. Danny would put him on his shoulders and take him into the water, where Charlie would ride on his back as if the hulking Marine had been a dolphin. And the dolphin also taught him how to breathe and kick.

Charlie was practicing his new swimming skills that day when Danny drove by in his truck. Charlie didn't see Danny, but Danny saw him, and he was waiting when Charlie returned to the barracks. "How was school today?" Danny asked.

"Good," Charlie said. "Learn lots."

Danny nodded solemnly, then reached over and ran his fingers through the boy's hair, still wet and full of sand. Charlie hung his head. He couldn't lie to Danny, but he really hated that school.

The Marines were worried; Charlie shouldn't be playing hooky. They marched him before Lieutenant Creswick. He'd gone AWOL, they told the officer, who mocked a stern face as the boy stood shamefaced before him. "I promised your father I'd send you to school," Creswick lectured. "If you don't go, I'll have to send you home."

Charlie told the lieutenant he didn't want to go to a Chinese school. He wanted to learn English; he wanted to go to an American school.

The problem was there wasn't one. He did actually want to go to school, for he'd taken to heart the lectures of his grandfather and father. It was how he could help lift China from decades of bondage.

During the years under Japanese occupation, Tsui Li Chin, his father, had been ashamed of his country. "China is so weak," he would say to Charlie and his three brothers. "We let the Japanese come into our homeland and treat us so bad. You must get an education and do something for your country." In his forties, of medium build, with kind eyes and a slight mustache, the older Tsui had been inspired by Mao's words, as had most Chinese peasants. The promise of food and property was more than he could imagine, and he did not trust Chiang Kai-shek.

Chiang's government was corrupt, extracted terrible taxes, and treated the Chinese people no better than the old emperors had. Also, Chiang had waited too long to stop the invading Japanese.

Still, Tsui Li Chin knew better than to get involved in the civil war between Mao and Chiang. He had learned, as had millions of peasants caught in the middle of so many different wars, that it was best to mind your own business. Their world went along unchanged by the machinations of kings and emperors, dictators and generals. Seasons passed, life remained hard, and there was poverty no matter who ruled. Tsui Li Chin never talked about politics; nobody dared to say anything. They never knew whom to trust. The Tsui family had learned that the hard way.

A brother of Charlie's mother had resisted the Japanese. As a double agent working for the puppets—the Chinese collaborators who served the Japanese, the most hated and feared soldiers of all—he smuggled weapons and shoes to a mountain village from where the Communist guerrillas ran their resistance against the Japanese.

Someone he trusted told a Chinese collaborator, who told the Japanese. The Japanese waited until he left one night with his contraband. They followed him to his village, surrounded it with tanks, and set it on fire. Everyone in the village died, and the body of Charlie's uncle was never recovered.

The family went into silent mourning. He was a hero, but it was dangerous to mourn openly. It was in their grief that Charlie and his brothers had committed themselves to helping their country. "What can we do?" they had asked their father.

"Get an education," he had answered.

As military personnel and U.S. civilians poured into Tsingtao in the months following the war, families of officers and businessmen began arriving, too. Soon there was talk of an American school opening. Creswick promised Charlie he would look into sending him, but in the meantime he'd have to continue in his Chinese school.

"Yes sir," Charlie said with a salute, a good Marine following orders, however distasteful.

But there were compensating distractions. The men frequently brought him to town on liberty with them. After two months, he was communicating regularly in broken English. He translated and negotiated with merchants for tattoos and dragon-embroidered silk jackets.

The men always got a better deal with Charlie along, though the merchants hated to see him—he haggled price in their own language and wouldn't let them cheat his buddies. When a merchant set a price, the Marines looked to Charlie. If he thought it too high, he'd wave off the deal. "No. No," he'd say in Chinese. "Two dollars, take it or leave it." If the merchant didn't budge, Charlie would say "Let's go," and they'd leave, the merchant running behind agreeing to the counteroffer.

Charlie spent a lot of time in town and sipped a lot of Cokes in different bars, waiting patiently while the men went upstairs to visit very friendly girls who seemed to spend a lot of their time in bars too. Best of all, though, was the movies. Of course he'd never seen one before, but when the projector began to rattle for the troops at the compound, Charlie was always in the front row, mesmerized. Especially by cowboys. Gene Autry and Roy Rogers were his favorites, and he would sit through every showing—two, three, however many times a day the films were shown—never taking his eyes off the screen. He sat through the talky ones too, and the ones that had kissing, though he didn't understand that.

America was the land of cowboys—campfires and harmonicas—and he memorized the songs the cowboys sang, all of them, especially "Home on the Range." That was the first one he learned when a Texan named Poncho Groves threw him a harmonica from his seabag. He sat on his bunk and practiced for hours, driving the men crazy.

One night Robert Fickle, the mail orderly, took him to town on liberty. They ate steak and eggs, then Fickle and Charlie went to a big house. Fickle disappeared into a room, telling Charlie to stay put. They didn't get back for taps.

"Charlie, where were you last night?" Fred McGowan asked the next morning.

"Me go on liberty with Fickle," Charlie answered. "We go into town. Eat steak 'n' eggs."

"Then what?" McGowan asked.

"We go to big building, lots of girls there," Charlie said. "Fickle and

Chinese girl go in room. Fickle said 'you wait out here.' I wait. Fickle no come out. I look in window. Chinese girl on bed." Then, to the Marines' delight and Fickle's embarrassment, he mimicked what Fickle had been doing.

"Fickle, you immoral SOB!" McGowan shouted. "You took the kid to a cathouse!"

One night soon thereafter when some of the Marines brought Charlie to town, McGowan stayed in the barracks to write letters. When he awoke the next morning, there was a young Chinese girl asleep in the upper bunk. "Where did she come from?" he asked the other guys.

"We brought her back from town last night," a hung-over Marine answered. "We thought Charlie needed a girlfriend."

After all, on 7 December, Pearl Harbor Day, he'd turned twelve.

Marines had always coveted China duty, ever since the 1850s, when Marines had first landed in China to fight in Shanghai, along the Pearl River near Canton. Then it was the Boxer Rebellion of 1900, which had been fraught with peril.

In this most recent Marine landing, the real war was over. While shore duty had its compensations, such as dragon-embroidered silk jackets and friendly girls, for men who had fought island to island in the Pacific, Tsingtao was a cruel delay to getting home. This Chinese civil war was not anything they understood. Communism was still a vague concept to them in 1945, and just a few months before, Russia had been an ally against Hitler.

President Truman's envoy, George C. Marshall, sent to Nanking in November 1945, managed a tenuous truce between Chiang Kai-shek and Mao Tse-tung, establishing a cease fire and halting all troop movement effective 13 January 1946. But that lasted only until March, when political and military differences split the country apart, and open warfare broke out.

Neither side honored the agreement, but Mao openly violated the treaty when he moved his troops into Manchuria. Soviet occupation forces, rushed into the area when Russia declared war on Japan before the bombing of Nagasaki, withdrew as Mao's troops arrived. The Russians turned over to the Chinese Communists weapons and munitions that the Japanese had left behind. While Mao built up strength in Manchuria, setting the stage for the eventual defeat of Chiang's Nationalists a few years later, guerrilla hit-and-run attacks against the railroads and Marine guard detachments continued throughout Shantung and Hopeh provinces during 1946, a period of massive Marine troop drawdowns.

Tremendous U.S. public pressure to send home combat veterans caused dramatic reductions in all units, and Tsingtao was no exception. In the beginning, the III Amphibious Corps consisted of units of the 1st and 6th Marine Divisions and the 1st Marine Air Wing, all under Lt. Gen. Albert Wedemeyer, commanding the China Theater. Their positions in Shantung and Hopeh provinces, along the route of Communist and Nationalist troop movements into Manchuria, put them squarely in harm's way, though they were not allowed any role except as uneasy spectators.

The drawdown added to their peril. The 6th Marine Division was disbanded, reduced to a reinforced brigade, then skeletonized further in 1946. By March the 4th Marines, the backbone of the 3d Marine Brigade, was the only infantry regiment in the Marine Corps to retain the World War II organization of three rifle battalions.

In May 1946, the China Theater itself was deactivated and its role assumed by U.S. Army forces in China. Operational control of Marine forces reverted to the commander of the Seventh Fleet, with a mission simply to "support the foreign policy of the United States in China," a nebulous directive at best. But the Marines' original mission had been accomplished: all Japanese troops had gone home. Their new mission was to provide "security of areas occupied by, or necessary for the support of, United States installations, property and personnel."[1]

Implied in this was a charge to assist United Nations' efforts in China, for China was the greatest beneficiary of the UN Relief and Rehabilitation Administration (UNRRA), set up to distribute food, clothing, and other supplies to victims of World War II. The relief personnel, including many Americans, arrived in China beginning in November 1945. Then other civilians and their families came, adding to the security burden of the Marines. The UNRRA operated in territory held by both Communists and Nationalists, and General Marshall

26

accordingly suggested that the Marines help deliver supplies in Communist areas. The hope was to foster better understanding, but the result was negligible. The Communists' harassing attacks continued, including against the compound in Tsingtao.

Seven Marines were captured in July 1946 and held prisoner for a week, until U.S. officials met Communist demands of an apology for unlawful entry into the "liberated area." But only five days later, a patrol escorting trucks from Tientsin to Peking was ambushed. Five Marines were killed and twelve wounded in the four-hour firefight. That clash between Marines and Communists prompted an investigation, at the urging of both Chiang and Chou En-lai, but the probe turned into a name-calling exercise, and General Marshall ordered the U.S. investigative team to withdraw.

By August 1946, China was plummeting into the chaos of all-out civil war. Without regard to the truce, both sides initiated military action, accusing the other of provocation. Nothing General Marshall did could stop the fighting, and the repercussions for the United States reverberate to this day. As a result of events in China, America found itself engaged in another civil war just a few years later, in Korea. Then, in another ten years, another generation of Marines got mired in Vietnam.

But for Lieutenant Creswick, McGowan, Lacey, and many others, 1946 signified the end of their war.

When Creswick got orders to go home, he felt that Charlie was a piece of unfinished business, and just before he left, he told Cpl. Jack Hutchins to look out for him. Easier said than done, for Charlie, like all boys, had a propensity for getting into things. And there were so many things to get into in Tsingtao.

There was that damnable school he had promised Lieutenant Creswick he would go to—but he hadn't promised to go all the time. So with a friend, the son of a wealthy Chinese merchant and the only other boy with a bike, he would often take off from school in the middle of the day to explore. They went to the markets and the port and to the beaches, though careful, now, to keep out of sight of passing Marine trucks.

There were also movies, and drills and marching, cleaning his gear, policing the barracks, practicing his harmonica, and trips into town with his buddies. Charlie didn't just pretend to be a Marine, he marched with his squad and stood inspection, falling in at the end of the line, standing stiffly proud. He went on hikes, too. On his first eight-mile hike, he couldn't make the fifth mile, but when the company commander stopped his jeep and offered a ride, Charlie answered: "Oh, no sir. I not ride with no officer." His buddies laughed—they wouldn't ride with an officer either—and one lifted him onto his shoulders and carried him the rest of the way.

There were frequent trips home to see his family. Proudly wearing his uniform, he would catch the mail truck going out to the airstrip, bringing the money he had saved and all the food he could carry back to Chukechuang. The family feasted on what he brought, and he gorged on food prepared by his mother, with lots of the garlic he loved. He and his friends would go to the village swimming hole, where he showed off the aquatic skills Big Danny had taught him.

After one weekend with his family, he returned to the compound with his uniform caked with mud and his breath reeking of garlic. The Marine sentries at the gate wouldn't let him pass. Only after much cajoling from Charlie did they finally call the barracks and reach Jack Hutchins. "We got a little gook here who says he's in your company," the sentry told Hutch.

Big Hutch could hear Charlie screaming in the background, telling the sentry: "I no gook. I U.S. Marine."

"Yep, that's him," Hutch said. "Send him over."

The sentry let Charlie pass, and after that he stuck close to Hutch. He was so big, and no one ever argued with him. There's a photograph of them together, both in khakis, with Hutch standing behind Charlie, his hand perched on Charlie's right shoulder, protective, and Hutch isn't smiling—he's looking straight at the camera, and he's serious. It was a year after Iwo Jima.

In the year since Iwo Jima, the world had become a dramatically changed place, much of its geography different. National boundaries had been redrawn, governments and monarchies toppled, and the continent of Europe carved up. On 15 March 1946, Winston Churchill gave a speech at Westminster College in Fulton, Missouri: "From Stettin in the Baltic to Trieste in the Adriatic, an iron curtain has descended across the Continent. Behind that line lie all the capitals of the ancient states of central and eastern Europe. Warsaw, Berlin, Prague, Vienna, Budapest, Belgrade, Bucharest and Sofia."[2]

The Cold War had begun in earnest, and the ally against Hitler became the enemy when the Soviet Union made it clear that it no longer intended to subscribe to the agreements reached at Yalta and Potsdam. The years of cooperation with the Soviet Union, a centerpiece of Franklin Roosevelt's foreign policy and a cornerstone in the war against fascism, turned to a get-tough policy under President Truman. New words entered the American lexicon—red menace, appeasement, pinko, fellow traveler. Communism became the bogeyman, Sen. Joseph McCarthy the hunter. He found them everywhere, even in the State Department, and soon the country was swept up in anticommunist hysteria. Not long after that, the United States entered a massive arms race when the Soviets developed their own nuclear capability.

In the Far East, with Japan defeated and Gen. Douglas MacArthur in Tokyo supervising the occupation, a new enemy emerged—the Communists of Mao Tse-tung. The first sprouts of the Bamboo Curtain poked the surface. Before this new Communist threat materialized, China was only a hazy part of the American consciousness, perhaps best identified through the writings of Pearl Buck. It was a faraway land, where hard-working peasants rejoiced in the good earth.

In World War II the China Theater had been a minor show, compared with the blockbuster productions in Europe and the Pacific. "Vinegar Joe" Stilwell, the China-Burma-India theater's commander, had fought Chiang's corruption and incompetence throughout the war, watching in disgust as the generalissimo's forces were defeated by the Japanese. Mao's troops were far more effective, he felt, and had the support of the people. Stilwell referred to Chiang as "the peanut" and saw no hope for him to defeat Mao in the civil war he knew would take place once the Japanese were defeated. But Stilwell was recalled and ordered to keep his opinions to himself.

Nevertheless, he declared that Marshall's mission to secure a truce between the two warring factions was doomed. "George Marshall can't walk on water," he said, and urged the United States to "Get out—now."[3]

But there was a powerful China lobby in the United States, including *Time* magazine publisher Henry Luce. The son of a missionary in northern China, Luce backed Chiang and urged support of his Kuomintang government. Events in China began getting front-page play, and suddenly the obscure civil war became an American concern, then an obsession. With fear of Communism growing, and at the vocal urging of the China lobby, half a million Nationalist troops were transported by the American military to Shanghai, Nanking, and key cities in North China and Manchuria during the year after V-J Day. Fifty thousand Marines landed to support operations, and the U.S. government supplied Chiang with $600 million in lend-lease arms, ammunition, and materiel.

But to no avail: corruption and incompetence were too staggering. Finally in July 1946, Marshall shut off the supply of arms to Chiang, saying that the generalissimo "simply does not know what is going on"—exactly what Vinegar Joe had said years earlier.[4] In the minds of most Americans, China was lost, though the death throes would continue for another three years. In this race against Communism, the United States was backing a losing horse and began to pull troops in droves.

Charlie saw his wonderful new life coming undone, his Marine family disintegrating as buddies left each month. First McGowan, going home at last to see his bride, and J. C. Lacey, who turned twenty the day he left China. On 25 April 1946 he boarded a slow-moving ship bound for Hawaii, and after him, others left with increasing frequency.

Ed Grady, the Dartmouth-educated Marine, got his orders. Each month he had been greeting Charlie's father at the compound, taking the twenty-five-pound bags of peanuts Tsui Li Chin brought on his bicycle from Chukechuang to repay the Marines for their kindness.

Charlie saw Grady off, as he did each departing buddy. "Good-bye Charlie," was all Grady said to him on a warm September day in 1946, the two standing on the front porch of the barracks in Tsingtao. "Listen to the guys and they'll take care of you. Be a good Marine."

"I will, Grady," Charlie said, trying not to cry. Then he saluted.

Grady marveled at how well Charlie spoke English and how much he had learned in such a short time. He was sure he would never see Charlie again, yet for thirty-five years Grady would wonder about him and whether he was even still alive. He carried a photo of the boy, and whenever his own children misbehaved, he would drive them crazy with stories of the perfect little Marine who could do no wrong. "Why can't you be like him?" he admonished.

Big Hutch left too. It had been a long war for him, and by the time he left China, Iwo Jima seemed a lifetime ago. "I'll be back," he said to Charlie. "I'm just going home on leave." He told Charlie about his home in Kentucky and the girl he hoped to marry someday, and he gave him the address where he could always be reached: John Randall Hutchins, Hazel Green, Kentucky, USA. Charlie put it to memory. But Hutch truly believed he would be back: his enlistment had another year to run. So there was no good-bye, just a see you soon.

But when Hutch arrived in the States, he learned that he was eligible for discharge. The long war was finally over, but the fact that he hadn't said good-bye to Charlie always bothered him. For ten months he and the boy had bunked side by side. He went home to the girl he'd left behind in Hazel Green—Eula Mae Buchanan. They married soon after he returned and had children right away.

As men left others arrived, a very different group of Marines. These men had not been in combat, but had been rushed through training to replace combat veterans aching to go home. Among them were two North Carolinians—William Bullard of Autryville and Don Sexton of Greensboro. Both would have a profound influence on Charlie's life in the years to come.

Bullard was born in May 1926, in a farming community near the Army town of Fayetteville, in a house not five hundred feet from where he lives today. A midwife brought him into a world that he never left except to serve his country. Drafted in 1944, Bullard reported to Fort Bragg ready to fight the Japanese, but the Army told him they couldn't use him. They never said why. He returned to Clement High School and graduated two months before the Japanese surrendered. After that he helped his father, a sheriff's deputy, on the family farm. But the desire to serve never left him. Moreover, he couldn't get over the sight of the previously chunky farmboy Isadore Williams returning on furlough all trim and pressed in his Marine blues.

Knowing how good he'd look in a uniform and realizing he'd make fifty dollars a month as a Marine rather than a hundred a year on the farm, Bullard ran off to Raleigh and enlisted. Four months later he was on Kyushu Island, Japan, guarding a U.S. installation near Sasebo. It wasn't the military career he'd planned, but soon his fortunes changed and he got his chance to fight—in Tsingtao.

Just as for Bullard, the war ended too soon for Don Sexton. He wasn't even seventeen on V-J Day. Born in November 1928 into a family that had a car and a home—rare those days, where he came from—Sexton had been spoiling to fight the Japanese. Fighting was in his blood. Like so many Southern white boys of the times, Jesus and fighting were the things he loved best. Sexton's father ran a service station, but that was lost during the Depression. He remembers a life of little money and meager food, when a good week meant bacon and eggs for Sunday breakfast.

Trouble came early for Sexton. In the third grade he got in a rock fight and put out the eye of another boy. Hauled before juvenile court, Don got a lecture from the judge about how it could have been his eye that was lost. His parents were ordered to pay for the injured boy's glass eye. The experience made a big impression on Sexton—not that he quit taking up for himself or stopped his frequent trips to principals' offices, but in the future, he thought twice about his method of defending himself.

He was thirteen when Pearl Harbor was attacked, and though the war was over by the time he was eligible to enlist, he joined the Marines as soon as he finished high school. He reported to boot camp at Parris Island in January 1946 in good shape. He had well-developed arms, from delivering soft drinks for his father to country grocery stores and service stations. There were twenty-four bottles in a case, and Sexton carried a case in each arm. He finished boot camp in March, got orders for China, and took a troop train across the country.

His temper went with him. One "Yankee" Marine made fun of the way he talked, so Sexton grabbed him by the back of his neck and forced his head out the window as the train barreled through Texas at 110 miles per hour. There weren't any more problems after that. After reaching California and then spending another eighteen days crossing the Pacific, he was in Tsingtao, China.

There he met Bullard and Jack Hutchins, the latter his new squad leader, greatly admired by the replacements because he'd survived Iwo. Stowing away their gear in their new unit, Bullard and Sexton watched in amazement as a little Chinese boy strolled into the squad bay like he owned the place, dressed head to toe just like themselves, his hair in a crewcut, his shoes shined. And he could speak their language and sing the cowboy songs they'd learned back in North Carolina. Wide-eyed, they looked at each other: "What in the world?"

That night, his first in China, Don Sexton found out exactly what kind of world he was in. Issued a rifle, he was told to guard a field dump, a gaping hole dug by bulldozers, holding hundreds of fifty-gallon drums of oil and aviation fuel.

Guard it from whom? he asked. "Chinese bandits," he was told. So in the darkness of a city that had become a seething black market, Pfc. Don Sexton paced his post, torn between exhilaration—this was his first real duty, there was the prospect of danger—and fear, spooked by the dark and the unfamiliarity of his surroundings. Training was over: this was real, everything he had prepared for, he told himself. And indeed, a real enemy was outside the wire, soldiers from Mao's army bent on stealing U.S. property.

Once a two-man post, the fuel dump had been reduced by the massive drawdown of Marines to using a single guard. It was too big for Sexton to protect by himself, and, in the early morning hours at one end of the perimeter, a gang of Chinese broke through the wire. They stripped sheet metal off a Quonset hut, an item that would bring a hefty sum on the black market. Meanwhile, at the other end of the perimeter, another group of bandits tried to make off with oil drums.

As soon as Sexton ran off one gang, the other struck. As he ran at them, shouting for them to drop the sheet metal, sniper bullets tore into the ground around him. He dove for cover and called for reinforcements, thinking that this field dump half a world away from home was not the grave he wanted.

It certainly wasn't Iwo Jima, and it was nothing like the John Wayne movies he'd seen. But that night Don Sexton became the newest player in the Cold War.

More than half of the hundred thousand men originally sent to China after the war had returned home. Some units had been deactivated and others gutted, needing to be reorganized. Because of the drawdown, it was no longer possible for the Marines to provide security for the coal fields and rail lines. That responsibility was turned over to Nationalist troops.

Gradually outposts were pulled in and troops concentrated in major cities, but the withdrawal emboldened the Communists to step up their attacks. They even hit the 1st Marine Division's ammunition supply point at Hsin Ho, six miles northwest of Tangku.

On 1 August 1946, 1st Marine Division directed forces in Tsingtao be reduced to a reinforced infantry battalion—3d Batallion, 4th Marines. The rest of the regiment was sent back to the States. The 3d Batallion would remain in Tsingtao under the operational control of the commander of the Naval Port Facilities, and Capt. Charles Robertson was ordered to form a rifle company from the men in the compound.

Robertson chose them individually, and the handpicked unit was designated Love Company, 3d Batallion, 4th Marine Regiment. Its charge: to guard 1st Wing facilities at Tsangkou Air Base.

When Robertson toured his new barracks for the first time, he found a little Chinese boy with a crewcut, in a miniature, very neat Marine uniform. Though his curiosity was piqued, he didn't say anything. When he returned the following day for a formal inspection of his troops, the boy was standing at attention before his bunk, shoulders back, uniform pressed, shoes spit-shined.

"What's the deal with the kid?" he asked the men.

When told, he merely shook his head in amazement.

"Can we keep him, sir?" one of them asked.

"He's not a pet," Robertson said.

"Oh no, sir. He's one of us."

Robertson considered for a moment, then nodded. "Just make sure he stays out of the way and doesn't get hurt."

So Charlie came to be part of Love Company.

A few days later the company was ordered to the air base to provide security. Charlie packed his gear along with the men. After his bike was loaded onto a truck, he hopped in and again bounced along with grim-faced Marines. This time they were going to face the Communists—armed and dangerous, as Don Sexton and the others now knew.

As he watched Tsingtao fade into the distance, Charlie cast a final, grateful glance at his school disappearing from sight. Would he ever get to go to an American school? he wondered.

He had no way of knowing that in the very near future, he would. Soon to arrive in Tsingtao was someone who would make his dream come true, a Nebraska-born nun named Sister Blanda.

3
Even as a young girl in Howells, Nebraska, in the early 1900s, Magdalen Johns had no doubts about her life's mission. She was one of nine children from a devout Catholic family and used to parade around her mother's kitchen with a dishtowel over her head, pretending to be a nun. Even so, she was shocked when at the end of eighth grade, her final year in Catholic school, her teacher, a nun, asked: "Magdalen, have you ever thought of becoming a sister?"

The child put her head on her desk and wept.

"Why are you crying?" the sister asked.

"I've waited and prayed so long for you to ask me that question. I didn't know if I was good enough."

That night at home, she asked her mother for permission to go to a convent in Milwaukee. But her father, Frank Johns, a bricklayer and carpenter, was off homesteading in Wyoming, and she would have to wait for his blessing until he came home at Christmas.

When her father did return, Frank Johns thought his fourteen-year-old daughter was too young to leave home. But by the summer of 1918, he'd left again for Wyoming. Magdalen left too, with a teacher and two other girls, for Milwaukee—just for the summer. The teacher and one girl returned to Howells at summer's end. Magdalen and the third girl, Johanna Becker, remained. Eighty years later, they're still there. Both are in their nineties. In the intervening years, a cavalcade of events unfolded in which Magdalen Johns became a most unlikely participant. Who would have thought the little girl with dishtowels on her head would go to China, become a prisoner of the Japanese, and teach her religion to a little Chinese boy being raised by Marines?

Her beginning hardly gave clues. Like all novitiates, Magdalen was on probation for her first year. She never wavered in her dedication and took her vows in 1920, given the name Sister Blanda (for an early saint) by the community of the School Sisters of St. Francis. She became a teacher and asked to be a missionary, but that prayer would not be answered right away.

After leaving Milwaukee, she taught first, second, and third grades in a two-room girls' school in Westphalia, Iowa. After that she went to Chicago for ten years, and finally back to Wisconsin. In 1929 George Weig, a German bishop from Tsingtao, visited the convent. He was looking for a religious order willing to send nuns to China to build a school. The Chinese poor, he told the sisters, had no control over their lives, because they had no education. "Until we develop education in China, the church will never have much of a hold there," he told them.

Sister Blanda volunteered to go. In 1933, at age twenty-nine, in the midst of the Great Depression, she and eight other nuns arrived in China to teach in an American school for Chinese girls. They built St. Joseph's Middle School at the same time an addition to St. Michael's Cathedral was being erected on the highest point of Tsingtao. The school quickly prospered, filling with twelve hundred girls who learned everything from English to biology, and Sister Blanda became fluent in Mandarin. She was happy and fulfilled.

Then, in 1937, Japanese troops invaded northern China. They kept the nuns under close watch but allowed the school to remain open— until 7 December 1941. Early on the morning of the eighth, Sister Blanda went to town to buy books and supplies. As she was walking back to the school, a Chinese man who taught math rushed up to her breathlessly. "Did you hear the news on the radio?"

He told her about Pearl Harbor, and about what his sons had seen while passing the school earlier: Japanese soldiers had it surrounded. Sister Blanda ran back and told the other nuns about the attack. The children were sent home, and soon armed soldiers with guns and bayonets converged on the school courtyard. The soldiers ordered the nuns to gather their belongings: they were being sent to a concentration camp in the morning.

Frightened because they had heard the stories of Japanese atrocities, the nuns woke the next morning expecting to be dragged away. But no one came. For nine months they lived in isolated fear, under heavy guard in a girls' dormitory, subsisting on almost nothing. The townspeople were afraid to approach them or help. Finally, in September 1942, they were brought to a Russian hotel outside Tsingtao. Six months later they were sent two hundred miles inland to a former Protestant missionary camp near Weihsien, used by the Japanese to intern foreigners.

Thirty-three women—five of them nuns—three dogs, and a cat lived in one cramped dormitory room without lights or running water. They survived on what they could grow or gather—spinach, leeks, and bitter leaves of chrysanthemums, with water drawn from what tasted like a cesspool.

After a year, the nuns learned that they were being sent back to the United States. Sister Blanda wanted to stay to help the Chinese, but the others convinced her that the Japanese would kill her or she would starve to death. In 1943, she boarded the Swedish peace ship *Gritsholm,* bound for America. Her life's mission was interrupted, but Sister Blanda knew she would be back someday. It took four years. By then the great war had ended, but a different strife consumed China. Sister Blanda was in New York, teaching in the tenements at St. Monica's School, near the East River when she got word that China had been reopened to missionaries, and her school would be reopening, too. She immediately volunteered to return. In December 1946, she got the call. By then she was in Glenville, Illinois, teaching kindergarten.

After Christmas at the convent in Milwaukee, she caught passage on a boat to Shanghai, arriving in February 1947. She stayed for three weeks, during which she was colder than she had ever been. Finally, a boat arrived to take her up the Yellow Sea to Tsingtao.

Soon she was back in the school she had left four years earlier. She moved into a house not far from the Marine compound, where it was unbearably cold, because the Japanese had wrecked the furnace. Tsingtao had changed drastically since she'd left, the ravages of war evident in the poverty and destruction. But it was still a bustling city of commerce and growth, centered around a new element with money to spend—U.S. sailors and Marines.

And spend it they did, though not always in a manner a nun could approve. One day she intercepted a young Marine pulling up in a rickshaw before a dilapidated house in the Iltus Hook section of Tsingtao. This was a German neighborhood where she was helping a priest to open a chapel, an annex to St. Michael's, so the residents would not have so far to go for Sunday mass. Sister Blanda had noticed that one particular house was always full of young women, White Russians who seemed to possess an uncanny talent for knowing when the naval ships had docked. Whenever the nuns saw the White Russian women flocking to the harbor, they knew that U.S. Navy ships weren't far behind.

"Young man, you shouldn't go in there," Sister Blanda admonished when she caught the young Marine climbing out of the rickshaw. "There is nothing but sin in there."

"Yes ma'am," said the chastised Marine, directing the rickshaw driver to leave.

Satisfied with having saved a soul, Sister Blanda reported the incident to another nun. "Oh, Sister, you are so naive," the other said. "You know the minute you left, he went right back."

Probably so, she mused, but after all, it wasn't her charge to save the world from that kind of sin. She had returned to China to teach the children. Accordingly, she was the first to raise her hand when a naval officer came shortly after her arrival to tell the nuns that the military was opening an American school. Were any of them willing to teach there?

By mid-1947, hundreds of wives and children of American officers and executives were pouring into Tsingtao. Also arriving that year was George McDonald, orphaned at eleven and raised by grandparents and half-brothers in Louisiana, then Houston, where he'd spent the war at a box company making special containers to ship bombs overseas. At age sixteen McDonald lied about his age to join the Coast Guard, and he was assigned to a Navy liberty ship transporting 830 horses from Texas and Mexico to Italy. During the war the country had been depleted of horses, which were needed for transportation and farming.

After Italy the ship returned to Newport News, where a friend persuaded McDonald to join the Marines. It didn't take much persuading, for McDonald had caught an itch to see the world. He enlisted in March 1947. Months later he boarded a ship bound for Tsingtao, along with four hundred wives and children of military officers and company executives. The ship, a German vessel captured in the war, was the first to take dependents to China. They stopped at Pearl Harbor for a week and then in Yokosuka, Japan. By the time they arrived in Tsingtao, the city had become an international magnet, drawing Americans, Germans, and White Russians on their way to Israel.

The first day Sister Blanda walked into her class, she was struck by the international character of her students. Fifteen countries were represented, including China. Marines, youths not long out of school themselves, had brought three Chinese boys. Months later more Chinese boys enrolled, and eventually there were seven in all: Smoky (the Marines had caught him smoking), Jingle Bells (found on Christmas Day by Marines), Michael, Patrick Smith (his father's name, he said), Jack (a Manchurian orphan found by Marines and brought to Tsingtao), Pie Chu ("beer," in Chinese), and one who was decked out in a crisp uniform cut to size—Charlie TuShu.

Tom Barclay of Love Company brought Charlie to Tsingtao American School that first morning. Word had been passed by headquarters that a school was opening, and that the Chinese boys adopted by the five different companies would be eligible to attend, provided each company paid the thirty dollars' monthly tuition. Love Company quickly raised the money and took up a collection each month thereafter, handing Charlie the money solemnly. He brought it to Sister Blanda.

Charlie, now twelve and older than everyone except Jack, started in first grade. Within a few months he skipped to third grade, and at the end of the year he was promoted to fifth. His dream had come true. He loved school as much as he'd thought he would, consuming math and English lessons. Sister Blanda taught her students the rhythm of English through songs, and soon her class was filled with the strains of "Mommy's Little Baby Loves Shortnin' Bread" and "Ave Sweet Mary," sung in a variety of accents.

Most of all, Charlie loved the nun—all the Chinese boys did. She called them her "little Marines." She was strong, caring, and had no favorites among the children, even if she did take a special interest in the Chinese boys, especially when she found them poring over an illustrated Bible in the library between periods. For in addition to teaching, her mission included bringing her religion to China, and now she had willing students. Sister Blanda began catechism lessons.

Charlie studied for those as diligently as he did for his regular coursework, even though, thinking back to the drought when he was ten years old, Charlie was unsure about the existence of a supreme being. "Sister, I not sure I can be good Christian," he told Sister Blanda one day. "I not sure I know God that well."

"That's okay, Charlie," she said. "It just means you're curious. But to understand God is beyond human comprehension."

Each day at the end of school, she reminded them to say their prayers and repeat the Ten Commandments before bedtime. They met for Bible classes on Saturdays in the office of a naval officer, or on Sundays at her home before mass. One day she announced that they were ready—it was time for them to be baptized.

So one Sunday at age thirteen, Charlie was baptized in St. Michael's by a German priest, Father Voys. Standing in the massive cathedral with its colorful stained glass, he felt an inner strength that would sustain him in the difficult years ahead.

Next, the proud Sister Blanda got right to work on teaching her "little Marines" the lessons they needed to receive communion.

Rumor had it that American cardinal Francis Joseph Spellman would be coming to Tsingtao after visiting occupation troops in Japan. The archbishop of New York City was one of the most influential religious figures in the United States. As vicar of the military, he was coming to Tsingtao to preach to Catholic Marines and sailors. But Sister Blanda had an additional duty planned for him.

One day she told Father Voys that she'd been preparing the Chinese boys for their first communion. "If Cardinal Spellman comes," she said, "do you think he would preside?"

"I don't see why not."

Spellman arrived the following Sunday. To the delight of Tsingtao's

Catholics, mostly Americans and Europeans, he brought Bishop Fulton J. Sheen to say the mass. Sheen's radio show, *The Catholic Hour,* had a national audience, and his books had made him the world's best-known spokesman for the teachings of his church. To Charlie, they were just religious men with big noses, like all Americans. He arose that morning with the Catholic Marines telling him to dress neatly and quizzing him on the process for communion.

The church was full when Charlie arrived with James "Dick" McIlvane, a Marine from a Pittsburgh suburb, as his sponsor. He sat in the front row with other children, his uniform as neatly creased as those of the Marine color guards who escorted Spellman and Sheen to the altar. As Charlie listened to Sheen's sermon, he was curious about one phrase: "God is our universal King." After receiving communion from Spellman, Charlie looked for McIlvane. "McIlvane," he said, "this word *universal* not familiar to me, what does it mean?"

"It means the whole world," McIlvane said.

Charlie had understood the phrase to mean that God was king of the university. The two sat on the steps of St. Michael's and laughed.

His English vocabulary still may have been lacking—he'd only spoken the language for two years—but school was never a problem. Charlie now never needed help with his homework. The Marines—Tom Barclay, mainly—signed his weekly folder, and they rewarded him for good grades on his report cards. When they went to PTA meetings and parent-teacher conferences, they heard only glowing accounts of his progress and his behavior.

The other Chinese students fared well too, though Smoky, the class clown, frequently got into trouble. One day when he tried to cut school, a Marine delivered him to Sister Blanda by the scruff of his neck.

"Sister, I got busted," Smoky said with a mischievous grin. "I go AWOL."

But Charlie never did. He never missed a day, even while he was at the air base with Love Company. Then he caught a ride in the mornings on the mail truck, and rode it back to the base every afternoon. He diligently did all his homework. He shined his shoes and polished his brass, marched with the men, and ate in the chow hall with them. But now, he also began to lecture them on their bad habits. He told them they shouldn't be going into town to visit the friendly girls. Now, when they went, Charlie admonished: "Prostitution is sin."

Charlie was worried about his buddies' souls, but soon physical safety was everyone's concern. And danger in the waning days of 1947 wasn't just limited to guard duty.

Don Sexton and two of his best buddies from his squad found danger in an alleyway in town. One payday, the three of them went into Tsingtao on liberty: Sexton, David Brooks—himself a hotheaded North Carolinian who would make the Marines a career—and Coke Sharp, a red-headed teenager from Arkansas who could dance like Fred Astaire. Aware of Charlie's newfound religion, they left him in the barracks to finish his homework. Besides, they were hoping they'd have to fight their way out of a bar this night, leaving a wake of wounded sailors. The boy would be safer staying behind.

Late leaving for town, they were afraid they'd have trouble catching a rickshaw. To their surprise, a cab pulled up in front of the compound. "We go on liberty. Uptown," Sexton told the driver.

The plan was simple, like that of many paydays before: with money in their pockets they would go for dinner at the Great Tsingtao Cabaret, one of the city's finest restaurants and a favorite haunt for sailors and Marines. There a dollar fifty bought a thick sirloin, and ten cents a Chinese girl to dance with to the American big-band tunes played by a group of White Russian and Chinese musicians. Afterward they would shop, then search for a bar promising the excitement of fights with drunken sailors. Brooks usually was able to stir up trouble. It didn't take much, just the wrong look and a right hook.

But this night, trouble began early. Instead of heading into town, the cab driver steered in the opposite direction. "Hey, buddy, you missed the turn, you're going the wrong way," Sexton shouted to the driver in his thick, liquid North Carolina drawl, but the driver ignored him and continued into a seedy section of Tsingtao, then into an alley. Suddenly eight Communist soldiers rushed toward one side of the cab while the driver fled on foot.

Outnumbered, weaponless, and having witnessed many others returning from liberty with busted skulls, even Brooks saw sense before

valor in the situation. He bolted from the other side of the cab, shouting to the others, "We best get our butts out of here. These guys don't
look like they're in a party mood."

Sexton and Sharp followed, streaking from the alley to safety and
catching a rickshaw that delivered them to their original destination.

Now their appetites were whet for some real action, which wasn't
long in coming. After Love Company returned to the airstrip, Communist activity picked up. Sexton was disappointed that it wasn't anything that could rival the beach landings and hand-to-hand combat of
which Pacific War veterans could boast. The closest Sexton ever came
to war was on the day his unit was called out to rescue a pilot downed
in Communist-held territory.

Captain Robertson ordered Lt. Robert McNeeley to ready his platoon for an insert. Three R5D transport planes took the Marines in full
combat gear to Weihsien, two hundred miles inland. Sexton and the
others were nervous; in skirmishes with Mao's peasant soldiers, several
Marines had already been killed, and some captured.

The best-known incident was when four Marines from Love Company had left the air base in a jeep to hunt rabbit and deer. Beyond
Tsingtao, deep in a forest, they were surrounded by Communist troops
who wanted their jeep, but the Marines burned it before it could be
taken. Pfc. Charles Brayton was killed in an exchange of fire, and the
others were held prisoner for three months before their release could
be negotiated.

This rescue mission wasn't nearly so adventurous. As Sexton and the
others jumped out of their aircraft and surrounded a field, searching the
tree line for snipers, they spotted the pilot they had come to rescue. He
was standing by his plane, mired in a sinkhole. He'd radioed that he had
landed in a friendly village, but his communication had faded before
Love Company could receive the message that he was safe.

Not all incidents ended as well. In the four years Marines were in
North China, twenty-two died in plane crashes and another twelve
were killed in skirmishes with the Communists.

As for Charlie's life, for the time being it had stabilized. He was in
school, learning Christianity, and was well cared for, living a life far different from the one he had left in Chukechuang eighteen months ago.

His village friends scarcely recognized him the first time he returned home after moving out to the airstrip. With his spit-shined shoes and tailored uniform with corporal's chevrons, his face and body filled out and his rigid bearing, they thought Chi Hsii had become an American citizen. They imagined that someday, he would be a great man helping his country. They had no way of knowing how much he would suffer, later, for his contact with the Americans. Had they known, they wouldn't have envied his new life.

Charlie had no way of knowing, either. At the air base, he lived in the barracks, went to school, studied, and worked out in the gym, lifting weights and jabbing a punching bag, putting muscle on his once-frail frame. He was a good boxer, and Roy Sibit, a smooth-talking, quick-tempered Marine from Ohio, made sure the boy knew his way around a ring. Sibit was among the final wave of replacement Marines sent to China as it began to fall under the control of Mao.

Sibit arrived in China in March 1947 and joined Love Company at the air base, assigned to Don Sexton's squad. He met Charlie the first day he arrived. The uniformed boy came into the barracks and challenged him to a friendly game of poker.

Though Sibit didn't socialize much with other Marines, he spent hours teaching Charlie how to lay jabs and hooks on an opponent. Boxing, almost as much as his studies and religion, became part of Charlie's routine. After Love Company returned to Tsingtao and the Marine compound, he and Sibit sparred in the company gym in the attic of the barracks, or at the Tsingtao YMCA. "Treat the punching bag as a foe," Sibit told him. "Mix up your punches": a couple of left jabs, then a surprise right hook. "Keep your balance, and never take your eyes off the other guy."

None of the other Chinese mascots were his match except Jack, who was two years older and many inches taller. Headquarters arranged a bout. But the day they boxed at the YMCA in town, no one from Love Company was there to watch Charlie fight Jack to a draw: they were standing guard.

As Charlie's boxing prowess developed, so did a cockiness that sometimes got him into trouble. Outside the air-base gate were two sentry booths, one for Marines, the other for Chinese Nationalists. Late one afternoon, Charlie watched as a Chinese coolie who swept the Love Company barracks tried to leave the gate toting two cans of left-over food that he'd taken from the company kitchen. The Marine sentries let him pass, but a Chinese guard stopped him.

"Who said you could bring things out of the base?" he asked the frightened coolie, as Charlie slipped closer to listen.

"I'm taking it to my family," the coolie explained. "It would only be thrown away."

The guard asked the coolie for a cigarette—an obvious bribe—but he had none, so the guard told him to drop the cans of food and leave. As the man walked away, Charlie picked up the cans and ran after him. "Take them and go," he said.

The guard was livid. "Who gave you permission to go against me?"

"He didn't take anything that was valuable, he only wanted food that would be thrown away," Charlie replied. "He wouldn't do anything to hurt the Marines. He works for us."

As Charlie tried to explain, the guard suddenly smacked the boy twice—one cheek with his forehand, the other with his backhand. Charlie had just turned thirteen and was still small for his age, but in the base gym he'd built strong fists and rapid-fire reflexes. Before the guard's hand could return for a third slap, he ducked, grabbed the guard's leg with one hand, and punched him in the solar plexus with the other.

As the sentry lay on the ground groaning, five other Nationalists surrounded Charlie. But seeing him in trouble, the Marine guards ran to his rescue. The Chinese backed off, heeding their orders not to do anything that could cause an international scene. Taking Charlie to safety, the Marines told him he was right to give the coolie food, but he must not offend the Chinese guards again.

"It's not smart to make enemies," one Marine said. "Do unto others" was the Christian way, he explained, but that was not the way the real world operated. "Don't tell Sister Blanda, but reality is payback, and payback is getting even. The best way to get along is to go along; if you mess with somebody, he'll get you back sooner or later."

Charlie learned that lesson the hard way. One Saturday morning with nothing to do, he decided to ride his bicycle out to see his family. The bike was stored in the barracks basement, but when he went to get it, it was gone. He thought one of the Marines must have taken it for a ride, but when he asked, they said no. He searched the base to no avail. He asked the sergeant on duty if he'd seen anyone riding it off base, but he hadn't; he knew the bike and would have stopped anyone trying to sneak it through the gate. They jumped in a jeep and circled the base, asking guards at each post if they'd seen it. Soon it became obvious that Charlie's beloved bike was gone. Someone had hustled it over the six-foot brick wall that enclosed the base.

Charlie was devastated, even though by this time the bike was dirty and worn, covered with scratches. He didn't understand why anyone would want it, especially since everyone on the base, both Americans and Chinese, knew how much he loved the bike.

Then it hit him. *Everyone* knew what the bike meant to him—including the Chinese guard he'd humiliated in front of his comrades. This was the payback he'd been warned about. The guard had gotten even with him after all. He had made an enemy, and it had cost him his bike. Charlie resolved not to make that mistake again. He wouldn't make *any* more enemies.

He would not realize until years later how many powerful enemies he was making without knowing it, nor how terrible their payback would be.

That was all part of the adult world Charlie knew little about. It was a world that grew more dangerous by the day, with many different enemies: the United States versus the Soviet Union, opposing forces in Korea, and the Viet Minh and the French in Indochina. Open warfare would break out in Korea in a few short years, a conflict unresolved to this day, while in Vietnam, war would rage for nearly forty years. It would take the United States and the Soviet Union nearly half a century to end their arms race.

But in China, hostilities came to a quick head. By January 1947, relations between the warring Communists and Nationalists had deteriorated so badly President Truman recalled his envoy, George C. Marshall. He initiated steps to withdraw all U.S. Marines from North China except for a guard contingent at Tsingtao, where Navy personnel were training Chinese Nationalist counterparts.

In April 1947, operation plans were completed for the redeployment of the 1st Marine Division and 1st Marine Aircraft Wing to Camp Pendleton, California. The last clash between the 1st Division Marines and Communist forces occurred that month. In the longest, most costly incident, 350 Communist troops again struck the isolated ammunition supply point at Hsin Ho, killing five Marines and wounding sixteen.

A new command, Fleet Marine Force, Western Pacific (FMFWesPac), was activated at Tsingtao under Brig. Gen. Omar T. Pfeiffer. The mission of the unit, which comprised the 1st Marines and the 3d Battalion of the 4th Marines, with air support from three squadrons at Tsangkou Air Base, was to provide security for U.S. naval-training activities and to protect the remaining U.S. lives and property in China.

On 1 September 1947, Tsingtao became the last Marine duty station in China, and FMFWesPac was ordered to have an infantry battalion ready at all times to be air-transported to Shanghai, Nanking, or Tientsin—wherever Americans needed rescuing. To prepare for any eventuality, surprise alerts and practice air lifts became a staple of training. Though woefully undermanned for the task of securing such a large area, combat training and patrols alternated with guard duty of the garrison and airstrip.[1]

William Bullard spent much of his last few months in China rescuing Americans—mostly missionaries—from the countryside. His squad would fly into areas surrounded by Communist troops. Landing in a village where missionaries lived, they would whisk them aboard R5D planes and take them back to the compound, out of harm's way.

Because of the Marine presence, there was a facade of peace in Tsingtao. Liberty was generously granted, and dragon jackets were bought, tattoos inked into arms, many girls visited. A recreation program was implemented, and off-duty education studies were encouraged. In keeping with postwar policy of reuniting military families whenever possible, a greater number of dependents were permitted to come from the States.

Tsingtao duty seemed much like that at any overseas station, except that just beyond the facade raged a brutal war. For Charlie, something even worse than that was happening that autumn of 1947—his new family was breaking up.

As orders arrived for more Marines to go home, Charlie's buddies— Sexton, Bullard, Sibit, McIlvane, Ray Brewington, Warren Evans, and Clayton Mattice—huddled in the barracks night after night, scheming ways to get Charlie out of China to America. They knew that unless they succeeded, he would be in grave danger once they were gone. They tried to get him sent to a U.S. school, but authorities quickly denied the request. There was only one sure way: they would smuggle him out in a seabag.

But in the end they gave up on that idea, too. "What if he got lost?" Bullard asked.

Sexton left in September. Saying good-bye to the other Marines was hard enough, but leaving Charlie was worse. Hugging him on the docks the day he left, waiting to board the USS *General Mitchell,* he told his young friend: "Be true to the spirit of the Marines, and remember what you learned from Sister Blanda. We'll do what we can to get you to the States. Semper Fi."

Then it was Bullard's turn. As he did with all his departing friends, Charlie went to see him off. On the landing strip, he and Bullard hugged. In eighteen months they had done so much together: trips into Tsingtao on liberty, eating together in the chow hall, watching Gene Autry Westerns. Before leaving, he gave Charlie his address: Route 1, Autryville, North Carolina. He told Charlie to write often.

"Bullard," Charlie shouted over the drone of transport planes, "You send for me, won't you? You bring me Stateside, won't you?"

"Yes Charlie, someday we'll come back for you."

With that he was gone. As the plane roared down the runway, Bullard saw Charlie through a window, standing at attention just off the runway, saluting.

Bullard couldn't see that he was crying.

Still, not all foreigners were leaving Tsingtao. Soon, as the fighting in China began tearing the country apart, a twenty-one-year-old mission-ary arrived: Miriam Matthews. She entered Charlie TuShu's life just as the one he had was falling apart. Together they would enact their own pauper's version of *The King and I.*

4

Johnstown, Pennsylvania, was half a globe away from Tsingtao. They also seemed to exist in different time dimensions, as if Tsingtao had been lost in a time warp (a new term that had recently been propounded by Albert Einstein, teaching at Princeton). Yet in an unlikely series of events, two people from these drastically different worlds—an idealistic young woman and a little Chinese boy—were brought together for a brief period, separated for decades, then reunited.

In 1947, the world of Charlie TuShu was as removed from that of Miriam Matthews as was the world of Genghis Khan from that of Marco Polo. In fact Matthews, the daughter of a dentist and a school-teacher, probably knew more about Marco Polo's world than she did about Charlie's. Her brothers had fought in World War II. Mercifully, they had returned unharmed, and, as did many others throughout the country, the Matthews' lives closed in on community again.

The United States in 1947 was a land of readjustment, a place seeking normalcy. John F. Kennedy and Richard M. Nixon had been elected to Congress; the electric clothes dryer had just hit the market; suburbia was born in the form of Levittowns. People read *The Robe,* sang the new jingle "Pepsi-Cola hits the spot," and tried to decide "which twin has the Toni" (neither, it turned out after a Federal Trade Commission investigation—they had both gone to a hairdresser).

50

Hundreds of thousands of soldiers, sailors, and Marines, including Iwo Jima veteran Jack Hutchins of Kentucky, went back to college, courtesy of the GI Bill of Rights. Because Hutch was married—to his old sweetheart, Eula Mae—in addition to the five hundred dollars yearly tuition grant, he got the maximum living allowance of ninety dollars a month.

Dwight D. Eisenhower went back to college too—as president of Columbia University. His counterpart in the Pacific, Douglas MacArthur, was in Tokyo, overlord of defeated Japan. In a few short years, both their lives would be touched by events in Asia. Eisenhower would be elected President of the United States, and MacArthur would be fired, forced to retire.

Events in Asia would also have a profound and immediate impact on a twenty-one-year-old senior at Wilson College, Pennsylvania. Miriam Matthews had heard a lot about China from the sermons of the Rev. Kirk West, pastor of First Presbyterian Church in Johnstown, where she had been baptized. West had been a missionary in China for fifteen years, living in Tsingtao with his wife, Helen "Tuck," a medical doctor, and their four children. Forced out by the Japanese during World War II and sent to Johnstown, West made it clear to his parishioners from the outset that he would return to China at the first opportunity.

As he spoke almost romantically about northern China, his sermons were filled with vivid pictures of life there, and descriptions of missionaries facing hardships that challenged their faith every day. What better way to do God's work, he would ask, than to help a downtrodden people in desperate need? There was boundless opportunity for Christian service in China, he said.

His sermons mesmerized Matthews, and after church on Sundays, she visited with Kirk and Tuck, listening to more China stories. Soon she longed to go there too and perform the work he so eloquently described. She was still in college when Kirk West received permission to return to China after the war. By the time she graduated in the summer of 1947 and got a job as program director for the YWCA in Johnstown, he was back in Tsingtao.

She wanted to go, too. China seemed so exotic, and the work of a missionary so important. She was young, unmarried, energetic, and athletic—Tsingtao seemed a wonderful place to go. So Matthews was excited when she got a telegram from Kirk West one day in early 1948: "Teaching position open at American School in Tsingtao. You should come." She immediately cabled back: "This is something I've wanted to do for years. I just didn't think it would happen so quickly."

Indeed, it came very fast. Through West's intercession, the Board of Foreign Missions of the Presbyterian Church wrote her on 29 March 1948, offering her a one-year appointment to the Tsingtao American School as a physical-education teacher. The salary would be $170 a month. Rooming would be free, and military commissary privileges available. The U.S. Navy would provide transportation; her cost for that would be $1.50 a day for food while on shipboard.

Her family wasn't happy, but Matthews was a headstrong young woman, and they knew better than to try to dissuade her. It wouldn't have done any good; the lure was too great. China offered the adventure of a lifetime, she felt. She would be able to do God's work in a foreign land, helping unfortunate people in their direst time of need.

In June, Tuck West wrote her a welcome letter describing the life before her and suggesting that she bring some "dressy formal things," as there was an active social life, and some "long red underwear," because "there was a fuel shortage last year and some of the teachers nearly froze to death." Tuck also wrote that she'd no longer be able to call Matthews by her nickname—Sis—because there were two nuns at the school, Sister Blanda and Sister Hiltrudis, both "excellent teachers" who were "regularly just called Sister."

Her assigned roommate, Regina Hoover, also wrote a welcoming letter. She suggested that Matthews bring a supply of toothbrushes, as they were scarce, and vitamins, because "the food is all thoroughly cooked and loses some of its nutrient value."

Altogether it sounded like a lark—safe and fun. And the journey out was a grand adventure: she took a Pullman coach across the country to San Francisco, where she stayed off Union Square. Then came the day of departure, 19 August 1948. Matthews sailed under the Golden Gate Bridge on the troop carrier USS *General G. M. Randall,* arriving in Honolulu just as the United States entered a new phase of history.

❧

The new young congressman on the House Un-American Activities Committee, Richard Nixon, was spearheading an investigation of alleged Communists. Newspaperman and recanted Communist Whittaker Chambers had accused Alger Hiss, former State Department aide to President Roosevelt, of spying for the Soviet Union. He had even produced microfilm that had been hidden away in a pumpkin. The witch-hunt for Communists in America had begun, and fueling the enterprise were events in China.

Oblivious to these developments as she sailed there, Miriam Matthews made friends with other young women—teachers on their way to exotic places and wives joining their husbands. It was a calm cruise, the ocean peaceful, a harbinger of times to come, she hoped. On board, there were games and lifeboat drills. Marines on their way overseas boxed on deck. She had not realized how much Marines loved to box. She knew even less about how one of them who was already in China, Roy Sibit, was perfecting the skills of one of her future students.

On Guam, Matthews caught a Navy transport plane to Shanghai. She sat "in bucket seats," as she wrote in her letter home, from where she could see the clouds and the stars. "I'm sold on planes now; best way to get anywhere—unless you're at your leisure, then there's nothing like an ocean voyage." Heady words from a young woman who one month earlier had been the YWCA program director in Johnstown.

After a short layover in Shanghai and a two-hour flight, she was in Tsingtao. Reverend and Mrs. West greeted her at the airport, but right away Matthews saw that things were not as she'd expected. The Wests looked so tired and seemed so overworked. In just the few months since she'd been hired, the situation in Tsingtao had deteriorated dramatically. Refugees had poured into the city to escape famine and the war that raged farther north between the Communists and Nationalists. Squatters and beggars were everywhere, and the Communists had sealed off Tsingtao. No supplies could get through. "Had I known it was going to be like this, I wouldn't have let you come," West told her.

In one of her first letters home, Matthews described a China very different from the China of Kirk West's sermons two years earlier. Her descriptions of events were different as well from those in U.S. home-town newspapers:

September 23, 1948

It's like watching a sick dog gasping for its last breath. As I walk to school, I pass small children in rags, or old, wrinkled up, dirty women—all picking twigs up from the ground, or digging into the ground hunting for bits of coal. Oh, there are many uninviting scenes—all leading to the same questions: Is there any hope for China? It is very clear why the masses are turning to Communism—at least they'll have something to hold on to. These people aren't even what you'd call existing. It is felt the Chinese Nationalists are driving this country into the ground.

How quickly the situation deteriorated took everyone by surprise. Even before the school year began, there were rumors that the Navy-run school would close and everyone be sent home. The city was being overwhelmed by refugees fleeing Manchuria, as it fell to the Communists.

After the end of World War II, Mao dispatched his leading general, Lin Piao, with 120,000 soldiers and 30,000 cadres, to Manchuria. In a move discouraged by U.S. advisers, supposedly neutral in the civil war, Chiang Kai-shek sent his troops to Manchuria also. There they bogged down, and Chiang's American support began to work against him—he was viewed as a puppet of foreigners, and his army blundered everywhere.

Still, for Chiang to lose the civil war took a remarkable achievement of mismanagement and battlefield incompetency. Originally viewed as liberators from the Japanese, his troops and administration behaved even worse, so badly that a major newspaper, *Ta Kung Pao,* appealed to the government: "Don't lose the confidence of the people completely. An infinite number of people once rejoiced deliriously at the victory over Japan, but now all of us cannot even keep ourselves alive."[1]

Corruption, graft, and mismanagement even more than military incompetence doomed Chiang—and, by complicity, America's fortunes in China. General Wedemeyer, finishing a three-month investiga-

tion in China for President Truman, reported "oppressive police mea-
sures, corrupt practices and maladministration of the National Government officials, the deterioration of the economy, the incompetence of
the military, the loss of support from the population." [2]

By mid-1947, Mao Tse-tung had mobilized North China's rural
peasants into an effective, rapid-moving army. He sent infiltrators into
the Northeast to indoctrinate the peasants and recruit troops to engage
in a long-playing people's war. Meanwhile, surrenders and desertions
further reduced Chiang's forces and his ability to wage war, and draft-
ing another million men at the end of the year didn't help. He wasn't
addressing the country's critical problems.

Mao had stated that "a people's war is not decided by taking or losing a city, but by solving the agrarian problem."[3] Chiang sealed his
own defeat by not dealing with that problem, and in 1948 starvation
and despair gripped the country. In April the U.S. dollar was worth
1.8 million Chinese dollars, and a pound of rice cost ten million dollars. That was ten thousand times more than it had cost the previous
year. In August Chiang banned all demonstrations and proclaimed "economic reform" under the direction of his son, Chiang Ching-kuo. The
Chinese dollar was pegged at four to the U.S. dollar, but in three weeks
it soared to twelve million to one greenback.[4]

That was the situation Miriam Matthews found herself in: A city
teeming with squatters living in tent dwellings made of sheets and discarded cardboard. She had to step over them every morning on her
two-mile trek to school from the house she shared with Regina
Hoover, walking past long lines of bedraggled refugees waiting for their
food ration—a half cup of grain a day—and warmed only by the blanket the missionaries gave them.

As winter approached, it looked increasingly likely that the school
would close, as dependents began to leave and children withdrew. On 3
October Matthews wrote to her parents:

Flour and wood are extremely scarce. Yesterday long lines of Chinese stood waiting for a little ration of flour—once a month. As to
wood—there's hardly a tree left standing. It's against the law to cut
down a tree if it's alive so the Chinese cut the bark off the tree

55

causing it to die. There's no grass either anywhere. Chinese pull it by the roots for food.

Matthews taught all physical education classes and coached the after-school sports, arranging soccer matches with the children of the Germans and White Russians. But the foreign legations began to withdraw their people also.

There was one special assignment that Matthews loved: tutoring English to a group of seven Chinese boys, the Marine mascots who showed up every day wearing Marine uniforms. There was never a problem with any of them. They seemed older than the others, more serious and less carefree. They were punctual, exceedingly polite, and hard-working. They were good athletes, too—they'd been taught baseball, football, and boxing by their older uniformed "brothers."

But the future looked grim that winter of 1948. Every day Matthews saw the impact of Mao's forces winning the civil war. Her letters home show just how grim it really was:

October 6

Last night curfew was enforced. Chinese police came around, searched our house for Communist imposters. All roads were blocked.

October 16

There is a terrific food shortage, not only in Tsingtao, but Peking, Shanghai, etc. Not only that, but Tsingtao has become the refugee city. Another 3,000 arrived from some cities and villages up north. About one block from our house is an old temple—there, 2 times a day, different shifts of refugees enter the gates and crowd on top of each other clutching a tin cup, wait in line to be served their one meal per day—porridge. The sad thing is that families are separated, children and parents. The look on their faces—forlorn, lost and helpless. As I brush shoulders with them daily, I wonder, How do they live? Every day, you can be sure some drop over dead.

Everybody should realize the tragedy taking place. The Nationalist Government is as good as fallen. Everybody feels there is no hope.

The Communists are out to win. It's merely a Peasant Revolution led by so-called Communists. As long as the Nationalists remain in power, the money will remain in the hands of the few. Perhaps China can get on her feet through Communism. At any rate, the total situation looks pretty hopeless. I really feel sorry for these poor, ignorant, helpless Chinese people. It's sad—nothing but very sad.

October 24

The critical thing is the food situation. There are many Chinese who have nothing. There will be many a change when the Government falls, but all for the better—the Nationalists have been in power too long, doing no good.

November 1

There is no such thing as coal on the Chinese market. The few remaining trees are disappearing; our wooden soccer goal posts disappeared. The fear of food riots is rising. The weather is becoming cold, food is becoming still more scarce, and more homeless and starving people! The beggars, wailing at doors!

In just months, Matthews saw the city disintegrate before her eyes. Fifty years later she would say: "I guess I knew from the beginning we'd have to leave. I just didn't want to accept it, especially after I got so involved with the children. What would happen to them if we left?"[5]

American involvement had come too late. But no amount would have helped; Vinegar Joe had been right all along. Still, few in the United States believed this, or they believed instead that it was an insidious Communist plot backed by the Russians. The witch-hunt for Communists had picked up steam and would reach hysteria in a few short months, when the Soviet Union detonated an atomic bomb. Their bomb had been built using secrets stolen from the United States, for which Julius and Ethel Rosenberg were executed.

Meanwhile, elections had been held in divided Korea. Syngman Rhee declared the independence of the Republic of Korea in the South, while a People's Republic was declared in the North. Both sides lay claim to sovereignty over all Korea, and tensions mounted. Many predicted the outbreak of war shortly.

In the States, the China lobby intensified its campaign to bolster support for Chiang, launching a massive propaganda offensive in magazines and newspapers that culminated in Madame Chiang's speaking tour that fall. All of it was to no avail.

On 10 November the U.S. consulate advised American civilians in Tsingtao to leave, because of "the rapid deterioration of the military and political situation." Five days later, the consulate warned: "Military developments make it appear possible that hostilities may spread, with result that normal transportation from Tsingtao may be disrupted." After noting the critical food shortage, the recommendation was that "unless you have compelling reason to remain you should consider evacuation from Tsingtao while transportation facilities remain available."[6]

Yet the social life continued, and Matthews put to use the dresses she'd been advised to pack. She was constantly asked to functions at the Officers' Club—after all, she was female, single, and attractive. The last days of Raj in India, a scene playing out on the same continent not far away, were probably similar. "Invited to Admiral and Mrs. Badger's reception," Matthews wrote home. "These fancy cocktail parties get me. These Navy people live on cocktail parties. Such social life, such superficiality—I never did see."

Yet it was like dancing on the deck of the *Titanic:* The end could not be forestalled. This feeling was evident in her letters home:

November 9

There is one sure thing—the Nationalists are fighting a losing battle. The Nationalists have lost all will to fight; the sense of loyalty has also long been lost. At the battle of Tsinsen, General Wang Yao, supposedly the best Nationalist general, turned Communist and handed over arms, equipment, Chinese troops etc. Same thing happened in Chiuchow. The complete collapse of China is merely a matter of time. This probably wouldn't be seen in American papers—the Nationalists are much more destructive than the Communists. It is obvious why the Chinese want to see Communism come in—anything to keep the money from remaining in the hands of a few. A lot of refugees are returning to their homes because they figure living under the Communists could be no worse.

As to taking a bath, we're getting as bad as the Chinese. All water and electricity are turned off 12 hours a day—even when it does come on, we seldom get water, and it's too cold.

November 17

Things are getting more serious every day. All Americans will be out of Tsingtao by January. The first evacuation ship leaves next week.

The situation everywhere is utterly pathetic. As to food and fuel riots—not much is seen of violence; the Chinese are more willing to continue getting weaker and weaker and finally lay down and die. Really, it's so sad!

December 8

Well, how's Madame Chiang doing in the good 'ole USA? Sure hope U.S. watches its step—so far most of the material aid given to the Chinese has fallen into Communist hands. We'd do best staying out of this hopeless mess.

The second evacuee ship left today. The one evacuating the White Russians, Poles and Jews is due Dec. 15—to Argentina via Shanghai. Then there will be one more evacuee ship.

Now most Chinese look upon us aliens in disgust, almost hatred. You have to get used to that as you walk the streets.

December 19

Message came through from Tientsin. The sudden capture of this city was a surprise to everybody. Peking is also gone, the best general of the Nationalists surrendering. No one knows what's going to happen next—maybe it will be Nanking.

The number of refugees, the poverty, cold weather, etc.—and all increasing. What sights! This place is no longer the beautiful city it used to be a year ago! However, this afternoon walked through Tsingtao Park, built by the Germans naturally, and could tell at one time it must have been magnificent.

Tsingtao had been magnificent once. Chiang himself had kept a summer home there. But no longer. The city, like the rest of the country, was in disastrous shape. In less than a year China would officially be a Communist country, and Chiang would flee to Taiwan.

By the end of 1948, the U.S. military had no illusions about the outcome. The end was drawing near, and the withdrawal of troops was quickening. Almost all the countryside had come under Communist control. Manchuria had fallen, and Mao's armies were putting a stranglehold on the major cities. Finally it was Christmas, and Miriam Matthews held a last party for the children. The school was closing for good, and she described it to her parents:

December 25

I entertained twenty grade schoolers. I originally planned just to have my Chinese kids, the mascots, for a popcorn roast because they had never seen popcorn pop. When the kids started to pop corn, they didn't put the lid over the pan soon enough, and popcorn popped all over the kitchen, hitting everybody and everything. We all laughed so hard, no one thought of rushing to put the lid on the frying pan.

Good music was on the radio so I started teaching them to dance. How I wish you could meet this gang—they're so appreciative! I was very surprised to receive so many gifts from them, even my Chinese mascots brought gifts: candy, manicure set, jewelry.

Last night, Christmas Eve, went to church at 11 P.M. What a beautiful service. The church was packed, only a few civilians, all the rest servicemen. Some of the latter came down the aisle for communion staggering, but evidently not as bad as last year, because 2 weeks ago a Navy rule was put into effect throwing any drunken serviceman in the brig. Thank goodness, because the drinking out here is outrageous.

Perhaps the troops were celebrating the new year early, or toasting the end of U.S. involvement and their return home, for that was Matthews's last letter from China. Her ship departed 10 January 1949, just as Peking was falling to Mao's forces. The Nationalist commander surrendered with all his troops and later received a trusted position in Mao's regime.

Entering Peking, Mao's troops rode American-made trucks led by American-made tanks. The Communists won the civil war using Japanese arms secured through Russian benevolence in Manchuria, as well as American-supplied arms captured through the Nationalists. The United States had delivered the armaments to Chiang along with military advice, but Chiang had taken only the hardware. In the end, he lost both it and the war.

When Peking fell, the evacuation of Marines and sailors accelerated, as did chaos throughout the country. As George McDonald, Tom Barclay, Clayton Mattice, and other remaining Marines broke down lines, blew up ammo dumps, and loaded up supplies, the former Nationalists swarmed Tsingtao Harbor on foot, by bicycle, on crutches, begging the Americans to take them from China and the punishment they knew was close behind, at the hands of Mao's troops.

McDonald, the New Mexico cowboy who had become close to Charlie in the final days, was abruptly ordered onto a troopship. "Where's Charlie? What happened to Charlie?" he shouted to anyone coming from the Marine compound. No one knew. No one had seen him. Hopeless and angry, McDonald thought he would never see him again. Like the other Marines before him, McDonald had plotted to smuggle Charlie out of China, in a seabag perhaps, but in the end he'd feared he might get lost, be discovered and sent back, or worse, punished as a stowaway. So now all he could do from the deck of the rapidly filling troopship was witness the desperate scene on the docks below. It sickened him to see the Nationalist soldiers and supporters below, many ill, wounded, or near dead, pleading for American help. After all, the men of Love Company had served alongside many of them. Some stepped in front of trucks in a final attempt to escape the danger they felt lay ahead, and at night McDonald could hear the sick and wounded moaning on straw mats in the street.

All his life, McDonald would never be able to purge the scene from his memory, nor the helplessness he felt for not being able to save the Chinese boy he'd come to love as a brother.

◦

Miriam Matthews's departure was less chaotic but just as heart wrenching. On the day she left, Sister Blanda brought all the students left in Tsingtao, Charlie included, to say good-bye. On board, she wrote:

January 11, 1949

Well once again I'm out on the beautiful Pacific.

No one knows what will happen when the Communists come. The rumor leaked out that our Marines were leaving—so their departure is being delayed, although they're all packed. The Navy has only enough food and supplies to last till Jan. 25. Many critics feel that peace will come to China much quicker if the U.S. Navy pulls out—yet if rumors are true that Russian troops are already at Cheefoo—oh, who knows? Anyway, we're glad to get out of such an uncertain situation—at least physically.

The whole remaining school came to see us off. It was hardest to say "goodbye" to my Chinese mascots because they'll never get to the U.S.

For the next thirty-five years, she would wonder what became of Charlie and the others.

With most of the Marines gone and their compound at the university closed, Sister Blanda gathered up Charlie and the six other Chinese mascots and took them to the Chinese school, where they slept on bunk beds and lived for weeks in the basement with other refugees the nuns took in from the streets.

Though the Navy had offered the nuns safe passage out of China because of worsening conditions, Sister Blanda and the others initially declined, feeling responsible for the mission's Chinese nuns, whom the Navy said they could not take.

In the basement of the Chinese school, Charlie and the other boys settled in a corner of the room, and at night Sister Blanda sat with them, discussing Bible stories. All the boys thought their predicament would be temporary. After all, the Marines had told them they'd come back. "Hey, guys, it's not going to be long," Charlie told them. He was the most diligent of students, and therefore, they all felt, the wisest.

"The Communists will never stay in power. It may take a couple of weeks. It may take a couple of months, but the Marines will be back."

He absolutely believed this. They had told him so. Also, each Sunday for the next month, three Marines who had stayed behind (Tom Barclay and Arthur Buckley were two of them) to help with the last of the evacuation came to see them. "Charlie, are you okay?" they would ask. "Are you safe?"

"I'm okay," Charlie would answer, offering a smile. "The sisters treat us real good."

"Don't be sad," Barclay would say. "I wish I could take you with me. We all want to take you with us, but there's nothing we can do. One day though, we'll be back for you and take you Stateside."

At the docks, Sgt. Jerry Hanson tried to negotiate with a naval lieutenant to let the boy smuggle aboard the USS *Pasadena,* a cruiser docked at the end of Pagoda Pier that would take home all but twenty-two Marines, including Hanson. "The kid is one of us," he told the lieutenant, explaining that Charlie had kept the neatest bunk in the entire company. But permission was denied.

Hanson, who would spend his career in the Marines, also tried to get the company dog, Lockerbox, on the ship. The dog that barked and snapped at anyone Chinese except Charlie had been with the Marines—first Love Company, then Charlie Company—for three years. The men couldn't part with him. But the lieutenant said no to Lockerbox, too.

As had the others, Hanson told Charlie they'd come back for him someday. Then one Sunday no one came to see Charlie at the Chinese school. In the distance he could hear heavy artillery shells exploding, and he knew the Communists were closing in. Sister Blanda told the boys not to leave the school, but Charlie had to see why the Marines hadn't come to see him. He ran to the port facility where the Navy was based and where the few Marines who remained had moved after the compound closed. No one was there. The barracks were deserted, the doors boarded up, the building wrapped in barbed wire.

The Marines were gone. He stood in front weeping. Finally he headed back to the Chinese school and Sister Blanda. "Now I must put my life in the hands of God," he said to himself.

But he was scared. Chiang had warned the Chinese that life would be hard if the Communists won the civil war, and now they had. Charlie also knew that any association with the Nationalist government or the Americans would be dangerous. Then he thought of Sister Blanda's lessons, that it was noble to die for your beliefs. That eased his grief, and he wasn't scared anymore. Besides, he had Sister Blanda to protect him. Certainly she wouldn't leave too.

But just weeks later, in the middle of March 1949, as Charlie stood at a window of the school before dawn one morning watching torrents of rain beat against the glass, a taxi pulled up to the school. Five women rushed out and climbed into the car. With his face pressed against the window, he watched the car pull away, then disappear down the street. Later that morning, the two Chinese nuns who'd been left behind, Sister George (named for the German bishop in Tsingtao, George Weig) and Sister Adolph (after the spiritual director at the Milwaukee convent), told the boys that Sister Blanda and the other nuns were gone. Their Mother General in Milwaukee had wired them to return, and they'd accepted evacuation on one of the last Navy ships to leave Tsingtao.

"But Sister Blanda didn't even say good-bye," Charlie cried.

"It happened so quickly," Sister George explained. "The Navy said they had to leave immediately. There is such upheaval."

Now Charlie and the others were truly on their own, strangers in their own country.

As a great darkness fell over Charlie's life, the only light he had was from wishing stars. Two years earlier Ed Grady had told him that shooting stars were lucky, and that wishes would come true if you made them when you saw one. For the next thirty-five years, whenever he saw a shooting star, Charlie made his wish: "Dear God, please bring the Marines back to take me Stateside."

The earliest known photo of Charlie with three of the
first Marines to bring him to Tsingtao from Tsangkou Air
Base. Names of the Marines, members of Fox Company,
are unknown. Photo shot in 1945.
Courtesy Don Sexton

Charlie, suited up in his cut-down Marine overcoat,
salutes in front of the barracks at the Marine compound
in Tsingtao, 1945.
Courtesy Don Sexton

One of hundreds of shots taken with his Marine buddies, 1946. These three are members of Love Company. Seated, from left: Don Sexton, the Greensboro, North Carolina, mechanic who would play such a large role in Charlie's life; David Brooks, the fist-swinging Marine from North Carolina, who after China duty and tours in Korea and Vietnam would die in a suspicious fire in Albemarle, North Carolina. Standing, from left: Jack "Big Hutch" Hutchins, the Kentuckian who survived the bloody battle of Iwo Jima, wounded three times (he would be Charlie's guardian for ten months before going home); Ray Rosenwinkle.
Courtesy Don Sexton

Charlie and Robert Golden of Fox Company, 1945. To his mother, Golden wrote on the back of the photo: "This is Charlie and me. He has a carbine on his shoulder. Damn cute kid. That's not my jeep."
Courtesy Charlie Tsui

Two North Carolina boys, David Brooks (left) and Don Sexton, on liberty at the Great Tsingtao Cabaret, 1947. Spiffed-up and slicked-back before fighting their way out of the bar.
Courtesy Don Sexton

Charlie and several of his classmates, 1947. The Chinese mascot wearing fatigues and a hat, holding a baseball bat, is Jack Tufaro, the kid from Manchuria whom the Marines found running around orphaned. Charlie is to the left, three rows up. No one knows what happened to Jack.

Courtesy Sister Blanda

Charlie with William Bullard on left, William Marsh of Chicago on right.
Courtesy William Bullard

The Tsingtao American School. *Courtesy Charlie Tsui*

Charlie and his class with Sister Blanda, 1947. With Charlie is Lockerbox, Love Company's dog. *Courtesy Sister Blanda*

Sister Blanda in front of the school in 1947.
Courtesy Charlie Tsui

Charlie and his classmates in Sister Blanda's class at the Tsingtao American
School, 1948. Charlie is seated, framed by the window.
Courtesy Sister Blanda

The twin-spired St. Michael's Cathedral, on the highest point in Tsingtao. Charlie's grandfather was a laborer during construction of part of the church.

Courtesy Charlie Tsui

Bishop Fulton Sheen delivers the sermon during services at which Charlie and other Chinese mascots receive their first Holy Communion at St. Michael's Cathedral. Charlie is seated in the front row, second from right. *Courtesy Sister Blanda*

Charlie receives his first communion from Francis Cardinal Spellman of New York City. St. Michael's, 1947. Love Company's James "Dick" McIlvane is his sponsor. *Courtesy Sister Blanda*

The student body at the Tsingtao American School, with Sister Blanda.
Courtesy Charlie Tsui

Love Company's barracks in Tsingtao at the Marine compound, a former women's university built by Germans in the 1800s.
Courtesy Charlie Tsui

View of Tsingtao from the coast, 1947.
Courtesy Don Sexton

Charlie and Clayton Mattice, 1948.
Courtesy Charlie Tsui

Love Company's Roy Sibit of Ohio, 1948. He and Ray Brewington of Michigan taught Charlie to box. Sibit would later orchestrate the campaign to bring Charlie to America, only to have a nationally publicized falling-out. *Courtesy Don Sexton*

Three Love Company soldiers, from left: George McDonald, James "Dick" McIlvane, Tom Barclay. On liberty at Tsingtao Beach, 1948. *Courtesy Charlie Tsui*

One of the last photos shot by the Marines, 1948. The pants he is wearing were dyed black by his mother, so that Communist authorities could not tie them to Charlie's past with the Marines. He would wear them on special occasions, including on his wedding day, his graduation from agriculture school, and on Chinese New Year's Days. He plans to wear them to the ceremony that will make him and his family U.S. citizens.

Courtesy Don Sexton

5 The taxi took Sister Blanda to the dock, on that cold March morning in 1949. There she boarded a naval vessel, the USS *Anderson,* berthed in the harbor, battered by the wind. It was the second time she'd had to flee China, and this time she knew she would never return. She'd first come to Tsingtao in the midst of the Great Depression to build a school and serve her God as a missionary. She'd toiled for ten years, after which the Japanese had held her captive during World War II before sending her back to the United States. Four years later she'd returned, in a miserably cold February 1947, filled with hope and determination. But her sojourn was cut short two years later by a dedicated enemy of her God—Communists determined to weed out Christianity and uproot her labor.

Her leaving came so suddenly that there'd been no time to say good-bye to her little Marines, but because of bad weather, the ship couldn't sail for two days. So they remained in port. She was brokenhearted to leave, but there was nothing they could do. So as the nuns watched for the weather to clear, they talked about their concern for the boys and Chinese nuns they wished they could take with them.

What would happen to them now? The boys had lived such rich lives with the Americans, and now that was gone. She knew they were in for a hard time. As the *Anderson* pushed off and the city that had been her home for much of her life drifted from view, Sister Blanda and the other nuns prayed that their Chinese friends' lives would be spared in the strife that was certain to follow.

Sister Blanda returned to Milwaukee and the convent. After several weeks of rest and three more of substituting for a sick nun at a Milwaukee school, she was assigned to a junior high school in Arlington Heights, near Chicago. It was Easter Monday 1949 when Sister Blanda resumed her life as a nomadic teacher.

She moved from school to school, and whenever there was news of China, she followed it eagerly, thinking of Charlie and the other boys. She paid scarce attention to the Cold War and the "red scare" politics that were consuming America, but she followed school rules, forcing her students under desks during bomb drills.

Back in the States also was Miriam Matthews, who'd arrived before Sister Blanda. She took the train across country, enrolled in Franklin and Marshall University in Lancaster, Pennsylvania, to get her master's degree, and became director of Christian Education at First Presbyterian Church. That spring she met a young graduate student named Ernest Haddad and they began to date, he telling her of his dreams to be a minister, she regaling him with stories about her mission work in China.

They married a year later, in 1951, in Johnstown, in the church where Kirk West had filled her head with romantic stories of China. Then the newlyweds moved to New Jersey, where Ernie enrolled in Princeton Theological Seminary. During their three years in Princeton, two sons were born; after moving to Ernie's first church in Round Lake, Minnesota, the Haddads had twins, a boy and a girl.

While raising her family, Miriam continued with her Christian education at the First Presbyterian Church of Round Lake. At night, as she tucked them in and the icy Minnesota winds rattled the windows, Miriam told the children stories of China and the Chinese boys to whom she'd grown so close, and who, she worried, were now suffering.

After Sister Blanda left and before Mao's forces marched triumphantly into Tsingtao, Charlie and the other mascots lived in the basement of the orphanage. There they were cared for by the two Chinese nuns, Sister George and Sister Adolph. It was a frightening time. The nuns had seen the boys become devout Catholics and knew the danger they faced once the Communists captured Tsingtao. Besides, they had been Sister Blanda's favorites, and she had left with one request: to look after them as long as it was safe, then see that they got home safely.

From the orphanage, they could hear artillery echoing in the Laoshan Mountains as the battle drew closer. Starvation gripped the city. Rumors of what would happen to foes swirled in the wind, casting an even greater chill, yet the orphanage provided a temporary haven, a few months' sanctuary—food, and a semblance of normalcy.

The letters from Jack Tufaro to Miriam Matthews tell the poignant tale. One of the seven mascots and the one for whom Matthews felt most sorry, Jack was a twelve-year-old refugee from Manchuria who'd been tormented by other children in Tsingtao. The Marines had saved his life, having found him in the streets being chased by other children. Had they not taken him with them, he surely would have died. But what would happen to Jack now? His protectors were gone.

His three letters were written in ink, with fine penmanship, on Marine Corps stationery, with the globe and anchor, embossed "Semper Fidelis."

February 9, 1949

Dear Miss Matthews.

Have you receive my letter yet?

Tonight I got my scold from Sister, I was fight with a small boy in my room when I stay now. I moved out of compound two Mondays ago. 12 of us live in one room in St. Joseph School, "Chinese Girl's School." The Chinese Sisters will taking care all of us. We are fine so far. Do you want to say anything to these boys? I have hurry finish this letter, before is bed time. I hope you can making out this letter.

In school we can't playing softball any more, not even basketball game, two children in each team we played today and yesterday. Not one of girl playing with us.

What ever we do, I hope it's coming just right. I am nervous, I hope that you are not mind. I can't write anymore on this one.

Jack

March 28

Dear Miss Matthews,

I received two letters of your's this month. I was glad to have letters from you. I also want to thank you for it. You know those letters that you wrote to me, Sister read it. After she read it then she gave it to me.

After school I have to study about almost three hours, before I can playing outside. I try make myself happy as I can, but some time I still feeling sad when I go to bed.

Sister also bought a pair glasses for me for school use. Now we have only two Chinese Sisters here. We been moved out of basement to a classroom. Four of us live in one room about 13 feet long 11 feet wide, one double bed in here. It's old and looking one too. I thinks things get worse all the time. Just got to get used to it. I don't know what's good for me since I moved out of compound.

Right here I got to the church everyday—sometimes two or three times in one day.

I haven't see any communist long's I know in the streets.

Did you get a job yet? Please answer soon, I'm get often lonesome in here. I hope you can understand this letter.

Good by
Jack

That was the last Matthews heard from Jack. No one knows what happened to him.

That February and March, Sister George and Sister Adolph made Jack and the other boys study hard. Their Chinese language skills had been neglected; in the years with the Marines they'd spoken mostly English, and their studies with Sister Blanda had been in English. Unschooled before the Marines had adopted them, they were essentially illiterate in Mandarin, their native language. They could not read or write Chinese, and their speech had become tentative. So the nuns drove them hard, knowing how the boys would be stigmatized when the Communists took over. They would not be considered orphans, but tainted children raised by Marines—foreign soldiers: the enemy.

Compounding the boys' problem was the fact they were now devout Catholics, anathema to the Communists.

Not a day went by that the boys didn't talk about—even pray for—the Marines to return and rescue them from certain punishment.

"I hope those guys keep their promise and come back for us soon," Pie Chu told Charlie one day.

"They will," Charlie said confidently. "Marines always keep their promises."

But at last, fearing for their safety and knowing they themselves could not protect the boys—and the boys' situation might in fact be more perilous in the orphanage—the nuns told Sister Blanda's little Marines to go home to their families. That night Charlie found Pie Chu crying in the room. "I don't know what to do," he sobbed. "I have no place to go; I have no home."

Pie Chu, a year younger than Charlie and from a village only five miles from his, had been like a little brother, and Charlie felt responsible for him. "You can come home with me," Charlie comforted him.

And so, two days before the Communists started streaming into the city, Charlie and Pie Chu stuffed their possessions into backpacks and duffel bags: including their uniforms, letters, books, photos, all the evidence of their Marine life. The nuns hired a two-horse wagon to take them the ten miles up Shilu Road to Charlie's village. Before leaving, they said their farewells to the others. "Be safe," they wished one another, "And don't forget your prayers," they added, just like Sister Blanda had told them at the end of each school day.

Then they were off, the wagon pulling the two boys up the bumpy road that Charlie had ridden countless times in Love Company's mail truck. Along the way they didn't talk; instead, Charlie studied the wagon, thinking it looked like the stagecoaches he'd seen in the cowboy movies at the compound. From his duffel bag he pulled out his harmonica and began to play "Home on the Range," the first song that Poncho Groves had taught him. The music cheered the two, breaking the monotony of the horses' clopping against the hard, potholed road.

It was a depressing end to an adventure that had begun nearly four years earlier, when he'd climbed into a coal-burning truck with grizzled warriors headed for the fabled city. There he'd lived a life of spit-shined shoes, marching, bikes and movies, swimming and school. But perhaps it wasn't the end, he thought. This is just a temporary separation, he consoled himself. His buddies again were just going back to their homes for a while, and so was he.

That prospect—seeing his family again—lifted his spirits as they approached the village. But the homecoming wasn't what he'd expected. When his parents saw him still in his Marine uniform, they were terrified, knowing the Communists would punish anyone whose ideology differed from theirs. Any association with the Nationalists or foreigners could lead to disaster. "You mean the Marines didn't take you with them?" Charlie's father asked nervously. "They've been gone a month. How come you didn't come home earlier? We thought you left with them."

Charlie told them about the orphanage, then introduced Pie Chu. "He was with me in the Marines. I feel badly for him; he has no place to go. I couldn't leave him on the street."

Though profoundly uncomfortable with this development—now there were two uniformed children—Charlie's family took in Pie Chu. But the next day the two boys walked back to Tsingtao. Maybe everyone wasn't gone; maybe some Marines were left, after all. They found no one, and hiked the ten miles back home. Then, two days later, they decided to walk into town again—just in case.

As they walked along Shilu Road, they could see Mao's vast army lumbering toward Tsingtao, soldiers on foot, horses carrying the heavy provisions and weapons. The peasant army never walked in the road, but along fields or through ditches, and they didn't bother the boys. The trip was futile that day, as it was two days later—they found no one at the compound.

Finally convinced the Marines were gone for good, they started home. Walking along the compound wall, they saw a man at the main gate desperately looking for someone, asking questions of everyone he saw. Suddenly Pie Chu turned in another direction. "What's the matter?" Charlie asked, holding onto his jacket.

Then the man started running toward them, calling out.

"Do you know him?" Charlie asked. "He seems to know you."

Pie Chu lowered his head in embarrassment: "He's my father."

The man reached them, a huge grin on his face. "I've come looking for you every day since the Americans left. Where have you been? I've been so worried."

Why had Pie Chu lied about having no place to go, Charlie wondered as the three walked back to Chukechuang in silence, Pie Chu unwilling to meet his gaze.

Later, after Pie Chu and his father ate with Charlie's family and before they left for their village, Pie Chu told Charlie that his family was so poor, and life with the Marines so rich, that he couldn't face going home to his old life. He apologized for making up the story, but now he could see his father's concern and that fate had brought them back together for a reason.

Charlie was proud of his own father's willingness to take in Pie Chu, but he saw his relief when he left: they would be safer now. Pie Chu would have caused trouble.

As it turned out, however, Pie Chu fared better than Charlie. Pie Chu joined the Communist Party and prospered. A different fate awaited Charlie.

Fate is often a missed connection—a moment's delay, a cab pulling to the curb as another leaves. In Charlie's case, there were still Marines in Tsingtao those days when Charlie and Pie Chu walked to town—twenty-two of them on Pagoda Pier, including Jerry Hanson.

It was Hanson who had unsuccessfully negotiated with the Navy lieutenant to smuggle Charlie and Lockerbox, the company dog, aboard a cruiser. After the Marines left China, Hanson and the others remained behind to mop up the evacuation. They ran a switchboard in the old U.S. consulate building, to keep naval officers on shore at the Edgewater Hotel connected to the ships.

By May 1949, order had been restored at the docks. The occupying Communist troops left the twenty-two Americans alone, though looters constantly hit the supply depot where the Americans worked day and night to load the ships. On 25 May, Hanson and the others boarded a cruiser. When it sailed from Pagoda Pier, the last Americans were gone, and the colorful era of the China Marines was over.

Gone too were the Chinese nuns. Sister George had family in Tsingtao, and as the city grew dangerous, a cousin persuaded Nationalist soldiers to smuggle the nuns out of the country dressed as soldiers, their habits in bundles. They caught a ship to Hong Kong and there had a difficult time convincing authorities that they were Catholic nuns. When their identities were proved, they were eventually allowed to emigrate. They went to Milwaukee and reunited with Sister Blanda and the other nuns. They too never returned to China.

It was good fortune that Sister George and Sister Adolph got out when they did: they would not have fared well under the Communists. It was lucky that Chiang Kai-shek got out when he did, too. The collapse of Nationalist-led China was like an implosion. Chiang's world crumbled before his eyes. Wherever he fled to escape Mao's armies, they fell upon him again.

Mao's army entered Peking in March 1949. Nanking, Chiang's capital, fell on 27 April. Wuhan was taken on 16 May, and Shanghai captured on 27 May, two days after Jerry Hanson and the last Americans in Tsingtao left the country.

By June, 1,500,000 Kuomintang troops had deserted the Nationalist cause, and another 700,000 would cross over to the Communists by the end of the year. Chiang fled to Chungking, then Chengtu, Kuangchow, Hainan, and finally, on 8 December, he left the mainland for Taiwan. But that was just a postscript; the real end had come months before.

On 1 October 1949, in Peking, Mao Tse-tung, standing on the Tien An Men—the Gate of Heavenly Peace—proclaimed the People's Republic of China: "The Chinese people have stood up . . . nobody will insult us again."[1]

Those chilling words would reverberate for decades, and they still cast a pall over U.S.-Chinese relations. For China's new leaders bore deep hatred for the United States because of its support of Chiang after the anti-Japanese war. Mao and the Communists were in power beholden to no one. They had won the civil war almost entirely on their own. The Soviet Union had given no significant help, and Stalin, with little faith in the future of the Chinese Communist Party after the end of World War II, had maintained correct diplomatic relations with the Kuomintang until the end.

Angry and isolated, China drew a "bamboo curtain" around itself. But China struck out only a few months later, when hostilities erupted in Korea. This formalized a feud with the United States that endured for decades. Only now, half a century later, is the curtain parting, though distrust continues and relations remain tenuous.

By the new decade, Communist troops from North Korea would cross the 38th parallel, and new legions of American forces would come between warring factions. In the United States, McCarthyism stirred anticommunist passions.

Jack Hutchins paid little attention. His war was over, Iwo Jima five years past, his wounds healed, and he was back in America contributing to the postwar baby boom.

Discharged from the Marines at Great Lakes Naval Base in Michigan, he asked a buddy to wait to send his seabag to Kings Mountain, Kentucky, until he got home first. But when he arrived at his parent's doorstep, his seabag had beaten him there and his parents were waiting for him.

That night, he and his father, Holt Lafayette, sat comparing their wars. The older Hutchins had lost the use of his hands in World War I, and his family had been told not to expect him to live. He did, but developed a dependency on morphine, given him by Army doctors to ease his pain. Ora Hutchins got her husband off drugs, but he transferred his addiction to alcohol. The night their son came home from China, little had changed—H. L. was drinking heavily. Still, he wanted to know about Iwo Jima.

"It was bad, Pa," Big Hutch said. "That's all I can say. A lot of friends of mine died on that island."

Then he told his parents about China, and little Charlie, though they already knew about him from Hutch's letters. Reaching into his seabag, he pulled out a photo album and showed them pictures of the two together.

"What's going to happen to him?" his mother asked.

Hutch shook his head. "There was no way to get him out. I talked to our chaplain about it, but he didn't think it would be possible. I don't know what's going to happen to him."

His mother hugged him. "We'd be glad to have him," she said.

The next day Hutch drove into Hazel Green to see Eula Mae. Three months later they were married and soon started their contribution to the baby boom with a daughter named Pamela. The young family moved to Berea, Kentucky, where Hutch went to college on the GI Bill, majoring in geology. He played a little basketball, until he decided that was taking too much time away from his family. So he concentrated on geology, becoming familiar with the minerals and rock formations of western and central Kentucky, a knowledge that would serve him well in the years to come.

He wrote Charlie faithfully and sent him clothes, and for a while Charlie wrote back, or there were reports about him from Marines just home from China, passing through Kentucky. But the stories grew grimmer, and soon the letters stopped. He wrote the State Department asking if there wasn't a way to get Charlie out. "Can I go over and get him?"

"With the Communists now in control, we can't get anybody out, much less get anybody into the country," a representative told him. "I suggest you forget about him."

He couldn't do that, of course. "That's my little brother," he told Pamela, showing her pictures. "You're going to see him someday."

But then his own letters came back marked "Undeliverable," and he began to fear that Charlie would die because of his friendship with Love Company.

Everyone who'd known Charlie left China wondering how he would fare after the country fell. But soon their lives and thoughts moved on. Sister Blanda was teaching junior high school; Miriam Matthews and her husband, Ernie, were moving from congregation to congregation, raising a family. Fred McGowan returned to Michigan, and instead of going on his long-delayed honeymoon with Mary Ellen, he went straight to work making refrigerators at the Gibson Frigerator Company. Their plans for a family put on hold because of the war, the couple got to work on that too, with daughter Carma born in the summer of 1947, David in 1949, and Patricia two years after that.

Discharged in June 1947, J. C. Lacey went home to Birmingham, and loafed for three months before reenrolling in his senior year at Jones Valley High School. He didn't get his diploma, dropping out again after three months, but he did meet Charlotte Bailey, and in January 1948, they married. J. C. used the GI Bill to train as a plumber and pipe fitter, then to get a low-interest mortgage to buy a house in Birmingham, where they raised five children—three sons and two daughters, all two years apart.

Love Company turned into Baby Company, with everyone doing more than his share. George McDonald came home in April 1949, and instead of going back to Houston, he moved to New Mexico, where he too used the GI Bill at New Mexico Western University in Silver City. With his new Mormon wife, Patricia, he raised eight children—four boys and four girls. For a while he toyed with airplane mechanics in California, but then moved the family back to New Mexico and McDonald started a business that serviced the oil fields straightening pipes.

In New Jersey and later in Connecticut, Ed Grady was climbing the corporate ladder of an electrical supply company. He and his wife, Mary, had three children.

David Brooks, the North Carolina boy whose idea of a great time was fighting sailors in drunken bar brawls, stayed in the Marines, naturally, married Mona Cranford of Albemarle, and they too started a family—two sons and a daughter—in between his assignments, first to Korea, later to Vietnam.

Charles Robertson also stayed in the Marines, but he'd started his family much earlier. In fact, it was in Tsingtao where he'd seen his child for the first time—in January 1947 when his wife, Betty, arrived to join him. His daughter Marsha was twenty-six months old, born while Robertson was in the Pacific. Another child was born in Tsingtao. In January 1948, Robertson left China for his new assignment as commanding officer, Marine Barracks, Naval Ammunition Depot, Fort Mifflin, just outside Philadelphia. To his surprise he discovered that his new command consisted of all-black troops, transferred from Fort McAllister in Oklahoma. Because of the still-pervasive racism of the times, the nearby town did not accept the troops' presence while on liberty.

For two years Robertson commanded one of the last segregated units

in the U.S. military. Though President Truman had ordered the desegre-
gation of the services, de facto integration would not come until the
Korean conflict broke out. In 1952 Robertson commanded some of the
same black soldiers again, but this time in a desegregated unit.

But Robertson didn't get to Korea as quickly as he wanted. Promoted to major, he was assigned to the 8th Marine Regiment, 2d
Marine Division, readying for Korea at Camp Lejeune in North Carolina, but he had to wait almost two years. His China service prevented
him from another overseas assignment so soon.

Don Sexton and William Bullard ended up in their native North
Carolina, too. Sexton, discharged 31 October 1947, arrived home in
his Marine dress blues late on Halloween night, surprising his parents,
who thought he was the last trick-or-treater. The three stayed up into
the next morning talking, but the main thing on Sexton's mind was his
girlfriend, Pauline Gunn. He'd written her faithfully in China and she'd
written back, but then the letters had stopped.

"She's married," his mother, Elsie, told him. "Fell in love with a
sailor, and they got married."

The news devastated Don. He'd known Pauline most of his life; she
grew up not two hundred yards from his house. When he joined the
Marines she promised to be faithful to him, saying she'd wait for his
return. Now she was married to another man—a sailor! Down in the
dumps and with no job prospects, Don went to work for his father,
Raymond. The elder Sexton had opened Sexton Wholesale Company
partly with money that Don had sent from China. Sexton Wholesale
was run from the home—combs, wallets, key chains, candy bars, and
penny candy delivered to country stores in the family station wagon.
Don worked eighteen months for his father, never getting a salary but
always an uneasy look when he asked for the station wagon to take his
new girlfriend, Arrie Ammons, to dinner and a movie.

Raymond Sexton was a heavy drinker, off on two-week binges
sometimes, and Don took responsibility for the business and for the
support of his mother, sister, and brother. As it turned out, the candy
and combs were a front for Raymond's real business—slot machines
and punchcards in a numbers racket that he ran. Don knew this was
illegal, but it was his family's main income. So with his father drinking

himself into stupors, Don delivered the machines himself, and brought broken ones back to the house for repair.

One day, federal agents raided the stores supplied by Sexton Wholesale and confiscated the slot machines they found. The older Sexton wouldn't go to retrieve the other ones, but he was willing to let his son get arrested, and he sent him.

After that, Don had had enough. He got out of the business and married Arrie in August 1949, the day after she turned nineteen (he was twenty). They joined the baby boom, too. When Arrie was in the hospital delivering their first child, Arlene, Don went to his parents' for dinner. As he drove up to the house, Greensboro police were escorting his father out in handcuffs. He'd been caught selling pornographic movies. Somebody had fingered Raymond, tipping the police that they could find movie reels on the back porch.

With his father in prison and a new family to support, Don moved from job to job until he settled on a trade learning to rebuild motors, for which the GI Bill paid him ninety dollars a month. His brother, Raymond Jr., had a race car, and in 1948, four months after Don's return from China, Ray, driver Melvin Glaston, and a pit crew that included Don raced a 1939 Ford coupe in NASCAR's (the National Association for Stock Car Auto Racing) first circuit. Don had always loved tinkering with motors. He got a job with Teasley's Garage making twenty-five dollars a week, rebuilding and modifying engines used on the racetrack—and engines used by bootleggers trying to outrun federal agents on Thunder Road. The cars, usually Fords, were rigged high in back with heavy shock absorbers: when they were loaded with moonshine, they hugged the ground.

Soon Don left Teasley's, to open his own four-stall garage. In his spare time he bolted a high-powered modified engine to his own 1939 Ford Coupe race car and taught Arrie how to drive it. Life was good. Don worked in the garage, Arrie in a beauty shop, and on weekends, they traveled from track to track. Business at his shop was good, too. In addition to modifying race-car engines for bootleggers, Don repaired vehicles for several used-car lots and two trucking firms.

Then he got a contract to keep the cars of the state Alcohol Beverage Control Board running fast. On some days he'd have state ABC vehicles in one bay, souped up to catch bootleggers, and in the bay beside it a bootlegger's souped-up car. Both the law and the lawbreakers were paying him. It was the best of all possible worlds.

It was not such a good world just down the road in Autryville. Little had changed when William Bullard returned to the family farm in October 1948 on leave. Planning to make a career in the Marines and hoping for another tour in China, where this time he'd get Charlie out, Bullard was joyriding in his 1940 Pontiac with a buddy on Christmas Eve when, rounding a sharp curve, the car jumped a ditch and hit a giant oak head-on.

Bullard lay unconscious in a Fayetteville hospital for twenty-one days, then was transferred to a Veterans Administration Hospital, where doctors told his parents his prospects for total recovery were not good. One eye remained closed for a year, and the events surrounding the accident remain fuzzy to this day. The only thing clear about the wreck was that Bullard's career in the Marines was over. So were his hopes of getting Charlie out of China.

In China, the tidal wave of Communism swept over even remote Chukechuang, forever changing the world of Charlie TuShu, and not for the better. Martial law was declared. Troops arrested thousands of people as counterrevolutionaries and put them in prison or summarily executed them. Fearing that the Communists would arrest her son and harm her family because of his friendship with the Americans, Charlie's mother told her husband to dig a hole behind their hut, where he could hide.

His father dug a three-foot-deep hole, and there Charlie lived for two weeks, sleeping on hay and covered by cornstalks, telling time by the light of day. Still dressed in the Marine uniform he'd worn home, Charlie shivered from the cold of the early 1949 winter, eating the food his mother smuggled out to him. At the end of the second week, ten Communist soldiers moved into the old garrison in the village, once manned by Japanese troops. Tipped off by a neighbor that Charlie was in hiding, three soldiers came to the Tsui home.

"We know your son is hiding," they told his mother. "Don't worry, we're not going to hurt him. We just want to know where he's hiding."

Reluctantly, Charlie's mother led them behind the house and called for Charlie to come out. She watched as the mound of hay and cornstalks rustled, then her son slowly pulled himself from the hole, body stiff and eyes squinting from the blinding sunlight, his Marine greens stained from the black dirt. Though his back ached and he had trouble standing, it was good to be out. But seeing the concern on his mother's face, his joy disappeared.

"The soldiers want to talk to you," she said. "They promised not to hurt you."

Facing the soldiers, Charlie nodded his head in courtesy but said nothing. Four years with the Marines speaking mostly English made him hesitant about his native language. He was afraid this would show if he spoke. The three soldiers appraised the strange, dirt-covered figure before them. "Don't be frightened," one finally said. "We know all about you. We know you were with the American soldiers and they left you behind. Now you have to start your life over. Our new government will protect poor people. We'll make sure everybody gets food to eat. There will be no more foreign invasions. The foreign soldiers are gone forever."

"The United States is your enemy now," another soldier said. "Make sure you obey the new laws and never speak or even think about your past."

The last sentence resonated in Charlie's head. He knew they were talking about the Marines. He was to forget them, all his buddies, all his past. Of course he couldn't do that, any more than he could his religion, and it took great restraint to keep from lashing out at the soldiers. After they left, Charlie's mother frantically gathered up her son's Marine possessions—uniforms, books, papers, even the notebook with all the American addresses of his buddies—and began to burn them.

"This is evidence they will use against you," she warned, tossing his Marine green trousers into the fire."

"No!" Charlie shouted, snatching them from the flames. "You can't destroy these. I won't let you do it."

Seeing her son's grief and understanding his loss, his mother relented. But to be safe, she dyed the trousers black.

6 Charlie knew the Marines had left Tsingtao, but God was still there. So each Sunday morning he rose at five o'clock and
walked the Shilu Road to be at 8:00 A.M. mass at St. Michael's. What
made the three-hour walk bearable was pretending he was on a hike
with the Marines, then seeing the twin spires of the cathedral looming
over the city. After mass he walked three hours back, a round trip of
twenty miles. One Sunday three months after returning home, he
found the church shut up, with two huge boards nailed crisscrossed in
an X over the front doors.

"What happened?" he asked several elderly men on the street.

Unwilling to answer at first, they whispered among themselves.
Then one said: "Don't talk about the church anymore. You'll be
arrested if you try to enter it again. It's against the law now to practice
religion."

Charlie walked home in despair. Everyone had deserted him; he didn't
even have a place to pray anymore. But that wasn't true, he realized;
they could close his church, but they couldn't take away his God. They
couldn't make him disbelieve. He would pray in English, he decided,
and with lifted spirits continued on, though it would be years before he
returned to Tsingtao. Why go back? His friends were gone, his church
closed.

Still, he could not reconcile himself to the reality his Marine buddies
were gone forever. There had to be a way to see them again. He saw his

chance a year later, when North Korea attacked South Korea on 25 June 1950. After the initial attack was halted and Douglas MacArthur counterattacked at Inchon, threatening to cross the 38th parallel into North Korea, Chou En-lai, China's foreign minister, warned that China would not "supinely tolerate their North Korean neighbors being savagely invaded by imperialists."[1]

Fearing that U.S. troops would defeat North Korea and perhaps cross the Yalu River into China itself, Mao put out a call for one million conscripts to aid North Korea. MacArthur's troops did cross the 38th parallel. They captured the capital, Pyongyang, and started a major attack toward the Yalu, the border with China. Spearheading the attack were U.S. Marines.

Surely, Charlie thought, if he volunteered, he'd be sent to Korea. There he could slip across the lines somehow and be reunited with his buddies—Hutchins, Grady, Sexton, Sibit, Bullard, McDonald—all of them. In his mind he envisioned them as before, unchanged, unaged, and they would welcome him as a lost brother. If his plan failed, he would return as a warrior for China, and the Communists would forgive his past. But his father disapproved. "I do not want you to risk your life," he said.

"Father, it's the only way to clear my name," Charlie replied. "The Communists don't trust me because I was with the Marines, but if I go to Korea and risk my life, I'll be an honorable citizen and they'll leave me alone."

Maybe he was right, his father thought, and gave his permission to sign up. In eager anticipation of seeing his buddies again, Charlie went to the county office to volunteer.

Korea had lain in a state of limbo after World War II, as had another Asian country, Vietnam, already bogged down in the French-Indochina War. Independent since the seventh century, Korea had been conquered and annexed by Japan in 1910. Promised a vague and general independence by the Cairo Declaration in 1943, the country was officially divided in 1945 by the Potsdam Conference into two separate occupation zones, under the auspices of the newly formed United Nations.

South of the 38th parallel, under the influence of the United States was the Republic of Korea, while the Soviets established the Democratic Republic of Korea north of the 38th parallel. To unify the country free elections were mandated, but Russia refused to allow UN commissioners into their zone, and no ballots were ever cast. Tension between the governments of Kim Il Sung in the North and Syngman Rhee in the South grew as each sought dominance. Charges of aggression and interference were hurled at one another, but a fragile peace held until June 1950, when General MacArthur reported from Tokyo that "North Korea struck like a cobra." Their army swept over the 38th parallel, overran all resistance, and captured Seoul, the South Korean capital, within four days.

"This is war against the United Nations," Secretary General Trygve Lie declared, and the United States rushed a resolution through the Security Council calling for armed resistance to the aggression. The measure passed only because the Soviet Union boycotted the meeting, and President Harry Truman immediately authorized naval, air, and ground countermeasures, all under MacArthur's command. Was America at war again so soon?

No, Truman stated: There was no war in Korea. He was asked at a press conference: "Would it be correct to call it a police action under the United Nations?" He responded: "Yes, that is exactly what it amounts to."[2]

It was a police action that ultimately would end in 100,000 U.S. casualties. Perhaps it was inevitable, for the temperature of the Cold War had been dropping steadily since the end of World War II. With the descent of the Iron Curtain, the separation of Germany into two countries, a Soviet attempt to starve out Berlin with a blockade, the loss of China to Communism, Ho Chi Minh's war against the French, and now a Communist attack in Korea, temperatures had dipped into the arctic range.

A hundred years after Karl Marx and Friedrich Engels had written that "a specter is haunting Europe, the specter of Communism,"[3] that specter became a hobgoblin for Americans. Indeed, there was levity in America in 1950—Milton Berle prancing and cross-dressing on the Texaco Star Theater (earning $6,500 a week); Gorgeous George wrestling in an ermine jockstrap, his golden ringlets falling over outrageous sequin-and-satin costumes (earning $70,000 a year); *South Pacific* in the middle of its record four-year Broadway run; roller derbies; the top-rated television show, *Your Hit Parade*. But a dark mood also gripped the country.

George Orwell's *1984* topped fiction best-seller lists, frightening readers with its totalitarian Big Brother, while on the political stage, real events proved even more threatening. On 5 August 1949, the U.S. State Department had issued a 1,054-page White Paper, announcing that the world's most populated country had fallen into Communist hands. That was not surprising news for Miriam Matthews and Jack Hutchins, Don Sexton, and the other Marines who'd been in Tsingtao. But a few weeks later, truly terrifying news was released.

"Are you sure? Are you sure?" Truman demanded when told that B-29 photographs of Soviet radioactivity material confirmed that the Russians possessed the atomic bomb, a full decade earlier than had been predicted. When the administration publicly released the news a month later, hysteria swept the land. People knew the destruction that the bomb could cause—they had seen the terrible aftermath of Hiroshima and Nagasaki. But now the Russians had the bomb and could wipe out American cities.

How had they gotten it? The only answer was espionage, and the Red Scare began in earnest, led by a young congressman on the House Un-American Activities Committee—Richard Nixon. In the hysteria, Nixon made Alger Hiss, a confidant of President Roosevelt, and Whittaker Chambers, a journalist and former Communist, household names. In January 1950, Hiss was accused of giving secrets to the Russians and convicted of perjury, leading many to believe that the Russians had infiltrated the highest reaches of the U.S. government. Congressman Robert Rich of Pennsylvania even accused Secretary of State Dean Acheson of being on Stalin's payroll. But that was just the beginning.

When Truman announced that work had begun on a hydrogen bomb that January, Albert Einstein went on television to warn that "radioactivity poisoning of the atmosphere and, hence, annihilation of any life on earth, has been brought within the range of possibilities. General annihilation beckons."[4]

Suddenly bomb shelters started to look like a good investment, especially after Scotland Yard announced the arrest of Dr. Klaus Fuchs, a British physicist, for selling American atomic secrets to the Russians.

Then madness took over. Joseph McCarthy, an obscure U.S. senator from Wisconsin, gave a speech in Wheeling, West Virginia, accusing the State Department of harboring 205 card-carrying Communists—he had their names and documentation of their treachery. Though the number changed to 57 and then 108 and eventually was never confirmed, it made no difference—China was gone, Stalin had the bomb, and spies were in the State Department.

A witch-hunt began for traitors. Black lists were drawn up. Delirium in the form of pathological fear of Communism swept the country just as North Korean troops swept over the 38th parallel. Seoul fell quickly. South Korea was overrun and nearly half its 65,000 defenders killed, wounded, or taken prisoner.

Only an immediate infusion of U.S. combat troops could save the country, MacArthur cabled Truman. They were sent, and in September the seventy-year-old general launched one of the boldest moves in military history, the amphibious landing at Inchon. By 1 October 1950, the army of North Korea was virtually destroyed—half captured, the other half struggling to get back home. But then MacArthur made one of military history's greatest blunders. Completely misreading the intent, and even verbal warnings from China, he sent his army across the 38th parallel to pursue the North Koreans, taking the capital and Wonsan. From there he announced a major pincer attack—Eighth Army one claw, Xth Corps the other—that would destroy the North Koreans and have his own men "home by Christmas."

Having warned after Inchon that China would not tolerate an "imperialist" attack, Chou En-lai formally told India's ambassador in October that China would enter the war if the Americans crossed the 38th parallel. The message was transmitted to Washington through New Delhi, Moscow, and Stockholm, and it was published in all the world's leading newspapers. Nevertheless, MacArthur dismissed the threat as "diplomatic blackmail" and assured Truman that there was little danger of Chinese intervention. Even if they did enter the war, there was nothing to fear. "There would be the greatest slaughter," he predicted.[5]

He meant, of course, the slaughter of Chinese, but that was because his intelligence reports were wrong. He thought there were 300,000 Chinese troops in Manchuria, with only 50,000 to 60,000 of them able to cross the Yalu. In reality, Mao had amassed 850,000 troops along the border and sent 120,000, the vanguard of his veteran Fourth Field Army, across the Yalu into Korea, with more slipping over nightly.

MacArthur had no clue. In fact, so confident was he that his battle plan would end the war, he made sure his troops got a hot turkey dinner that Thanksgiving, the day before the attack. He boldly stated that they would all "eat Christmas dinner at home."[6]

But three days later, on 26 November 1950, Omar Bradley, chairman of the Joint Chiefs, telephoned Truman. "A terrible message has come from General MacArthur. The Chinese have come in with both feet."

Thirty-three divisions of 300,000 men attacked, overwhelming UN lines and trapping the 1st Marine Division at the Chosin Reservoir.

Sgt. Jerry Hanson, assigned to the 1st Marine Division after leaving China as one of the last twenty-two Americans in Tsingtao, had participated in the landing at Inchon. He had taken MacArthur at his word: In a matter of weeks, he and his men would be home decorating their Christmas trees.

But now, nine miles from the Chosin Reservoir and suddenly surrounded by Chinese troops, he didn't see how that was possible. For, as Gen. Chesty Puller had described it: "The enemy is in front of us, behind us, to the left of us, and to the right of us. They won't escape this time."

For Hanson, wounded on Guam in World War II, there seemed no end to fighting in Korea in the early months. The days blurred with constant battles and skirmishes, and the troops were always on the move. Clues that it wouldn't be the cakewalk MacArthur had predicted came early. After the landing at Inchon, Hanson and eleven other Marines, along with a Navy lieutenant who was fluent in Korean, were ordered to swim the Han River and take control of three hills on the other side. There, he and three Marines left the group to scout the hills. But in a village, North Korean troops fired on them, and they fled a hundred yards across a rice paddy as bullets nipped at their feet all the way back to the river.

Hanson expected the cheering North Koreans to pursue them across the river, but the Navy officer said they were just celebrating. Then his voice dropped and grew in astonishment. "Uh oh," he shouted, "they're coming after us!" The thirteen hit the water, splitting up in threes and fours and swimming as fast as they could.

Hanson didn't know it at the time, but things would get gravely worse. Two months later near Koterie, on the way to the Chosin Reservoir, American and South Korean troops found themselves outnumbered ten to one by Chinese troops. U.S. Army officers still refused to believe that the Americans had made contact with Mao's army. They fought for days, then word came to make a break for it. They would go to the port of Hungnam, then be evacuated by ship. But getting out was harder than getting in. They took awful casualties.

From Hungnam, they went to Pusan and then Masan, to resupply and get replacements. It had been a hell of a way to spend Christmas 1950. If the Chinese hadn't jumped in, Hanson would have been home. But he stayed another year in Korea and made the first combat helicopter landing, taking Hill 886, the "Punchbowl," just above the 38th parallel.

That landing established how another war on the same Asian continent would be fought a few years later—with Hanson, David Brooks, and Charles Robertson in Vietnam, too. For Marines, war isn't optional attendance.

Maj. Charles Robertson was itching to get to Korea: "It might be a lousy war," as the Marine saying goes, "but it's the only one we got."

The problem for Robertson, a veteran of World War II and attacks from the Chinese Communists in China, was that he wasn't eligible to go to Korea, having come back from an overseas assignment just two years before. He had to wait his turn, along with others at Camp Lejeune. By the time he got to Korea in October 1952, staged from Camp Pendleton in California after cold-weather training up at Bishop, he'd missed the great battles—the landing at Inchon and the battle of the "Frozen Chosin," where the famous line was spoken by the Marine commander, Oliver Smith: "Retreat hell! We're just attacking in a different direction."[7]

Though Robertson had missed the big action, Korea started hot and stayed that way for his entire tour. His first day in combat was a thirty-six-hour reconnaissance patrol. His unit, 3d Battalion, 1st Marines, was set in a defensive position holding the main road from the border to Seoul. Their mission was to try to contain four Chinese armies attempting to break through.

The police action had turned into a bitter stalemate. After the Chosin Reservoir fiasco, MacArthur wanted to pursue the war into China itself. He requested permission to cross the Yalu with a half million Chinese Nationalist troops from Formosa and two Marine divisions, after which he planned to drop thirty to fifty atomic bombs at strategic points in Manchuria. He was denied, and in April 1951, President Truman fired him.

MacArthur returned to address a joint session of Congress, leaving his audience in tears with his "Old soldiers never die, they just fade away" speech. He was given a ticker-tape parade in New York City, where 2,859 tons of litter were dropped, four times the previous record for General Eisenhower.

Gen. Matthew Ridgway replaced MacArthur as supreme commander, Allied Powers, and commander in chief, UN Command. He held the Chinese at the 38th parallel. By May 1951, the war had settled into a grim endgame going nowhere, a seesaw contest, with both armies anchored near a little village called Panmunjom, and there they stayed until the armistice agreement was signed on 27 July 1953. No one spoke or shook hands. After thirty-seven months and two million dead—fifty-four thousand of them U.S. soldiers—the result was a return to status quo. Nothing had changed: Korea remained a divided country.

When Charles Robertson and Jerry Hanson returned home, they were greeted not by parades, but by a public that knew little about their overseas police action. Korea became America's forgotten war.

With the armistice in Korea, Charlie's hope of reuniting with the Marines ended. Though he never got to Korea, two men from his village died fighting there.

His own request to join the army had been turned down: the Communists did not trust him. "Did you think our government would accept you into our army with your relationship with the U.S. Marines?" asked Li Sho Tan, Chukechuang's ranking Communist official. "Our purpose in North Korea is to *fight* the Americans."

Realizing that his past would continue to haunt him, that he was not considered an ordinary citizen, Charlie knew he'd have to watch his step and do nothing to arouse suspicions. But what could he do? He was seventeen, essentially illiterate—barely able to write his name correctly in Chinese—a farm boy from a poor village who faced a life behind a plow. The prospect was unbearable. He had been to Tsingtao, learned to swim in the Yellow Sea, learned to speak English, been to school. He had become a Christian.

A friend three years older, Li Zhon Hong, came to his aid. Go back to school, he urged, and promised to tutor him. He even talked the principal of the grade school into enrolling Charlie in the second half of the fifth grade. The principal felt sorry for Charlie and told him he'd help him relearn his language and catch up in his studies, if he worked hard. Charlie promised he would. But to go to school, he needed permission from his grandfather, the family patriarch.

The old man loved his grandson but felt that the family needed help in the fields more than Charlie needed an education. While Charlie lived with the Marines, the old man and Charlie's father tended the farm. But now, as Mao placed larger demands on production, his grandfather wanted Charlie at home. Much as he believed in the value of education and wanted it for his family, he also knew that the family would be punished if their harvest fell short.

"You need to work to grow food for your family," he told Charlie, "and if we can save money, we're going to arrange a wife for you. You need a wife, but we need to make sure you have enough money to support one."

Charlie wasn't interested in a wife; he wanted more schooling. He countered that he would never live a normal life, not with the baggage of his past. "It's only going to get worse as I get older. The only way to survive is with an education. If I study hard enough, I can catch up with everybody; it won't take long."

He explained to the old man that the Communists encouraged people to go to school. Finally his grandfather relented, and at the age of seventeen, Charlie became a curious sight sitting alongside other fifth graders. Some of his younger classmates snickered and asked how far he expected to go in school, at his advanced age. Others, more sympathetic, told him they respected his drive and understood that because he was poor, he hadn't been able to go to school until the Communists had taken over. It was a tribute to the new party to have him in their classroom, they said.

His classmates knew about his time with the Marines and forever asked about Americans, particularly during history class when their teacher credited the Russians with every major invention. The airplane, the teacher said, was invented and first flown not on a dune in coastal North Carolina by two Ohio brothers, but by Russians. Though many students knew better, they never dared argue.

Charlie kept his promise to the principal and worked hard to catch up, often studying through the night. He read books by the light of a kerosene lamp, since his family's hut had no electricity. At daybreak he helped his father and grandfather in the fields, his face blackened by the smoke of the lamp. He worked outside until it was time to head to school.

A year and a half later, at nineteen, Charlie graduated from elementary school. On graduation day, he did what would become a ritual reserved for important events: He wore his Marine green pants, the ones his mother had dyed black.

At this rate he would be twenty-five before he finished high school—if he could even get in, which was doubtful. His grades had been poor, mostly Cs, and after taking a competency test required for middle school, he failed every subject except math. What was he to do? If he couldn't continue his education, he was doomed to spend his life in the fields. He would never get to America.

Li Zhon Hong came to his rescue again. "Don't give up," counseled Li, now in the Teachers College of Tientsin. "You don't need to go to high school to apply to college. You can read the books and take an equivalency exam. I'll help, and when I have to go back to school, I'll get someone else to help you."

Charlie spent the next two years studying high-school courses. Every other night he and Li met to study, and when Li left for college, he arranged for friends to tutor Charlie. During the daytime he helped his grandfather and father on the farm, pulling out a book during breaks. His grandfather marveled at his perseverance. "I have a special grandson," he told his son. "I know he is going to make something out of himself. He studies so hard."

Charlie passed the high-school equivalency test in 1956, four years earlier than he would have graduated, and immediately registered for a college-entrance exam, listing medicine as his preferred course of study.

On the Saturday of his test, he rose early to walk to Tsingtao for the five-hour test at a high school two blocks from the old Marine compound. It was just across the street from the YMCA where he'd learned to box. It was his first return to the city in six years, but little had changed. Seeing familiar sights swept him back to another time and fortified his resolve to succeed.

A month later his results arrived. He'd passed, but didn't qualify for medical school. Instead, he was assigned to study agriculture in Jinan, two hundred miles inland from Tsingtao. Though he wanted to be a doctor to help people, agriculture school was still a great honor, and his parents and grandfather burst with pride. He was only the third person from his village to go to college.

Agriculture school was two years, free under the Communist system, with six hundred students. He slept in a large dorm room with eleven others, like he had with the Marines. He was assigned to study mulberry-tree cultivation. Because of their function as the sole diet of silkworms, mulberry leaves were of tremendous value in a country where silk, the only animal fiber of importance other than wool, was a major source of revenue. In making a cocoon, a silkworm can spin a half-mile thread of silk. China was too poor to develop the technology for synthetic fibers like nylon and rayon, and the government wanted to see if the silk industry could be expanded to prosper in northern China, which was much colder than in the south, where mulberry trees grew.

Classes stretched from eight in the morning until six. At night Charlie studied and seldom went out. He didn't know who he could trust, and to say the wrong thing could end his dreams of a college diploma. So he said nothing and whispered his prayers—always in English. He got his college diploma in 1959. In his class picture he's seated in the front row, wearing his Marine green-dyed-black pants.

After school he went to work for the Chinese agriculture department in Shantung Province as a research assistant. But immediately he got caught up in a massive political upheaval—Mao's Great Leap Forward, which had begun the previous year.

During Mao's first five-year plan for 1953 to 1957, China underwent a major transformation into a socialist country, nationalizing industry and agriculture and aligning itself with the Soviet Union, though relations soured when Nikita Khrushchev moved toward rapprochement with the United States after Stalin's death. In 1958 Mao launched the Great Leap Forward, an ambitious program of economic development that would make China less dependent on its Soviet ally and overtake Britain industrially, within fifteen years.

The aim was rapid expansion of industrial and agricultural production. In the Great Leap, peasant farms that had been forged into "mutual aid teams" in 1953 and then merged into cooperatives, followed by collectives, now became huge communes. In addition to making China wealthy overnight, the purpose of the Great Leap was to transform the Middle Kingdom into the world's first truly Communist society. Communes were to be the engine of this social revolution, with the explicit purpose of eliminating the family as an institution.

These communes, the cornerstone of the drive to expand the economy, were charged with overcoming the critical shortage of iron, essential for industry and weapons. Production left no one out. Farmers and peasants left their fields. College students were sent to communes, along with government workers. Cities shut down. Factories turned into giant smelters.

As Mao revised the goal to catch up with Britain—instead of taking fifteen years, it would now be done in two—thousands of small, crude, backyard furnaces were built throughout the country. Everyone took turns fanning coal fires to melt government-supplied ore in great pots. The air filled with the odor of burning ore, as the fields went untended and crops rotted.

Charlie's mulberry-tree-and-silkworm research was put on hold. Sent to the countryside as a member of a four-man team driving coal to the communes, he could barely see his way, some days, with all the smoke in the air from the furnaces on both sides of the road, Red Chinese flags flying at each. Even on the brightest days, the blue sky was lost in a haze of smoke, causing Charlie's eyes to sting as he drove past smoldering furnaces.

For months, farmers, students, and government workers slept in the fields by the furnaces, constantly feeding coal and fanning them with windboxes. But the backyard furnaces didn't generate enough heat to melt the ore into iron. It came out in large unusable lumps, useless as the crops rotting in the fields. Though it became clear that the Great Leap Forward was failing, Mao pressed on with the disastrous policy until poor planning, gross miscalculation of production goals, and natural disasters led to a devastating famine.

Only today is the magnitude of that catastrophe emerging. The exact figure of those who perished will never be known, but Chinese census figures indicate that perhaps thirty million people died from "excess mortality" between 1959 and 1961, a toll greater than any previous in history. Despite unspeakable horror—people eating dogs, cats, and insects; parents feeding their dying children a mixture of their own blood with hot water; widespread cannibalism—officials denied the famine. Instead, they doubled grain exports and cut imports.[8]

China's leadership concealed the tragedy from the outside world, blaming poor production on an unusually wet winter. Within the country, the government obstructed farmers' attempts to save themselves. An internal passport system and vigilant security force were instituted, and anyone caught fleeing a stricken locale was sent back.

In the midst of this man-made disaster, Charlie was thrust into a new role, one that would cause severe repercussions for him in the next cataclysm to sweep China—the Cultural Revolution. Fearing dissent, and knowing that resistance movements that toppled governments were usually organized by intellectuals, Mao ordered China's best-educated into national-disaster teams to go to the farms and villages to coax farmers into increasing productivity.

So Charlie found himself in the role of an unwitting government agent, a non-Communist placed in the political section of the agriculture department. Assigned to cover four villages in Shantung Province, he was part of a team headed by a dedicated Party woman. His job was to assess local conditions and report weekly the number of people who were starving or ill. His figures were the basis of the government's distribution of rations for those four villages.

The job was not easy, for farmers were bitter at having been forced from their fields and being now expected to meet unrealistic production goals, with only verbal assistance from the government. As Charlie traveled through the province, he saw the results of starvation—meager food supplies were given to children and the elderly, while others sat listlessly at home, too weak to work.

"Don't give up," he urged them. "Our government is good. Chairman Mao cares about us. You must go back to your farming."

He was met with resentment. One village leader told him: "We have nothing to eat. How can we work when we're hungry? What kind of government would allow this to happen? A bad government."

"You're wrong," Charlie said, giving the Party answer: "We didn't harvest any food because of natural disasters."

Both Charlie and the villagers knew better, so he promised to help them if they would return to their fields. It was a promise that would come back to haunt him.

The amount of grain rationed barely kept people alive, so Charlie falsified the numbers in his weekly reports, inflating the statistics of those starving in order to increase rations. If eight thousand were starving, he reported twelve thousand, so that those in the communes he served got larger portions of grain—mostly corn and wheat. In return the farmers began to produce more, and they petitioned that Charlie remain as their governmental representative. He felt he was doing some good, rehabilitating himself to his government while helping thousands in need. But an awful day of reckoning was approaching.

Times were hard in China, but not so in most parts of the United States. There were still serious problems with poverty, racism, and inequality, but for the majority of Americans, life in the 1950s looked pretty good, as President Roosevelt had hoped when he'd signed the Servicemen's Readjustment Act of 1944, the GI Bill.

War in Korea was over. In Vietnam, though, the French tricolor was lowered in Dien Bien Phu in 1954, and the country was split in two. American military advisers began arriving, a trickle that would swell to a tidal wave in the next decade.

Republicans returned to the White House after twenty years, with Gen. Dwight David Eisenhower defeating Democrat Adlai Stevenson in a landslide. Joe McCarthy's Communist witch-hunt finally ended, brought down as much as anything by attorney Joseph Welch's plaintive cry: "Have you no sense of decency, sir? At long last, have you no sense of decency?"

The Red Scare wasn't over, but things had calmed since Russia had detonated its atomic bomb in September 1949. The Rosenbergs were executed at Sing Sing for what J. Edgar Hoover called "the crime of the century"; the U.S. nuclear arsenal was well-stocked; and a sixty-five-ton H-bomb was exploded on Eniwetok atoll in the Marshall Islands, opening a 175-foot-deep canyon on the ocean floor and a new arms race—propelled further in 1957, when the Soviets launched their sputnik.

Stalin was dead, the Davy Crockett craze swept the United States, and Marlon Brando and Grace Kelly won Oscars. *Dragnet* and *The Honeymooners* ruled the airwaves in a new technology that swept America—television. And a family of four could get by on sixty dollars a week.

Jack Hutchins was doing much better with his own family of four. He and a friend named Brady McCubbin had just struck it rich, with a geyser of crude oil blowing from a well they'd drilled in central Kentucky. It was their first strike in a business they'd started on the side—Big Hutch with his knowledge of Kentucky rock formations, McCubbin with his brilliant salesmanship.

As a state employee, Big Hutch had helped to map Kentucky topographically—the first state in the country to do so—but he'd also used his maps to help wildcatters find suitable formations for drilling. When he and McCubbin decided to try their luck in the fifties, Hutch knew where to go. And McCubbin knew how to negotiate with farmers for the land. They found a likely place near Greensburg and dug a well, but they ran out of money and dickered with an Alabama man to sell it. At the last minute he turned them down, thinking it too much of a risk. As he walked away, a twenty-foot pillar of saltwater shot through the flow pipe.

Standing with the well between him and the setting sun, Hutch saw a yellow streak of water grow darker, suddenly turning to oil. He and McCubbin jumped and hooted in the spew, black crude soaking their clothes—it was like a scene straight out of *Giant,* released a few years earlier.

From then on the oil business was feast or famine for Hutch. He quit working for the state and turned to drilling oil full time, sometimes making a fortune and sometimes losing one.

About that time in North Carolina, Don and Arrie Sexton gave up weekend racing for church and religion. Don loved the cars and speed, but Arrie thought there was more to life. Something was missing, she told him after one weekend trip.

One day a used-car dealer whose cars Sexton serviced asked the two to his church. That night Don and Arrie started on a new road: church. They went Sunday mornings and nights, Wednesday night for prayer meetings, and Saturday nights for Youth for Christ rallies. Soon their drinking friends joined them, and they all began driving three hundred miles round trip for prayer meetings and revivals, teaching Sunday school classes, singing in the choir, ushering, and serving on the church board. In between all that, the Sextons began a family: a daughter was born in 1956, a son in 1959, and a second son ten years later. With each birth Sexton was taken back to another time, to a boy he'd left behind in China, and he wondered if Charlie was still alive.

7

The fifties segued into the sixties with no fanfare of the discordance to come, a cacophony that became one of the most tumultuous decades in the history of both China and the United States. Hints came early, though—in November of 1960.

Sister Blanda, teaching in Arlington Heights, just outside Chicago, thought that God was finally taking a long-overdue interest in American politics. Surely it was His doing that John F. Kennedy had been elected the country's first Catholic president, though others might have suspected it had more to do with some ballot-box machinations of Chicago Mayor Richard Daley. Nevertheless, God or Daley, Sister Blanda was pleased with the results.

Charles Robertson, swept up early in the events of the decade, was pleased, too: a Marine lieutenant colonel stationed at Camp Lejeune, he was assigned to beef up the defense perimeter around the naval base at Guantanamo Bay, Cuba. There were stirrings down there. Fidel Castro, after overthrowing the dictator Batista, declared himself a Communist. In retaliation for that move, Cuban exiles, with U.S. backing, launched the disastrous Bay of Pigs invasion. Their aim was to free Cuba of Castro, and it was the low point of the new Kennedy administration.

Robertson was given thirty days to buttress defenses, but it took only ten. That was a good thing, for soon afterward, the world teetered on the brink of nuclear war during the Cuban Missile Crisis. It was close, this clash between the two superpowers—between Kennedy and Nikita Khrushchev. Americans followed the events with fear. In Greensboro, Don Sexton roughed out plans for a bomb shelter that he and his sons would dig beneath the house. On Okinawa, Jerry Hanson's return home to his wife and three small children was put on hold, as replacements for his unit were rerouted to Cuba.

The replacements, along with Charles Robertson and his Marines, spent six weeks afloat off the Cuban coast, ready to engage the Russians—until, as Secretary of State Dean Rusk put it: "The other fellow blinked." In the end, Kennedy stood up to Khrushchev, and the Russians dismantled their missile sites in Cuba.

There was no blinking at home in the Civil Rights movement, however. Barricades were manned, jails filled, marches undertaken. In the Deep South, the days of Bull Connor and George Wallace, with their "Segregation now, segregation forever" mentality, were coming to a riotous end. When Martin Luther King was arrested in Birmingham, Alabama, Kennedy called out three thousand troops to quell the disturbance. In Greensboro, North Carolina, four black college students from North Carolina Agriculture and Technology University sat down at the counter of Woolworth's department store and ordered lunch, launching a new strategy—fill up the jails and break the city police budget—in the movement for equal rights.

Like most white people in Greensboro, Don and Arrie Sexton knew little of the Civil Rights movement. Previously, Arrie had walked the block from her beauty shop to Woolworth's for lunch, but she stayed away during the lunch-counter protests. The demonstrations in Greensboro and elsewhere grew larger, culminating when two hundred thousand Freedom Marchers descended on Washington.

Globally, the hot line installed between the White House and Kremlin was getting good use; while in South Vietnam, a military coup overthrew the government, killing President Diem and his brother in a van behind a church where they'd taken sanctuary. Kennedy sent military advisers and economic aid.

It was a wild beginning for a decade, but the sixties hadn't even hit their stride as Miriam Matthews Haddad and her husband, Ernest, listened to the car radio while traveling to a wedding in Daytona Beach, Florida, on 22 November 1963. The Haddads, now with four children, had been Floridians for four years—since Ernie had been sent to start a Presbyterian church in Ormond Beach.

Don Sexton was in his auto-repair shop in Greensboro, tuning the modified engine of a Ford, when the same news report broke into regular programming, to describe events in Dallas, Texas. Sexton dropped his wrench and rushed home, bursting into the kitchen just as Walter Cronkite interrupted *As the World Turns* on CBS to tell the nation that Kennedy was dead. Arrie watched it at Moses Cone Hospital, where she sat with Don mother's, Elsie, who'd just undergone surgery to remove a kidney. Arrie and Elsie wondered, along with a lot of people, whether this was a Communist plot. Who else was involved?

All anybody knew for sure was that Camelot died that day. In Chicago, Sister Blanda watched the horror on a black-and-white TV that her class had bought with S and H green stamps. Two days later she was cleaning her classroom with the TV turned on when President Kennedy's accused murderer, Lee Harvey Oswald, was murdered too. Where was God now? she wondered.

In China, Charlie was asking the same question, though for an altogether different reason. He knew nothing about John F. Kennedy or the politics in America; he was caught up in the politics of China, emerging from the disastrous Great Leap Forward and about to enter another calamitous period—the Cultural Revolution. When Kennedy was assassinated in 1963, Charlie was a prisoner of the Communists. His nightmare had come to life.

After the Great Leap Forward and the famine it wrought were officially declared over in 1962, Charlie was reassigned to an agriculture research group two hundred miles south of Jinan, in Lao Chun, testing fertilizers and overseeing a program to replenish trees lost during the Great Leap. He was working there, his life normal for the first time in years, when his parents wrote to tell him about a girl from a good family in Chukechuang. Her name was Zhu Jin Mie, they wrote. She was a teacher in the village, and he should come home to meet her during his next vacation.

Though he hadn't thought of marriage—and the idea of marrying a woman who wasn't Catholic didn't appeal to him—he dutifully traveled the two hundred miles home that Chinese New Year holiday to meet her. They met at a neighbor's house. She was a small woman, smart, with a gentle, shy smile—someone who would make a good mother, he thought. But, of course, it made no difference what the suitors thought: it was, after all, an arranged marriage.

Her family liked Charlie; he was educated and came from a hardworking family. They knew of his past with the American Marines, but they found no crime in that. Indeed, her father, Zhu Shan Moo, had experienced his own run-in with politics, government, and trouble. In a village of peasants, he'd held one of the few prosperous jobs during the Japanese occupation—as a driver for a trucking company that a relative owned in Tsingtao.

The company had a contract with the Nationalist government to haul supplies and ammunition to troops fighting the Japanese. Once, near the end of World War II, with hostilities resuming between the Nationalists and Communists, Zhu took ammunition and food to the front line, where a company of Nationalists faced off against the Japanese. As he approached, a regiment of Communist troops burst out of the woods. Zhu found himself in the middle of a three-way battle: Japanese, Communists, and Nationalists all firing at each other to get the truckload of ammo and food.

Zhu jumped from the truck and ran, not caring who got it. He quit driving and went to safer employment as a mechanic, then returned to farming. So he understood troubles shaped by politics, and he gave his blessing to the marriage. It was arranged: Charlie would return to work and ask for a ten-day leave to get married.

It was a simple ceremony at a friend's house in the village. Charlie wore his best suit coat and his Marine pants. The night before, he folded them tightly into a square and placed them under his pillow to give them a crisp, sharp crease for his wedding day.

After the ceremony, the newlyweds lived with Charlie's parents until he returned to work in Lao Chun. Jin Mie continued teaching and looked after her aging parents. She and Charlie wrote often, and he asked her to look in on his own aging parents. Married, it was easier for him to get time off from work to go home. During a leave in

1962, their first child was conceived, but when he returned to Lao Chun, he got his first whiff of the trouble ahead.

Though he'd avoided political involvement, many his age joined the Communist Party. One morning after their monthly meeting, his friend Chou Le Min approached him with concern. "Your name came up last night," Chou said. "I think you're going to have trouble. It has to do with associating with foreigners when you were young."

Charlie explained, "When I was eleven, American Marines came to Tsingtao. They took me in and sent me to school. There were a lot of us like this."

"I don't see anything wrong with that," Chou said. "I don't know why the government is investigating you, but they say you have an unclear record."

Charlie didn't panic; it was news he'd been expecting. "I'm innocent of everything," he told Chou. "I've been faithful in my job and done my best. I'm from a poor family and haven't done anything against the Communist Party."

"Just be careful," Chou cautioned. "They're watching you."

They were watching everyone; it was just the beginning of the seismic changes sweeping the country.

After Mao was forced to back off the Great Leap, prodded by his old comrade Deng Xiaoping and by President Liu Shaoqi, he felt threatened. Increasingly paranoid, he accused Deng of snubbing him and screamed at Deng and Liu in 1962: "You have put the screws to me for the last time! Now, for once, I am going to put a scare into you."[1]

He did—with the Great Proletarian Cultural Revolution. It started ominously, with Marshal Lin Piao, the defense minister, introducing intensified political training in the People's Liberation Army. The great Chinese general promoted the cult of Mao with the little red book *Quotations from Chairman Mao*. Every soldier carried it; then every citizen.

It was the end of political moderation in China and the triumph of Party zealotry. In a few years Mao's wife, Jiang Quing, would lead the Gang of Four in a total "reform" of Chinese culture.

Charlie became one of the first victims of the incipient revolution, and though he didn't know it at the time, he was lucky. By 1966 the

Red Guards terrorized the country, and no one was safe. President Liu's leg was broken and he died in jail of pneumonia; Deng was paraded in ridicule through the streets and was spared only because he had been with Mao on the Long March of 1934.

Had Charlie not been arrested in the very beginning, before the tumbrels rolled in earnest, he likely would have perished. In the beginning, the purge was limited to those with "unclear records." Later it turned on dissidents for crimes such as "running with the capitalist dogs," and in the case of Deng, for "catism"—an indictment of his famous axiom: "It doesn't matter whether the cat is black or white, as long as it catches mice."[2]

By 1966 it mattered very much which color the cat was, but in the winter of 1962, the focus was on those with ties to old enemies. Dredging up the specter of foreign foes was a good way to divert attention from domestic problems—the starvation deaths of millions. And what greater foe was there than the imperialist dogs of America, who still backed Chiang Kai-shek and the traitors on Formosa, supporting their claim to the offshore islands of Quemoy and Matsu? In the late 1950s, the Communist Chinese had shelled these islands, and President Eisenhower had threatened nuclear war over them.

A few days after his encounter with Chou, Charlie was called to the office of his department boss, Kou Mon. Charlie liked Kou; though a loyal Party member, Kou had been fair to him and seemed to appreciate and admire his work. But this day, seeing his personnel file on Kou's desk and remembering what Chou had said, Charlie sensed that his boss wanted to discuss something other than his work.

"I notice from your file that you have an interesting history," Kou began, leaning forward on his desk. "What do you think of our government's politics?"

"They're good," Charlie replied.

"But we have many enemies," Kou said, leaning back into his chair and folding his arms. "America is our worst enemy. Whatever we do, they don't like. If there is a war, like in Korea, they are against us."

Charlie nervously thumped the side of his chair with his thumb, waiting for Kou to get to his point. Then came a request he'd anticipated.

"We would appreciate it if you'd be part of our educational team," Kou said, looking Charlie squarely in the eye. "We want you to tell people who our enemy is, and why we should be careful of the United States."

Charlie listened quietly.

"With your knowledge of Americans and having lived with them, you can describe all the crimes their soldiers committed in our country. They robbed our people. They beat them. That is why we must hate Americans and why you must tell our people."

Charlie clenched his fists; Kou was talking about the Japanese, not the Americans. Older Chinese wouldn't believe such lies, but younger ones might. The time had come to test his faith. If he did as asked, he knew he'd be rewarded; he could return to Jin Mie and be left alone to live a good life. But Sister Blanda's lesson resonated in his ears: It is noble to die for your beliefs. He would not betray the Marines, or his faith.

"I did have an experience with Americans," he responded carefully. "But it was such a long time ago and I was so young at the time that I don't remember much. I'd like to help you with your campaign, but I can't remember anything clearly. I'm sorry."

Kou nodded politely, but Charlie sensed that his boss knew he was lying. Two weeks later he was told that the department was overstaffed; he was dismissed and sent home.

Charlie boarded a train to Tsingtao, saddened but not surprised by the turn of events. He didn't understand why this was happening and didn't know what the Party would do to him, but he understood that his predicament was perilous. In addition to his past with the Marines, they also had evidence that he'd inflated the numbers of starving farmers during the Great Leap Forward. On the train he tried to sleep, but he could only ponder the unfairness of the politics that had affected him. As the train rolled east that winter of 1962, each day growing colder and darker, he feared that the Party was building a case against him. So he began to plot his own survival. If anyone noticed him on the train, all they saw was a troubled man lost in his thoughts.

No one said anything when he returned home, though everyone in the village knew he must be in terrible trouble if he'd been fired. Jin

Mie was eight months pregnant. Charlie looked at her and wondered what the future held for their child if he was imprisoned. All he could think about, as he worked his parents' field, cultivating sweet potatoes and corn with his father, was the punishment hanging over his head. He couldn't even go to his grandfather for strength and wisdom; the old man had died while he was away.

In January 1963, Charlie became a father, his son born in the same mud hut where he'd been born. They named him Yin Whee. As he cradled his baby at night, Charlie wondered what good he would be as a father locked behind bars, for many with "unclear records" were being hauled off to prison. There had to be a way to save himself. Remembering a conversation he'd had with a black-market silk dealer while the two waited at Lao Chun station to board trains, he began to devise a plan. The dealer told him that you could get out of China by going to Hong Kong; no one could touch you there. But it required a lot of money.

One day, Charlie told Jin Mie he was going to Guangzhou, a city across a wide river from the New Territories of Hong Kong, to visit old friends from his university days. When he arrived two days later by train, he gathered information for his escape. A fake passport would cost 3,000 yen—about 750 American dollars. Smugglers who would get him across the border charged the same; they would hide him on the bottom of a boat and row across the river to the city where thousands of Chinese were fleeing.

The plan was terribly dangerous—the border patrol waited on the other side, and being caught by them meant certain execution. He couldn't completely trust the smugglers, either: they might take his money or, worse, turn him in. He could go it alone, attempt to swim across, but many had drowned trying.

Gradually his fears about what would happen to him if he stayed overcame his worries about escape. His mother, sick with asthma, sensed her son's concerns. Fearing that he might try something foolish, she sent her brother-in-law, Charlie's uncle, to talk to him. Charlie reassured him that he wasn't about to risk his life; after all, he was a new father. Tell my mother not to worry, he said. After a second trip to Guangzhou, Charlie decided the risk was worth taking. Life constantly worrying about arrest wasn't worth living. He would go to Hong Kong, get a job, and send money to Jin Mie, then try to reunite the family in the free world.

But where would he get the money to leave? He had no savings. All the years he'd worked for the government, he'd sent half of his money to his parents and a smaller amount to a younger brother in school, reasoning that Jin Mie had a good job and could support their son. On the train back to Tsingtao, he devised a plan. He would tell his mother and wife that he was going to Jinan, where he'd spent years studying and researching mulberries, to see a friend. There he'd go to a store and steal ten watches. Watches were easy to conceal, and the smugglers and passport counterfeiters would take them in lieu of money.

Nothing had prepared Charlie for what he was about to do. All his life he'd worked hard and lived by the rules. As a boy he'd brought the Marines peanuts and wood instead of begging, like other village children. He'd learned hard work and following orders; he'd kept a taut, squared-away bunk and spit-shined shoes. He'd earned everything he had received, from the food to the miniature uniforms with corporal stripes, the bike, swimming lessons, and school.

But now he was going to break God's commandments. He was going to steal. What would Sister Blanda think? Surely she'd understand; the Bible was filled with stories of desperate men. And he was desperate—if he didn't try to escape, it was only a matter of time before he faced a firing squad. It was happening all around him. Everywhere people were looking for ways to escape. Watches would bring a handsome sum, but more important, they would bring him freedom and a chance of survival.

Freedom and survival ran through his mind early one March morning in 1963, as he dressed in a light blue suit, the one he'd worn in Lao Chun for work meetings. Holding his three-month-old son, he told Jin Mie he was going to Jinan to visit friends for a couple of days. Nine hours later he entered the government-run department store in Jinan; watches were on the fifth floor.

Just before closing, he slipped into the elevator shaft and climbed onto the top of an elevator. His plan was to wait until everyone was gone, then take the watches from the display counter and catch the train to Guangzhou. At eleven o'clock he heard security guards making sure that doors and windows were locked. Then there was silence.

As a wisp of breeze blew up through the elevator shaft, he slipped through a grate back into the store. When his eyes adjusted to the dark, he went to the jewelry department. Reaching into the glass case that held the watches, he felt all around . . . but the case was empty.

Fear seized his heart. The watches were gone! He hadn't considered that the guards would remove them at night to lock in a safe. His perfect plan had gone wrong! And he had no alternate plan. But he'd risked so much already; he couldn't leave empty-handed. On the same floor, next to the jewelry department were expensive fabrics worth more than watches. Charlie knew silk: two bolts would bring the money he needed after all.

From a stack rising to the ceiling, he pulled two hundred-yard bolts, three feet wide. They were cobalt blue—popular in China for scarves, robes, and jackets—and would easily bring two thousand yen apiece. But now how would he make his getaway? The security guards had locked the doors to the lower floors.

Finding a window covered by eight-foot-long curtains, he tore them into strips and tied them together. Wrapping this around the bolts, he lowered them to the ground, then scaled down five stories. His escape had worked; within days he would be in Hong Kong. Charlie flagged a rickshaw and told the driver to take him to the train station, not realizing that the driver had watched him climb out of the store.

Guards arrested Charlie as he was buying a ticket for Guangzhou. They took him to a detention center, where other officers questioned him for an hour. He told them the truth—half of it, anyway—he'd just lost his job, his baby son was only three months old, his mother was sick. He needed money and knew the store from his days as a student at the university. He didn't mention that he was fleeing the country.

"Stealing is no way to solve your problems," an officer told him.

"But my family is very poor; I needed money to support them," Charlie replied.

The next day Jinan police sent an agent to Tsingtao to check Charlie's background and inform local authorities of the charges against him. The agent went to Chukechuang to tell Jin Mie and Charlie's family that he was in serious trouble. They didn't believe him.

"There is no way he would do that," Jin Mie said. "He went to see friends. There must be a misunderstanding."

The village leader agreed. Nothing in Charlie's past or in anyone's recollections suggested that he could be capable of stealing. He'd never disgraced his family or shamed his village. "You caught the wrong person," the leader said.

Yet when Jin Mie sent her younger brother to check on Charlie in jail, he told him that they hadn't caught the wrong person. "I deserve to be punished," Charlie said solemnly, as a guard listened nearby. "I was desperate. I have a new son and a sick mother. And no income."

Three days later he stood before his jailers, who were also his judges. The stealing charge alone wouldn't have sent him to prison—the goods had been returned unharmed and unsold—but an investigation had uncovered his "unclear record." He'd lived with American Marines for four years, had become a Catholic, had falsified government reports. He had refused to take part in an educational campaign to warn people about their American enemy. His loyalties were obviously questionable.

He was convicted on the charge of being a suspected spy, sentenced to seven years in the state prison at Jinan. Charlie was prepared. He'd always known he'd be punished for his friendship with the men of Love Company, but his conscience was clear. He was ready to take Sister Blanda's teachings to prison. Still, seven years seemed such a long time for a young father whose son was only three months old. He would not see him grow up.

8 No one had ever escaped from Jinan prison in Shantung Province. It was a maximum-security facility for two thousand prisoners convicted of serious crimes—murder, rape, robbery—and for those with "unclear records," like Charlie and former officials of Chiang Kai-shek's Nationalist regime. Many tried to escape, but those who weren't shot or electrocuted climbing the fence that surrounded the compound were shackled in double-leg irons and placed in solitary confinement. The prison, built just after the turn of the century and used by the Japanese to imprison those who resisted their occupation, was a massive facility with government-run farms and factories that produced steel and iron, cement and generators.

The first signs of spring were breaking the ground when Charlie entered it, that March of 1963. Given three sets of bluish-gray prison uniforms, a blanket and pillow, he was assigned to a bunkhouse with forty other inmates who slept on hay spread on the damp floor. Staking out his own spot, he meticulously unbuttoned the blue jacket he'd worn during his failed heist, folded it and the matching pants, then stowed them under his pillow and changed into his prison uniform. His fall had ended. He'd hit bottom, so he thought, a bleak prison two hundred miles from home. He wondered what would happen to his wife and son.

To keep up his spirits, he prayed in English, convincing himself that this was part of his God's plan. Sometimes he dreamed of Big Hutch and the other Marines mounting a rescue.

With his degree in agriculture, he was assigned to work on the two-hundred-acre farm supplying vegetables to Jinan. It was a menial job weeding, irrigating, and fertilizing rows of garlic, cucumbers, corn, and sweet potatoes. His mail was censored and friendships forbidden, but the political prisoners drew together nevertheless, covering for those too sick or old to work and giving encouragement when the work became too tedious or the homesickness too overwhelming.

One prisoner sentenced to life had been a general in Chiang's army and had sat in on high-level meetings. Now seventy and unwell, the guards gave him easy jobs. He seemed drawn to Charlie and would lament how much he missed his family, his voice dropping to a whisper as he said, "I'll never see them again."

Charlie wondered if he'd ever see his own family again. But he tried not to dwell on that—it would lead to madness. Yet he couldn't drive his family from his thoughts or dreams. He yearned for them terribly. So much that he began to plan an escape.

Like animals padding their cage back and forth looking for a way out, prisoners keep their sanity by plotting escape. It's only in hell where all hope is abandoned.

He watched prison officials, studying how they entered and left through the main gate just under a tall guard tower. They walked through attracting little notice, in gray civilian clothes, usually with folded papers tucked under an arm. The road outside the prison led directly to Jinan. Thirty yards outside the gate stood wooden guards' quarters, and twenty yards beyond that were white houses where prison officials lived with their families. Past that and thirty yards more to the road, a bus would take him to the train station in Jinan—and to freedom.

One Sunday four months after arriving, Charlie attempted his escape. Facing another six and a half years in prison, he was so depressed that a firing squad didn't seem an altogether bad fate. He'd spent weeks mapping his strategy: he would make it to the road, catch a bus to the city and train station, board a train to Tsingtao, then a bus to Chukechuang. There he'd say good-bye to his family, go to Guangzhou, swim across the river to the New Territories, and finally be free. From Hong Kong he'd go to America and find the Marines. Once settled there, he'd bring his family over. Prison might have warped his reality, but not his focus.

On Sundays, prisoners were allowed to dress in the clothes they'd worn to prison and read books or newspapers in the library. That morning Charlie put on his light blue suit, his four-pocket jacket buttoned closely around his neck. He scribbled a note and left it in his prison clothes: "I am begging for a couple of days off, a leave of absence. I promise I will be back within five days, so you don't have to look for me." If he was caught, the note would provide evidence, he thought, that he had no intention of staying gone for long. It was only a temporary escape.

He took a newspaper from the library, tucked it under his arm, and walked right through the gate, head down, his steps deliberate, just like he'd seen prison officials do so many times. None of the guards questioned him; he was sure none had even seen him leave. He walked past the guards' quarters, then the houses for the prison officials. He got to the bus stop before he realized he had no money for the bus.

So he walked two miles into town. On his way to the train station, a thought stopped him: he had no money for train fare back to Tsingtao, either. He needed money. The first time, when he'd stolen the silk, he had almost gotten away. Why not try it again? This time he'd steal something smaller and be more careful with his getaway. He went into the same department store, slipped into a women's bathroom, and hid in a stall. An hour later a store clerk came in and went into the next stall. Charlie sat as still as he could, but he stayed so suspiciously long that she alerted a security guard.

A policeman called him out. By then prison guards were searching the city for him, and three stormed into the store. They grabbed him in his blue suit, the newspaper still tucked under his arm. On the way back to prison, one guard asked incredulously, "Why did you do such a stupid thing? You knew you couldn't get away. No one has ever gotten away. And to go into the same store where you had been caught before—why would you do that?"

Charlie could only stare at his feet. "I missed my family so much. I was going crazy I missed them so much."

"You were lucky," the guard said. "If the guards on the gate had seen you walk out, they would have shot you. You've got a college education. I can't believe you would do something so stupid. Even if you had gotten away, you would have been caught sooner or later. Now you have made matters even worse."

Charlie said nothing on the drive back. All he could think about was the punishment facing him: a firing squad or leg irons. When the warden called for him the next morning, he too was incredulous. "How did you expect to get away with such a dumb stunt?"

Charlie hung his head. "My son is seven months old; I wanted to see him."

The warden studied him, then opened his personnel file and read it. When he finished he looked up, curious. "Tell me about those Marines you lived with."

"I came from a poor family. When the Japanese surrendered, U.S. Marines came into our town. I was eleven. I brought them wood for their fires and they gave me food for my family. Then they took me to Tsingtao and sent me to school."

"Who taught you in this school?"

"Catholic nuns and a missionary."

"What did they teach you?"

"How to read and write. And about Christianity."

If that didn't get him shot, nothing would, Charlie thought, but the warden didn't say anything. He stared at him for a long time, then finally nodded dismissal.

Charlie was stunned. He had no explanation for why he was let off; neither did the other prisoners. They were as surprised as he, but awed, too, not just for his daring escape, but because he wasn't shot after he was caught. All Charlie could think was that God had intervened and sent him an angel—this time in the form of a prison warden. He reasoned that if Marines could be angels, perhaps prison wardens could be, too.

Indeed it seemed so, for two days later Charlie was transferred to the prison's iron factory, still in Jinan. It was a promotion of sorts, because the factory was a moneymaker for the government. Consequently, the workers ate better.

~❖~

Jin Mie knew nothing of what was happening to her husband. At night she rocked her baby and cried until there were no more tears. Days after she received word of Charlie's arrest, she went to his parents. "My husband has been a good son to you. You need to help him."

But what could they do? They had no money and no connections. Because they didn't help, Jin Mie moved with her son to her own parents' house and barely spoke to Charlie's family again. It was a rift that continued until his parents died twenty years later, and it was aggravated when Charlie's younger brother, Tsui Chi Da, the brother to whom Charlie had sent money for school, denounced him when he joined the Party.

Jin Mie's family stood by her, counseling her not to give up hope. He's an innocent man, they said, punished unfairly. Soon the government will discover its terrible mistake and send him home. But weeks, then months passed, and Charlie didn't return.

Nights were the hardest. After the baby fell asleep, Jin Mie sat with her mother and they cried together. Yet life had to go on: she had to support her child. Leaving her son with her mother, Jin Mie went back to teaching school. Working helped; first and second graders kept her from thinking of Charlie and the sad turn their life together had taken.

One day the principal called for her. He told her she was a good teacher and he wanted to keep her, but this was becoming increasingly difficult with her husband in prison for spying. "It's causing problems," he said. "It doesn't look right for a teacher of our children to have a husband in prison. If you divorced him it would make things easier for everyone."

Jin Mie was stunned. Charlie needed her support; she had never considered abandoning him. Yet now she was faced with a horrible choice—standing by her husband or supporting her son. Buying time, she told the principal she had to consult with her family. That night when she discussed it with them, they were as dismayed as she.

"Your husband is a good man," Zhu Shan Moo said. "It isn't fair what's happening to him. It's hard enough for him without this. If you divorce him, he will lose his will to live."

Jin Mie always listened to her father. But with a son to care for, she told him she had to do what was best for him.

Zhu shook his head. "I don't know what the future holds for you and your son if you remain with your husband, but I know for sure that if you divorce him, you will kill him."

So together they hatched a plan. They would make the Communists think that she was divorcing her husband. She would go to the local court and file papers but send word to Charlie that it meant nothing—they would remarry as soon as he was released.

Charlie got the divorce papers but nothing from Jin Mie—her letters had been censored. Though he knew what kind of pressure she must be under because of him, he was crushed. He had never felt more alone and hopeless, not even when the Marines had left him in Tsingtao.

A guard in his unit sensed his grief and offered sympathy when Charlie told him what had happened. "How was your relationship with your wife?" he asked.

"We got along well," Charlie answered. "We never quarreled."

"Then don't sign the papers. You can't get divorced unless you sign the papers agreeing to it. Even though you're in prison, you still have rights. Write a letter to the court saying you don't agree to it."

Charlie thanked the guard and wrote the letter, explaining that he was a new man since his failed theft and escape. Once out of prison, he would join his wife and together they would work for a greater China. That was a lie, he knew, for ever since his failed escape, he'd been working on a new plan. As soon as he got out of prison, he was determined to leave China with his family.

Though Jin Mie's plan hadn't worked as she'd designed, now the principal could tell Party officials that she'd tried to end her marriage. She kept her job—for five years.

It was a turbulent five years. The sixties had hit their stride at last, and China and the United States were caught in the maelstrom.

LBJ declared war on poverty, committed his administration to civil-rights reform, and sent thousands of troops to Vietnam. It was an era of sit-ins, love-ins, draft-card burnings, long hair, flights to Canada, assassinations—Malcolm X, Bobby Kennedy, Martin Luther King—body bags, and napalm. It was a psychedelic age in the truest sense, one that took trips on LSD at Woodstock and to the moon on Apollo 11.

Yet in China, events were even more riotous. In an attempt to recharge the waning fires of his Marxist-Leninist revolution and avoid the morass that had befallen the Soviet Union, Mao launched the Great Proletarian Cultural Revolution in 1966. His goal was to replace those he felt had strayed from the revolutionary spirit and purge the Communist Party of practical reformers like Deng Xiaoping.

Hoping to give the country's youth a flavor of the revolutionary spirit, Mao encouraged them to organize into groups called Red Guards and ordered the Party and the military to leave them alone. The Guards were to revive the revolution by attacking traditional values and the drift toward bourgeois complacency, but instead they triggered a firestorm that swept out of control.

Anarchy spread as Red Guards terrorized the country. In deifying Mao, they turned on one another, each claiming to be the true believer. Paralysis gripped the major cities and spilled into the provinces. In 1968, it finally even filtered down to Chukechuang. The Guards took over the village school and told the principal to dismiss Jin Mie.

"They say they can't have somebody whose husband ran with the capitalist dogs teach the children," he told her. "You must go."

Jin Mie had never done anything but teach. Walking home after her dismissal, she worried about the disgrace she'd brought her family. Her father had made achievers out of his children: an older brother drove a truck for the city of Tsingtao, another was a carpenter, an older sister had graduated from a technical school, another worked in a rubber factory, and her youngest sister was a nurse. But she was unemployed. Fired.

Word spread quickly, and that night a friend came to the house and urged her to join a group of women who grew hop vines and dried the ripened flowers, with their bitter oils, for the Tsingtao Beer Company. Though the work was hard, she enjoyed it; she rose early every morning to walk to the fields. There she weeded, fertilized, harvested, and, after the leaves were dried and processed, loaded the powder into hop sacks for the brewery.

As the date for Charlie's release drew closer, she grew more anxious, for the Red Guards had become increasingly radical. How would they treat someone who had run with the imperialist dogs? What would they do to his son?

113

꙳

Though turmoil continued in China, the sixties were lurching to their exhausted end in America. It was as if a marathon had run its course, with the participants dropping at the finish. The light at the end of the tunnel in Vietnam still wasn't visible, but Richard Nixon had been elected president with a "secret plan" to end the war, and he began the first U.S. troop pullout in 1969.

That was the year Charles Robertson became a general, promoted to assistant division commander, 1st Marine Division, in Da Nang, South Vietnam. His ties to the country went back to 1965, when he had been assigned to the Joint Planning Group, Eastern Regional Team.

The Marines viewed the conflict as a counterinsurgency war, one in which "winning the hearts and minds" was crucial. But the Army saw the war as a conventional one and pursued it with tanks and mechanized armor. Reports for the National Intelligence Board indicated that when faced with overwhelming odds, the Vietcong would simply disappear—fade away until a more propitious time. According to the board's research, it would take a huge commitment of troops twenty years to make the South Vietnamese self-sufficient enough to withstand the North's aggression.

In 1967, Robertson was assigned to the J-5 planning staff of Adm. Ulysses S. Grant Sharp, commander in chief in the Pacific. In November he sat in on a briefing that Gen. William Westmoreland, commander of the U.S. troops in Vietnam, gave to Sharp. It was a preview of the one he was to give in a few days to the press corps in Washington. In a remarkably upbeat appraisal of the military situation in Vietnam, Westmoreland virtually dismissed the Vietcong and North Vietnamese as threats.

But Sharp expressed misgivings, and he had Robertson file those doubts with the Joint Chiefs, stating that he believed the enemy retained a "dangerous capability." He urged moderation in Westmoreland's optimistic report. Nevertheless, Westmoreland gave the speech unchanged.

Two months later the North Vietnamese and Vietcong staged the Tet Offensive. Though not a military victory, it was a press victory, largely because Westmoreland had led the public to believe them incapable of

114

such an attack. Later in 1968, anticipating withdrawal of U.S. forces from Vietnam, Robertson and his staff began planning for that eventuality. It started the year following Richard Nixon's inauguration.

That year Robertson went to his third war. Twenty-five years earlier he'd commanded a platoon in World War II; now he was commanding officer of the 5th Marine Regiment in Vietnam—a very seasoned warrior. He believed that experience and intuition gave soldiers a sixth sense, one that helped him on Mother's Day 1969, when the North Vietnamese attacked one of his battalions. Thinking it was a diversion, he ordered his own headquarters unit to prepare for an attack. It came thirty minutes later, with the first enemy artillery round landing five feet from his bunker.

In February 1970, he was promoted to brigadier general and made assistant division commander. He left in August with the withdrawal well under way, believing that Vietnam hadn't been lost in battle, but in the States.

By the time Jerry Hanson left Vietnam, he'd been promoted to master sergeant. This was to be his last war, too: he went home to retire in January 1969. So did another China Marine, but an unhappy fate awaited him.

In early 1969, David Brooks hung up his uniform after twenty-four years. The hot-tempered Marine from North Carolina had enlisted in December 1945, spent two years in China, fought his way through Korea and Vietnam, and retired as a first sergeant.

He went home to Albemarle to a marriage on the rocks, grown children he hardly knew, and time on his hands that he filled by drinking. As in China when he'd enjoyed fighting his way out of bars, it didn't take much to trigger Brooks's temper. He argued with his oldest son, who he felt was straying into drugs and booze, and he fought with a man he accused of having an affair with his wife.

Early one morning nine months after Brooks retired, a state trooper driving by his house noticed smoke. Peering through a window, he saw Brooks sprawled on the floor, but heavy smoke prevented him from going in. Brooks's brothers, Edward and Stony, and his sister, Marjorie Higgins, thought the fire had been set. At the funeral home, when his casket was opened, they saw bruises and three cuts on his cheek, as if

115

someone had tried to make sure he wouldn't escape the fire. They hired a private detective, but foul play was never proved.

About the time Brooks was buried, Charlie marked his seventh birthday passed at Jinan. He was in his mid-thirties but looked and felt older. Prison had etched its toll on his face and grayed his hair. He noted each passing Chinese New Year in February, when inmates were given steamed dumplings and two days off from work.

After his escape had failed, Charlie had been transferred to the iron factory and trained as an electrician. Hard labor was reserved for those who had committed terrible crimes; political prisoners were treated better. All he had to do was replace faulty wiring, obey the rules, and serve out his time.

Jin Mie wrote every few months. News of the outside world was censored; all he learned was that she and his son, Yin Whee, were in good health, the boy growing tall and curious. He was looked after by her parents while she worked in the hop fields.

One day not long after his thirty-fifth birthday, just before Christmas 1969, a prison official told him to pack up. His heart racing, he gathered his blue suit, toothbrush, and a few other belongings and wrapped them in a towel. In the prison-release office he signed papers, then listened to the official's lecture: "You served your time well. If you continue as you have, no one will ever bother you. Prove yourself by showing people you're willing to do whatever is required." He handed Charlie a train ticket to Tsingtao and pointed to the front gate, the same one he'd fled out of six and a half years earlier. "You can leave now."

As he walked through the gate, Charlie felt like a bird released from its cage. He was free, wings spread. Or so he thought.

Riding the train home with his face pressed to the window, staring at every tree and every post, every wall, he wondered what his son would look like, what the boy had been told about his father and his whereabouts all these years. In Jin Mie's last letter, she wrote that he'd started school.

9 Charlie returned to a much-changed Chukechuang, after seven years in prison. The chaos and economic destruction of the Cultural Revolution were over. Villagers had jobs in new factories. They'd started families and built houses of brick and stone, not mud, with cement floors instead of dirt, tiled roofs instead of hay. And, to Charlie's amazement, the houses had glass windows. Mao's promise of prosperity and property was coming true, though life was still tightly controlled—no longer by Red Guards, but by a militia of villagers, farmers, and factory workers.

When Charlie got off the train at Tsingtao, he caught a bus for the ten-mile ride up newly paved Shilu Road. As a dutiful son, he went first to see his parents. A neighbor ran to tell Jin Mie in the hop fields, and she rushed to the school to get her son. "Your father's home," she told Yin Whee breathlessly. For years he'd asked about his father but was told only that he was away—"working for the government; someday soon he will come home." Now Yin Whee hid shyly behind his mother when he saw his father for the first time.

Reuniting with his wife and son, joy and relief swept over Charlie—but also the realization that they were strangers, and he an outsider. He'd spent more time in prison than he had with his wife, but now they were back together, a family. The first priority was finding a place to live. Jin Mie returned to the fields and Yin Whee to school, urged by his

117

father to succeed, admonished how precious education was, even though it had caused him trouble.

For two years Jin Mie's brother and sister had squirreled away materials—cement blocks, brick, stone, and windows—to build a house once Charlie returned. He'd had no glass in his home as a child; now, with the help of relatives and friends, he set to work building a classic three-room house, with a central wok for cooking, walls of stone and brick, a tile roof, a dirt floor—and windows.

One day as the walls were going up, the village militia arrived. The captain, a man of Charlie's boyhood acquaintance, called him forward and told him he was stripped of his rights as a citizen and under house arrest. "We are appointed by the government to protect our village," the captain said. "You must not do anything to break our rules. We will monitor your activities. You can't go anywhere without permission and aren't allowed to leave the village. You can work to support your family but can't associate with anybody except the people at work, then you must go straight home. After you've proven you're no longer a security risk, we'll end your house arrest."

After listening to this speech in silence, Charlie went back to mixing mortar. There had been nothing apologetic in the captain's voice; after all, Charlie was a suspected spy. So there was nothing he could do. Defying the militia would land him back in prison. He had hoped to start a new life with his release, but his troubles continued—with no end in sight.

He had exchanged one prison for another, for the militia drew a circle with an invisible fence around him. He was allowed only to work in the fields and walk the ten minutes home, then not leave for any reason. At least he was with his family, and sometimes he sneaked over to his parents' house, a couple hundred yards away. They were elderly and needed help, and he didn't think the militia would punish him if he was caught, but he remained cautious nevertheless.

Jin Mie became pregnant with another son, Yin Tao, born a year after Charlie's return. Charlie and Jin Mie were happy together, but they wondered if their troubles would ever end.

Then, in the summer of 1971, before Yin Tao was a year old, an amazing rumor swept the entire country. Like all peasant villages,

Chukechuang was without newspapers, television, or radio. The only line of communication was a rudimentary intercom system with wires into each home, tied to speakers. It was run by the Party, offered government-sponsored music, and served for special announcements. The rumor, unconfirmed by the intercom, was that the American president, Richard Nixon, was coming to China to meet with Mao and Premier Chou En-lai.

It would follow two stunning events that year and served to show the world that the Bamboo Curtain was beginning to part, if even slightly. In April 1971, the Chinese learned of a coup attempt led by Lin Piao, the Red Army general considered Mao's heir-apparent, and of Piao's death in a mysterious plane crash. Not long after that they were dealt another shock, seemingly insignificant, but with international consequences. China invited the U.S. table-tennis team to visit. There were eight players, five coaches, and two wives, along with three American journalists who covered the tour.

The Americans visited the Great Wall and Chingua University. There, eighteen thousand Chinese turned out to witness a match between the Americans and a Chinese table-tennis team. It was the first public meeting of representatives from the two countries in more than two hostile decades. Everywhere people kept up with the matches with fascination, and ping pong's popularity swept China. Even in Chukechuang, a crude table was set up in front of the Communist Party office. The tabletop was flat stone, the net imaginary. Paddles were whittled from wood, but few had time to play.

Seemingly, table tennis had opened new relations between the two countries. During the ping-pong tour, Nixon announced that the United States would relax a twenty-year trade embargo against Communist China, in order to improve relations. At a reception for the American players, Chou told them, "You have opened a new page in the relations of the Chinese and American people. You have made a start here, and I believe in the future more American friends will come to China." He concluded by saying that Americans and Chinese would "in the near future be able to have many contacts. I believe it will not be slow in coming."[1]

Then in July, Nixon revealed that he had accepted an invitation from

Mao to visit China the following year. It was a visit that had been arranged during a secret trip to China by Henry Kissinger, the U.S. national security adviser. This was a high-level visit that couldn't come soon enough for Charlie, who labored in the government-run fields under house arrest.

The presidential visit was all workers talked about in Chukechuang. One morning before daybreak in February 1972, they heard the astonishing news: Nixon had arrived. Though the Nationalist government in Taipei protested vehemently, Nixon met briefly with Mao, then spent hours in talks with Premier Chou. In a remarkable reversal of policy, the United States dropped its long opposition to admitting the People's Republic of China to the United Nations.

Charlie followed all the news in stunned disbelief. Why was Nixon in China? he asked other field hands. "Chairman Mao hates the United States. America is China's number-one enemy."

That night Charlie heard the news for himself on the intercom: Nixon was indeed in China. He, Mao, and Chou had talked of opening diplomatic relations. At a state banquet, Chou En-lai toasted Nixon, saying normal diplomatic relations could now be established. Nixon responded with his own toast: "As we discuss our differences, neither of us will compromise our principles. Although we cannot close the gulf between us, we can try to bridge it so that we may be able to talk across it."[2]

The two countries were facing political reality. China, its alliance with the Soviet Union deteriorating, had become concerned about its isolation from the world. The United States, having backed Chiang Kai-shek for decades, finally realized that he was never going to liberate the mainland, where a fourth of the world's population lived. Nixon and his wife, Pat, visited the Great Wall, toured the tombs of the Ming dynasty, and entered the Forbidden City, the old imperial palace in the center of Beijing (formerly known as Peking).

A new era was opening, despite a myriad of foreign-policy differences. The war still raged in Vietnam, with China backing the North Vietnamese and the United States the South; there was disagreement over the role of Japan in Asia; problems lingered over divided Korea; and there was bitter conflict over the recognition of Chiang's government. Still, the two countries, in a communiqué from Shanghai, pledged to work for closer relations in an atmosphere of peaceful coexistence.

In America, many had grown increasingly restive with Nixon's failure to extract U.S. troops from Vietnam. They saw his trip to Beijing as nothing but election-year politics. Still, in November 1972, just back with his successful diplomacy in China and with "peace at hand" in Vietnam, Nixon was reelected. His presidency, meanwhile, stood on the brink of disaster because of a coverup scandal involving a burglary at the Democratic Party headquarters in the Watergate Hotel.

Reading about developments in China in his morning newspaper in Greensboro, auto mechanic Don Sexton turned to his wife, Arrie, and asked: "Do you suppose we could find Charlie?"

Over the years, Arrie had heard countless stories of the boy her husband's Marine company had befriended. But now, decades later, she shook her head at the prospect of locating him. "Of course not. They wouldn't know him as Charlie, and you wouldn't know where to start looking."

Half a world away from his old bunkmate, listening to reports of Nixon's visit, Charlie was thinking similar thoughts. The prospects of clearing his name and getting word to Sexton and his Marine buddies that he was alive—and yearned to come to America—had never been better.

Turning off the intercom, he closed his eyes and tried to picture the face of each Marine. Over the years, he'd ended his prayers every night with a word or two about them. He figured that many of them had been sent to Korea, then Vietnam, and he had asked God to protect them.

One morning, he met an elderly neighbor on the way to the fields. "Did you hear the news?" Charlie asked.

"Oh, yes, it's very exciting," the man said. "And good news for you; we are very happy for you. Now maybe the government won't consider you an enemy. Maybe now you'll be free."

But freedom would not come quickly. Charlie's life continued as before—working in the fields of sweet potatoes, corn, and peanuts, then returning home. A year after Nixon's visit, Watergate dominated the news, and talk of new relations between China and the United

States faded into silence. Charlie and Jin Mie added a third child to their family, a girl they named Yin Chao. Their lives remained nothing more than hard labor, with Charlie at the government-run farms and Jin Mie in the hop fields.

In 1973 a Vietnam cease-fire agreement was signed in Paris, though fighting continued. Watergate brought down the Nixon presidency. Several White House aides were sent to "Club Fed" prisons, and Nixon himself was secretly indicted as a co-conspirator. In August 1974 he resigned, as a House committee pushed impeachment and tapes showed presidential involvement in the coverup.

But all that was lost on Charlie and his family. They only knew that talk had stopped of Americans coming to China and Chinese going to America. He and Jin Mie raised their children as best they could, a task made more difficult after Jin Mie's parents died. They had looked after the younger children—the daughter a baby, their second son only three—now Charlie and Jin Mie had to leave them unattended as they toiled in the fields. Jin Mie checked on them once a day during her morning break when she walked ten minutes from the fields to feed the baby.

One day she found the baby barely conscious after a fall from bed. After that, to keep her from falling, Charlie tied a rope around her waist and the other end to a bar across a window. Charlie worked only the jobs no one else wanted. He dug wells to irrigate the fields, and ditches to drain them. He cleared new roads. But the worst job was carrying human waste in a cart to fertilize the fields.

After Nixon's visit the schools taught English, and Charlie's friends urged the village school to hire him; he'd lived with Americans and could speak and write the language better than anyone else. But the school wouldn't hire a target of the militia. He remained a pariah in his village, even to those he'd known all his life.

One day as Charlie walked through the village to the fields, a bus stopped to let off passengers. One was his old friend, Li Zhon Hong, who had tutored Charlie and encouraged him to go to college. Now a doctor in Tsingtao, Li was making his weekly visit to his parents. Their friendship had cooled with Charlie's persecution. Once Charlie had received militia permission to visit Li in Tsingtao, but Li had made it clear he wasn't welcome. This day, as they passed one another on Shilu Road, Li turned his head and pretended not to see him. Charlie had always viewed Li as a brother; now, shunned by him, he wept. They would not speak for years.

Charlie and Jin Mie weren't alone in their suffering. One day in 1975, their oldest son, now twelve and in the sixth grade, came home and announced to Jin Mie that he was quitting school. He knew better than to go to his father with the news. Jin Mie was shocked. "Why? You're too young to quit school."

Yin Whee told his mother that other students made fun of him, calling his father a puppet of the Americans. Also, even though his grades were good enough to merit the red scarf that the best students wore, Yin Whee's teachers wouldn't give him one. He felt ostracized for something that had happened before he was born. He was even threatened that if he didn't behave, his father would be punished. When Charlie returned home and heard this news, he and Jin Mie tried to convince the boy to stay in school. They didn't care about the scarf, they said. All they expected was good grades. They wanted him to learn.

But Yin Whee was adamant and did not return to school. Instead, he helped his family around the house. It broke Charlie's heart to see his oldest child ostracized, suffering because of him. There seemed no end to the misery.

By 1976, the last chopper had lifted off the U.S. embassy roof in Saigon—renamed Ho Chi Minh City by the victorious North Vietnamese—and Richard Nixon was in his long exile. Americans elected a new president that year; Jimmy Carter, a former Georgia governor and peanut farmer. Curiously, the new president and Charlie could have passed one another on the streets of Tsingtao twenty-seven years earlier, when Carter was in the Navy. Years later Carter's life, influenced by China, would have a major impact on Charlie's.

As a boy in Plains, Georgia, Jimmy Carter, a devout Baptist, had grown up with stories of Baptist missionaries working in China. From their slide programs, he came to view the Chinese as friends who were in dire need of hospitals, food, schools, and Christianity. Then, as a naval officer in early 1949, he went to China.

His ship cruised up the coast from Hong Kong to Tsingtao, with stopovers in the last cities still occupied by Chiang's Nationalist troops. They docked in Tsingtao, where Jerry Hanson, Lockerbox, and the last few Marines guarded Pagoda Pier. Then Carter and his shipmates went into the city, to find storefronts boarded up. On the streets of Tsingtao, Jimmy Carter saw young boys no older than Charlie and elderly men being recruited into the Nationalist army at bayonet point. He knew then that Chiang's downfall would not be long in coming.[3]

With this background, restoring full diplomatic relations with China—picking up where Nixon and Kissinger had left off—became a logical priority for Carter's administration. But China was in turmoil. For the same year of Carter's election, both Mao Tse-tung and Chou En-lai died, throwing the country into political chaos.

The infamous Gang of Four, headed by Mao's widow, purged Deng Xiaoping and other moderates from power, instituting yet another reign of terror throughout the country. When they themselves were purged, a power struggle emerged between Mao's hand-picked heir, Hua Guofeng, premier of the People's Republic, and the once-again rehabilitated, seemingly indestructible Deng Xiaoping. It was a clash between rigid Maoist dogma and economic and social moderation. By July 1977, Deng had gained the upper hand. It took him and his backers another three years to win total victory, allowing them to institute practical economic and social reforms.

Until then Deng had to play a hedged hand in foreign policy, for hard-line Maoists resisted any compromise with the United States. In addition to the political crisis in China, restoration of relations was hampered by the Nationalist government on Taiwan, as well as by diehard anticommunists in the United States who had picked up the banner of the old China lobbyists. Even before Carter's election, a flood of invitations for all-expense-paid trips to Taipei came to his relatives and neighbors in Plains. Those who went received expensive gifts and were urged to tell Carter to forget about mainland China.[4]

Forty years of close ties with the Nationalist government could not be suddenly severed; American foreign policy dictated that Carter assure Taiwan of protection from Communist China. But for their part, the Communists demanded that the United States terminate its defense treaty with Taiwan, withdraw its troops, and establish diplomatic relations with Beijing instead.

Carter invited Hua and Deng to visit the United States, but they refused as long as there was a Taiwanese ambassador in Washington. However, on a trip to China in May 1978, Zbigniew Brzezinski, Carter's national security adviser, found them surprisingly eager to discuss trade, technology, and diplomatic relations. The next month, the Party's official newspaper announced that China would explore joint ventures with U.S. oil companies and described Brzezinski's trip as positive and useful.

In November Carter told the Chinese that for relations to occur they had to agree that the United States could maintain its defense treaty for another year, that the Taiwan issue be settled peacefully, and that military sales to Taiwan could continue. He invited Deng to Washington and set 1 January 1979 as the tentative normalizing date. Deng accepted, and in December 1978 the two governments issued a joint communiqué. Carter said to the American people on 15 December 1978: "The United States of America and the People's Republic of China have agreed to recognize each other and to establish diplomatic relations as of January 1, 1979.

"The United States recognizes the government of the People's Republic of China as the sole legal government of China. Within this context, the people of the United States will maintain cultural, commercial, and other unofficial relations with the people of Taiwan."[5]

American businessmen rushed to China to tap into the world's largest market. Word spread quickly to Tsingtao, even to Chukechuang: enemies were now friends.

Eight months later, in the fall of 1979, while Charlie worked in the fields, the militia told him and his coworkers to come with them. When they got to the village basketball court, they met five other men who had been under house arrest, like Charlie. Standing on the front bumper of a truck, the militia leader announced to the growing crowd: "I have something to tell these men. The Party has decided they have performed their duties well, that they have not given us any problems. They are no longer under house arrest. Their citizenships are restored."

After seventeen years, Charlie was a free man. Though he knew this day had been drawing near, he was overwhelmed. All the trials and horrors of the past fell away; it was as if he had been born again. But what was he to do with his new life? Go back to the fields? No. Now he would look for his American friends.

That friendship had been costly, but Charlie couldn't shake the idea of seeing the Marines and Sister Blanda again. Besides, even with his restored citizenship, life promised little for him and his family—they had already suffered irreparable harm. One day soon after his release as he walked openly to his parents' house, he met Lee Fu Ye, a friend who was an accountant in a government-run textile factory in Tsingtao. Lee told him that all people talked about in Tsingtao was the newfound American friendship. Lee thought that Charlie could benefit from it, and Charlie invited him inside to discuss the matter.

"There are many Americans in China on business," Lee said over dinner cooked by Charlie's mother. "If you contacted your old American friends, maybe they could help you as they did before."

"I don't think I can reach them," Charlie answered. "After all these years, they may be dead. Or they might not remember me."

When Lee left, Charlie asked his mother what she thought about trying to find the Marines. She looked concerned, no doubt remembering him hiding in the hole his father had dug, and then having to burn all his clothes except for the trousers that she'd dyed black. He had suffered so much for his loyalty to the Americans. "I am afraid it will only bring you more troubles," she said at last.

But all his life he'd taken risks, he told his mother, starting with the day he'd gone over the fence at the airstrip and then returned daily, with peanuts and kindling. To see the Marines again he would try anything. "I don't know what will happen. I don't know if I can reach them, or if they're still alive. All I know is that a long time ago they were my brothers."

So the next morning he went to the county office to ask permission to write to his friends in America. Everyone knew about Charlie's past and the trials he'd endured. They told him they would consider his request. He waited for two days and then went back to file another request. When no answer came after another two days, he returned and renewed his request. It went like that for two months.

Finally, a Party official responded: "You suffered terribly because of these men, yet you want to contact them again? We'll let you write letters, but don't blame us if it turns out badly; we aren't responsible."

After all, he was a citizen again, with rights just like any person to write to China's new friends. Charlie marveled at his good fortune. For thirty years he'd wanted to see the Marines again. Now it might be possible.

But how would he find them? His address book had gone up in flames when his mother had burned all evidence of his past. How could he remember addresses from thirty years ago? That night he prayed for God's help. In the morning, an address came to him: John Randall Hutchins, Hazel Green, Kentucky, USA.

He wrote a letter and rode his bicycle to Tsingtao to post it. But he never heard back from Big Hutch. Then four more addresses came to him: Tom Barclay in San Francisco; Roy Sibit in Tallmadge, Ohio; Arthur Buckley in New York; and William Bullard in North Carolina. In painstaking but extraordinarily neat penmanship that Sister Blanda and Miriam Matthews had taught him, Charlie wrote letters. Only one of these other four made it: to Route 1, Autryville, North Carolina, USA.

10

In William Bullard's impaired memory, the boy he'd left crying at Tsangkou airfield thirty-two years earlier was always twelve years old, standing smartly at attention in a cutdown Marine uniform with precise creases, his tie knotted to perfection, his corporal chevrons overlapping the left sleeve of his jacket. That was how Charlie looked in the black-and-white, mahogany-framed photo that Bullard had kept all these years on his dresser on the family farm in Autryville. Never could he imagine Charlie as a grown man in peasant clothes.

That terrible car accident on Christmas Eve 1948 that had robbed Bullard of memory, hadn't taken away his ability to work, although he'd decided against farming full time. He sold life insurance for the Western and Southern Insurance Company throughout southeastern North Carolina, and he married Lorraine Martin. Together they raised a son, William Jr., and a daughter, Susan, in a house he built next to his parents' wooden farmhouse. The house in which Bullard had been born and raised was now a shambling wreck, used mainly for storing farm supplies.

Like his father, a deceased former deputy sheriff, he raised hogs and farmed tobacco, corn, and soybeans. Whenever Bullard looked at the photo on his bureau, he wondered if Charlie had survived all the terrible events he'd read about in *Time* magazine over the years. His own children, their aunts, uncles, and cousins—the entire farming community—had heard his stories about the boy. If ever William Jr. misbehaved, he was lectured about the perfect little Marine. There was another photo, too, of him and Charlie sitting together. Bullard had sent it to his mother, Betsy, from China; she'd kept it on her dresser.

One Sunday before receiving Charlie's letter, Bullard had stood at the pulpit at the Clement Baptist Church, where he was a deacon, and sermonized about brotherly love. Referring to Charlie, he'd begun to cry. Every Christmas, when appealing for the Lottie Moon Fund—named for a missionary who'd starved to death in China while helping the peasants—Bullard described the horrible conditions he'd seen there as a young Marine. He told about Charlie and the poverty the Marines had found his family in; then tears fell, and every year the Lottie Moon Fund grew bigger.

It had always bothered Bullard that he couldn't keep the promise he'd made to Charlie to bring him to America, but by the time doctors had released him from the hospital after his car wreck, returning to China was politically impossible. All he could do was look at the photograph and plow through the scrapbooks, wondering what had happened to him.

Then, one day in mid-May 1980, on his way home from repairing hog fences with a friend, R. J. Stewart, Bullard stopped at his mailbox. Sifting through the stack of mail—mostly checks from policy holders—he came across a letter that sent a shockwave through his body. On the envelope, across the flap, was written: "From: Tsui Chi Hsii, Chukechuang Litsun Laoshun County, Tsingtao, China."

Bullard tore open the letter with trembling hands. At first he just stared at the penmanship. Could it really be Charlie? Then he began to read.

April 13, 1980

Do you remember your old buddy in China? Did you ever think of little Charlie? Yes, here I am writing to you. I know this would be quite a surprise to you. But needn't so, thanks to God and the deed of pure friendship between our two great countries that we are able to get in touch now.

Thirty years over, it's really a miserable long, time. In all these times my heart was like on fire from day to night. I was always thinking of my old buddies.

I pray for the day for us to meet. Do you think it would be possible? I could never forget how you and my other buddies support me to school and treat me as your own brother.

With many hugs,
Charlie

"R. J., he's alive, little Charlie's alive," Bullard shouted, leaning against the mailbox post. Stewart looked puzzled, until he realized it had to be the Chinese waif he'd heard about all these years. Bullard drove straight to Clement Elementary School to tell Lorraine, then he called everyone he knew in Autryville. And that afternoon he phoned the Goodyear Rubber and Tire plant in Akron, Ohio, and asked for Roy Sibit.

Sibit was the only China Marine with whom Bullard had kept in contact. Years earlier when returning home with his new bride, Jean, from a vacation at Myrtle Beach, Sibit had stopped at the Bullards. This became a tradition, and every summer the scrapbooks from China came out of the closet and the stories were retold and stretched—of Charlie, of fights with sailors that had landed them both in the brig, of challenging their squad leader, Don Sexton, to a fight after he'd ordered lights out. That had landed them in the brig, too.

"Are you sitting down?" Bullard asked when Sibit came on the line. "I just got a letter from China. Charlie's alive!"

Months earlier, Eula Mae Hutchins had run into her house with a letter addressed to Mr. John Randall Hutchins, Hazel Green, Kentucky, USA. "Jack, it's a letter from Charlie!"

Her husband looked up from the newspaper. "Charlie who?"

"You know, Charlie! Your little friend in China. He wrote you a letter."

Hutch shot out of his chair and snatched the envelope, filled with strange Chinese markings stamped in the upper-left corner. It can't be, Hutch thought. Not after thirty years. Holding the letter, his mind traveled back to China. He saw himself, so youthful and strapping, walking down Tsingtao beach with Charlie as he explained about life in America, and then he remembered one of his last days in China, when he'd gone into a jewelry store with Charlie to buy a bracelet for his mother and one for Eula Mae.

The store owner had yelled at him angrily; then Charlie and the merchant had begun shouting at each another in Chinese. Finally Charlie had grabbed Hutch's arm and pulled him toward the door. "Let's go Hutchie. Him don't like Marines."

Now Big Hutch sank down in the chair with Charlie's letter.

June 7, 1979

Buddy, more than 30 years has past, it was a very long time. In all these time, I was always wondering how you and all mine other buddies were. I think of you every morning and dream of you every night. Some time I even magically murmur to the wishing star to grant me the chance to hear or see you. Could it be possible for us to meet each other again someday?

I'm not as little as 30 years before. I'm 45 years old now. I have wife two sons and little girl. . . .

Buddy please answer me immediately. Write me a long letter tell me everything about yourself and family.

Hutchins immediately penned an answer expressing how stunned he'd been to hear from his old friend. He put it in a box packed with clothes and goods and mailed it the next day. The package never arrived.

Rarely does a story spread through the media as wildly as did the story about Charlie and the Marines.

It began with letters: Bullard and Sibit wrote to every China Marine they could locate. In June 1980, Sibit drove to Autryville to map a strategy with Bullard, who had already contacted the U.S. Immigration and Naturalization Service in Raleigh. Together they drove to the INS office, where officials were encouraging. The officials said that if Charlie and his family were allowed to visit, they would need a place to live. Then they met with an immigration lawyer named Jack Pinnix, who initially could offer them little help but later would play a role in the story of Charlie Two Shoes.

While driving back to Autryville, Bullard decided to fix up the old family farmhouse. As is still the custom in rural North Carolina, friends and neighbors met after work on long summer evenings and on weekends to help out. The costs would mount to ten thousand dollars, most out of Bullard's pocket. Bullard opened a fund drive to help Charlie and his family, if they were allowed to visit. He and Sibit made the first of what would be hundreds of calls to politicians in Washington.

Both men told Charlie's tale to hometown newspapers. The story was picked up by larger papers in Ohio and North Carolina; then reporters from all around the country got it from the wire services. CBS correspondent Charles Osgood and a film crew traveled to Autryville to film Bullard and his friends "painting and propping up" the old house, as Bullard and Sibit told the remarkable story. Strangers read of Charlie or saw his story on television and sent money. "Hundred-dollar bills come with no return address on them," Bullard told Osgood.

In no time, the trickle of letters to Washington in support of Charlie turned into a flood. Bullard and Sibit maneuvered the maze of red tape and Washington bureaucracy, co-signing the official invitation and necessary sponsor forms that made them financially responsible for Charlie and his family.

In the beginning, Charlie knew nothing of what was developing. He didn't even know his letters had arrived. He never got Hutch's letter and package, there was no reply from Sibit (the letter to him never arrived), and months went by without a response from Bullard. He was growing increasingly discouraged, wondering if all his buddies were dead—or if they even remembered him.

Bullard's return letter to Charlie almost never made it, either. Bullard sent the letter to the return address, but no one could read it at the main post office in Tsingtao: the lettering was unknown to them. Who was this Tsui Chi Hsii? And where was this Chukechuang Litsun Laoshun County? They only understood Chinese script. But postal officials assigned a carrier to ride a motorcycle throughout Tsingtao to find the recipient, and if he couldn't find him in the city, he was instructed to ride village to village until he did. They wanted to know who had contacts in America in this era of warming relations.

Two weeks later the carrier sputtered into Chukechuang, stopping at the village office. "Does anyone in your village have connections to the United States?" he asked the ranking Communist, showing him the letter.

"I don't think so," the village leader said, studying the indecipherable address. Then he paused. He was a boyhood friend of Jin Mie's older brother and remembered hearing about Charlie's life with the Americans. "We have a man who lived with American Marines in Tsingtao long ago, but certainly this couldn't be for him."

It was worth a try, the carrier said: it was his only lead so far. The village leader offered to deliver the letter himself, but the carrier told him he'd been charged with the mission and that he'd already spent two weeks riding the countryside looking for the recipient. He would go to Charlie's house himself.

A motorcycle was a rare phenomenon in Chukechuang. Everyone heard it draw nearer, and no one was more surprised than Charlie when it stopped in front of his house and the carrier knocked on his door. "Do you recognize the name and address on this letter?" the carrier asked.

Charlie looked at the envelope. As he read the return address— from the USA—his eyes brightened in disbelief and joy. His face spread into a wide, consuming grin. Seeing Charlie's reaction, the postman smiled, too: he'd found his man. "This is my letter," Charlie said. "It's from William Bullard, my friend in America."

"I am happy for you," the carrier said. "I am happy for myself; my mission is complete. I can go home." He saddled his motorcycle and was off in a cloud of dust, leaving Charlie with his letter and memories.

Charlie's life had come full circle. The Marines knew he was alive and where he was; surely they would remember their promises and send for him now. Word about the letter spread throughout Chukechuang. Many of Charlie's neighbors were happy that his old friends had found him. Others saw the letter as confirmation of their long-held suspicions: Charlie was a spy for the Americans. Otherwise, why would they be writing?

Those suspicions had prevented him from getting a job even after his house arrest had ended. He'd tried to get a position teaching English, but no one would hire someone with a prison record. So he farmed with his father, though the rift persisted between his family and Jin Mie.

Now, every day he carried his letter to the fields and read it over and over again. Then another letter arrived, this one from Sibit, who wrote that the Marines had not forgotten him and assured him they would figure out a way to get him to the United States. He enclosed a photo of his family. Charlie wrote back immediately:

Dear Sib, no word in mankind can describe how happy I felt. I press your picture of you and your family over my heart and thank the angels of God for bringing the picture and letter to me.

My body is Chinese but I was raised and grown up by you and our other buddies . . . my soul is really yours. For this I have suffered a lot. I have no bit of money. May God grant possible for me to come to America. May you and our other buddies do as you did in the old days help me to succeed. I beg you to rescue me.

Charlie didn't know it, but he'd already become a celebrity in the country he so desperately wanted to move to. His story had taken on Hollywood proportions, and he even had a new media name: Charlie Two Shoes, a logical extension from Charlie TuShu.

The story mushroomed, taking on a life of its own. As Sibit and Bullard negotiated visas, other Marines—some who hadn't even known Charlie—called or wrote with offers to help. George McDonald of New Mexico, one of the last members of Love Company to leave China, called with an offer to do whatever was needed. A Medal of Honor winner sent Sibit a check. Schoolchildren sent nickels and quarters.

Sibit contacted the Chinese embassy in Washington. His wife sent out petitions urging Congress to support Charlie's visit; they came back with hundreds of signatures. A millionaire named Leon Toups called from St. Louis, where he ran a Fortune 500 company. He told Sibit that his family had decided to make their yearly cause the Marines' cause, offering to pay plane fares for the entire family if visas were obtained.

In Chicago, Michael Sneed, a young female reporter for the *Sun-Times,* was one of the first to write the story. She captured the imagination of thousands of readers, including a former Marine and veteran of Guadalcanal—Duke Bingham. When he spoke to Sneed, she told him about Sibit and Bullard and suggested that they might need his help.

The story instantly appealed to Bingham, who'd spent time in naval intelligence and had worked undercover for the St. Louis Police Department. He was still a Marine to the bone, and this story had Marine written all over it. He also had a great affection for Asians. He'd married a woman of Korean descent and had hired a young Korean woman to help him with his computer-software business. He made frequent trips into Chicago's Chinatown to a Catholic church, where he played gin rummy with Father Schmidt and Father Chun.

Bingham called Sibit and Bullard, telling them he'd had experience bringing Asians to the United States. They said they needed all the help they could get; they were already mired in bureaucracy. To the ex–undercover cop and naval intelligence agent, getting Charlie to America became a challenge.

By this time, Bullard and Sibit were talking to Charlie on the one phone in Chukechuang, in the village security office. Whenever a call came for Charlie, a clerk ran to his house to get him. Bingham wrote to Charlie with his telephone number and told him to call collect. He did, every two weeks, or else Bingham called the village. He just said "Charlie" to whoever answered, and in a few minutes, Charlie was on the line.

After Sneed's story appeared, people all over Chicago wanted to help, and word was out that Bingham was the contact to call. A Charlie Two Shoes Fund was established to defray expenses. Chinatown organized a committee, and a group of military men, mostly Marines, began meeting at Glenview Naval Air Station to discuss strategies on how to bring Charlie and his family to America. While Bullard and Sibit worked their congressional contacts, Bingham saw Charlie's extraction from China as a military operation.

The number of men meeting at Glenview kept growing, often with forty to fifty discussing elaborate plans: swooping the family out of the country in a seaplane to Japan or Taiwan, or even straight to the United

States, and then dropping into Lake Michigan, with reporters waiting. They even discussed renting a submarine, for fifty thousand dollars, and smuggling the family aboard.

To Bullard and Sibit, those plans sounded like something out of an adventure movie. Still, Bullard appreciated Bingham's interest. Sibit grew increasingly distant, perhaps feeling that Bingham was intruding. "Everything is being handled from here in Tallmadge," Bingham remembers Sibit telling him.[1]

In the late summer of 1981, Sibit traveled to Autryville to inspect the work that Bullard and his friends had done on the farmhouse. He left without commenting on it. Bullard could see that Sibit was growing distant, but he didn't know why until September, when he received a letter from him.

By now Sibit was getting calls from TV-network officials and representatives from movie companies interested in Charlie's story. Sibit's letter was a contract to form a financial partnership to bring Charlie to America, laying out a plan for speeches, books, and movies. The contract authorized Sibit to make speeches and films about Charlie, speak to the media, and write stories. It stipulated that "nothing in this agreement restricts or restrains me from accepting any compensation that may be offered which I deem to be appropriate." All expenses as well as compensation would be split with Bullard.

Bullard was shocked—and not interested in the proposition, to which he did not respond. Six weeks later, Sibit wrote again, this time officially withdrawing his offer of a partnership. It was the end of a thirty-year friendship. From that point, Sibit and Bullard worked separately to bring Charlie and his family to America.

In Chukechuang, Charlie sensed something was wrong. It seemed that Bullard, Sibit, and Bingham weren't working together any longer. On Bullard's advice, Charlie went to the police department in Tsingtao and applied for passports for the family. Three months later, without a response, he applied again. Three months after that, Charlie was told that no passports would be issued. "We can't approve passports because you don't have any family ties in the United States," a clerk told him.

"You don't understand," Charlie responded. "These friends in the

United States are like brothers. They want me and my family to visit."

"That's not how the system works," the clerk said.

Charlie wrote Bullard that the Chinese government had denied his passports but he wasn't giving up. He also called Bingham. "They won't let me leave," he said.

"Don't worry," Bingham said with his customary confidence. "We'll get you here. There are a lot people who want you to come."

Charlie returned to the passport office every month to reapply. Finally the clerk told him to get lost. "There's no use coming back," he shouted. "Policy is policy."

Friends and family urged him to forget his dream; his persistence would bring more trouble. Discouraged, he called Sibit and told him that his only hope lay with the Chinese embassy in Washington. In October 1982, Sibit drove to Washington to meet with embassy officials Ji Chaozhu and Pung Jinray. Ji's brother had been an interpreter for Mao and Chou En-lai. Sibit told them how the Marines had come to know Charlie, and that they wanted to see him now that relations between the two countries had been reestablished. He asked for their assistance in securing passports for Charlie and his family. In a follow-up letter, Sibit wrote to Ji:

> Many similar relationships were created through mutual needs of American soldiers and young Chinese children; however, Charlie became special to many service men and created a lasting friendship as indicated by the attached letters. . . .
>
> Financial support and housing has been obtained for Charlie and his family for and during a visit to the United States.
>
> On behalf of Charlie and all his United States friends, I beg your assistance in making such a visit possible.[2]

Ji was encouraging, but he told Sibit that one or two passports might be all he could get.

Seven months passed with no word, disheartening Charlie and the Marines. Charlie pleaded with Sibit to go back to the Chinese embassy; passport clerks in Tsingtao had heard nothing from anyone in Washington. Sibit did meet with Ji again, and he told him that Charlie still didn't have his passports. Ji said he would check into the holdup. Two months later, a messenger came to Charlie's house with word to go to the passport office in Tsingtao. There, two officials questioned him about his American friends.

"Can these Americans be trusted?" one official asked. "Are you sure they'll take care of you?"

"Oh, yes, we were like brothers," Charlie responded.

"Do you want to take your family? Do you want to stay in the United States?"

"Yes," Charlie answered fervently. "I want to stay and educate my children so they can help build a better world."

When Charlie returned home, he told Jin Mie that they would be leaving soon. Yet three more months passed without word. Finally, in March 1983, he was told that passports were ready for his whole family. Later he learned that the embassy in Washington had pressured Beijing, noting, "This man has a lot of friends. We need someone like him in the United States."

Now all that stood in Charlie's way was getting visas from the formidable U.S. State Department. Sibit told him to go to the American embassy in Beijing for visitors' visas; he was certain they would be ready. Bullard assured him that the State Department wouldn't give him any trouble, now that he'd gotten passports.

So, passports in hand, Charlie took a train to Beijing and the American embassy, a twelve-hour trip. He arrived on Women's Day, a national holiday, to find government offices closed. The stress was unbearable. He checked into a cheap hotel, where, unable to sleep, he paced the floor all night. Though never a heavy smoker, he went through three packs of cigarettes trying to calm his nerves.

In the morning, a clerk at the American embassy told him that visas could not be issued because an affidavit of financial support had not been filed. Charlie called Sibit with the news, and Sibit said he would go to work on the document immediately.

Charlie went home to wait. Two weeks later, the affidavit arrived and Charlie took another train to Beijing, where he was told that only one visa would be issued—for him alone. Officials were concerned that if the whole family went to America, they would never return to China.

"But your government told my friends in the United States my whole family could go," Charlie said.

"This is all we can do," the clerk told him. "Take it or leave it."

He had feared this would happen. Years ago he'd left Jin Mie and an infant son, but he couldn't leave his family now and go to the United States. On the clerk's desk, he saw a file with his name. It was stuffed with newspaper clippings about the efforts to bring him to America, and he realized that his passage had become very political. He begged the embassy official to let him take his youngest son, at least: "My little boy is very smart. I know he will do well in school and get a good education."

The clerk told him he would talk with the chief consul, but when Charlie returned the next day, the answer was the same: one six-month visitor's visa, for him alone. He called Sibit again. Take the visa, Sibit advised. "You come first, then we'll work to get your family over."

Charlie took the visa. It stipulated that he must leave the country by 30 June 1983. On the long ride back to Tsingtao, Charlie worried about what he would tell his family. At home, it wasn't any easier than he'd thought it would be: to his daughter's tears and his wife's dismay, he announced that he was going to America alone. He told them not to worry—he'd get them over as soon as he could.

So it was arranged: Charlie would leave on 10 May 1983 from Beijing. The ticket was paid for by Leon Toups, as promised. On the day before he left, Chukechuang's leader and a security officer came to his house to tell him that China's central news agency had approved a request by NBC-TV newsman Sandy Gilmour to interview him. They advised Charlie to watch what he said and not to criticize the Chinese government.

Gilmour had opened the network's Beijing bureau in 1981, as soon as U.S. journalists were allowed into China. He was preparing to go home in June, when editors in New York sent him a magazine story about Charlie, describing his upcoming reunion with his Marine buddies. The New York people thought it would make a moving story. Gilmour agreed and put his researcher, Eric Baculinao, a native Filipino fluent in English and Chinese, on the hunt to find Charlie. The magazine story had used pre-Communist spellings, so Baculinao was at a disadvantage. However, it did say that he lived in a village near Tsingtao.

Baculinao had been in China since summer 1971, when he had come with a group of college students for a three-week visit. But while there, conditions at home had worsened under President Ferdinand Marcos. Baculinao, blacklisted as a dissident, was concerned that he would be arrested if he returned. He and the other students decided to wait for tensions to ease, but then Marcos declared martial law, and the students were stranded. Baculinao would not return for fifteen years—until Marcos went into exile in 1986. By that time he had married a Chinese woman and started a new life in Beijing. He was one of the first people Sandy Gilmour hired when he opened the NBC Beijing bureau in 1981, just after the United States and China restored diplomatic relations.

Baculinao imagined the closest modern Chinese sounds for the old spellings and used long-distance operators to connect him to the likely places. He worked first on the county, then the city, and finally the village. It was early evening in his office at the Qianmen Hotel, Beijing, when he was connected to the village leader in Chukechuang. Baculinao asked if he knew of any villager who was traveling to America.

"Yes, a man in our village is leaving for the United States soon."

Gilmour was working on another story when he heard Baculinao yell, "I found him! I found Charlie Two Shoes!"

Several minutes later he was talking to Charlie in Chinese. Charlie sounded cautious and reserved, but when Baculinao switched to English and used the names of his Marine buddies, he opened up. When they hung up, Baculinao telexed the foreign-affairs office in Tsingtao, requesting permission for Gilmour to interview Charlie at his home in the village. He cited the cause of Sino-American friendship, and permission was granted.

While Gilmour and a translator set off for Tsingtao, Baculinao called Roy Sibit in Ohio to get information about Charlie's schedule and plane arrangements. Sibit, wanting to keep Charlie's trip a secret, appeared to become "really mad," according to a surprised Baculinao, and said there could be legal consequences if "NBC's intrusion into Charlie's story messed up things."

In Tsingtao, Gilmour was not allowed to go to Chukechuang after all, so he sent a van to bring Charlie and his family to the Foreign Hotel in the city. The hotel was on the beach where Big Danny had taught Charlie to swim long ago, and where he'd been caught skipping school. Gilmour was the first American Charlie had seen in thirty-five years, and the first one his family had ever met.

After the initial interview, Charlie took Gilmour and his translator, Mr. Cao, around Tsingtao to tape interviews in front of all the places that had meant so much to him as a boy. They went to the Marine barracks; to the school where Sister Blanda and Miriam Matthews had taught him English; to the YMCA, where he'd learned to box; to St. Michael's, where he'd found his faith; and to Pagoda Pier, where his buddies had left him saluting and crying. Heeding the advice of his village leader, Charlie said nothing about his years of persecution. When Gilmour asked why he hadn't been back to St. Michael's since 1949, he told him he'd been too busy to attend. He said nothing about the boarded-up front doors. Nor did he mention prison; to do so could put his family at risk, separating them permanently if he left the country by himself.

Gilmour asked why he still loved his Marine buddies.

"My Marine friends, in the old days, they treat me like their own brother—they love me very much and took good care of me," Charlie said, squinting into the camera. "I took them as my father, or my elder brothers and I love them from my deep heart. Because of our great love, and after all these thirty-five years, I have never forgotten them. In my dreams, in my prayers, I always meet them."

That evening Gilmour treated the family to the best meal they'd ever had. Waiters brought course after course, dish after dish of Chinese food. They had Coca-Cola to drink, which Charlie had sorely missed and his family had never before tasted.

Slurping it down, Yin Tao, Charlie's younger son, whispered, "Dad. Will this make us drunk?"

The next day, as Charlie's train readied to pull out of Tsingtao station, his daughter, Yin Chao, broke down in bitter tears and could not be consoled. Charlie hugged her four times. All he could say was that they would be together soon. Still, he wondered if he was doing the right thing. What kind of man would leave his young daughter to pursue his own dreams? Yet surely, he thought, with the help of Bullard, Sibit, and Bingham, they would be apart for only a short time.

But this thought gave him no consolation as the train chugged out of the station with Yin Chao running alongside. On the train, Charlie and oldest son Yin Whee, who was accompanying his father to Beijing, sat quietly in a bench car, each with his own thoughts. Gilmour, in another car, decided against interviewing him further. There were so many armed guards, he didn't want to bring trouble to Charlie.

When they arrived in Beijing, Baculinao took Charlie to the Pan American desk at the Beijing airport to get his ticket. He also gave Charlie his business card, asking to be alerted when his family left for America—he wanted to tape their departure also. The next day at the airport, when his father boarded the plane for San Francisco—completely unaware of the intrigue swirling around him and the trouble ahead—Yin Whee dropped to his knees and began to wail.

In Cleveland, Roy Sibit also was boarding his first flight ever; it was bound for San Francisco too. Worried that Duke Bingham was going to divert Charlie to Chicago, he wanted to be there to prevent it.[3]

Bingham told Sibit Charlie's story would get better play in the Chicago media, aiding their cause to bring his family to America. He'd told Charlie that businessmen in Chinatown were willing to help him settle and give him a job; a parade was planned.

But Sibit had worked too hard for Charlie to go anywhere besides home with him. So, taking no chances, he was winging his way to the West Coast to rendezvous with the friend he'd promised to bring to the United States thirty-five years earlier.

The last photo that Charlie had made of him and his family in front of their house in Chukechuang, 1983. Charlie left for the United States soon after.

Courtesy Duke Bingham

Eric Baculinao in front of the American embassy, Beijing. Baculinao helped Jin Mie and the children get their visas to come to the United States in 1985. He was the NBC researcher who found Charlie for NBC Beijing correspondent Sandy Gilmour to interview.
Courtesy Pamela L. Moore

Charlie with NBC correspondent Sandy Gilmour and his wife, Karen.
Courtesy Charlie Tsui

Charlie and Sister Blanda after Charlie's confirmation
in Tallmadge, Ohio, 1985. Sister Blanda was his sponsor. Roy Sibit is in the background.

Courtesy Sister Blanda

Charlie after his confirmation. Behind Charlie, from
left: Ed Grady of Redding, Connecticut; Roy Sibit;
Ray Brewington of Michigan.

Courtesy Charlie Tsui

Charlie on the day he and his family arrived in Greensboro, North Carolina, 1986. To his left is William Bullard of Autryville, North Carolina; to his right, Don Sexton of Greensboro.
Courtesy Don Sexton

Surviving members of Love Company and other
former Marines at the 1991 reunion, Charlie's
restaurant. Seated, from left: William Bullard,
Ed Grady, Neil Kinner, Dominick Liberatore,
George McDonald, Charlie, Don Sexton, Earl Parks.
Standing, from left: Frank Liberatore, Charlie
Ritterburg, Warren Evans, George Powers,
Berwyn Bragg, Dick Matthews, Bob Donovan,
Bob Smith, Ken Bailey, Jesse Gorman, Jim Sweeney.
Courtesy Don Sexton

Charlie playing his erhoo, a two-string Chinese instrument, for his Marine buddies at a 1991 reunion at his restaurant. *Courtesy Charlie Tsui*

Charlie with Jack Hutchins and his wife, Eula Mae, at Charlie's Tsingtao Chinese Restaurant, Chapel Hill, North Carolina, 1991. *Courtesy Charlie Tsui*

With retired Brig. Gen. Charles Robertson at Charlie's restaurant, 1991. Robertson was the Marine captain who formed Love Company and let "regulations be damned" when he allowed Charlie to remain with the company. *Courtesy Charlie Tsui*

Charlie and his family. Jin Mie is seated; standing with Charlie, from left:
Jeff, Susan, David. *Courtesy Don Sexton*

11 No media event occurs without a camera and a script. For the story of Charlie Two Shoes, a story that made national headlines and network television and captured the hearts of Americans everywhere, Roy Sibit wrote the script. He also called the reporters and arranged for the cameras. He created the event and the star, becoming the manager of the event and agent for the star. But the event became a circus, with the star dressed in a Chinese peasant outfit shilling for coins.

As Sibit flew to the West Coast to rendezvous with Charlie, he had no idea what lay ahead—for Charlie, for himself, for Jean, and for their sons, Shawn and Darrin. If he could have seen the future, he probably would have let the story die in China. But in the beginning it all seemed so perfect: He was fulfilling a promise and reuniting with a long-lost friend. He had a great story to tell and a star who was well known in America even before he arrived.

Roy Sibit grew up in Akron, a company town run by Goodyear Rubber and Tire. He was the son of hard-working Italian immigrants who raised one daughter and five sons. Roy had a fraternal twin, Russell. In the mid-1940s, during the war, the twins were starting offensive and defensive guards—Roy on the right, Russell on the left—for the Garfield High School Presidents. They were city champs in their senior year, 1946. Roy was All-City, and though not particularly big for his position, he earned a reputation for fearlessness that won him a football scholarship to Miami of Ohio University, in Oxford.

Roy and Russell boxed, too. In their senior year they entered a tournament at Garfield High. There were twenty contestants, but the twins defeated everyone. They faced each other in the championship. Roy won.

The day after graduation, he left for Oxford and football practice. But he grew restless, and without telling his parents, he and a friend hitchhiked to Fort Pierce, Florida. They bummed around for two weeks, then hitchhiked home, where Roy went to the Marine recruiting office. He'd always wanted to be a Marine—he liked the way the recruiters dressed, with their uniforms so crisp, their step and demeanor confident and disciplined.

It was while trying to enlist that he discovered Roy Sibit was not his legal name. He was Ray Cipiti, son of Rosario Cipiti, the name his father brought from Sicily. After a thirty-day wait to legalize the name he'd used all his life, he was in boot camp at Parris Island. Then he shipped out to Camp Pendleton, where he awaited his first assignment—Tsingtao. His unit of replacements left San Francisco in February 1947. The troopship didn't make it past the Golden Gate Bridge before Pfc. Roy Sibit, a rifleman, heaved his guts over the side. It took forty-eight seasick days to get to Tsingtao by way of Pearl Harbor, Guam, Manila, and finally Shanghai.

Disembarking at Pagoda Pier, Sibit went by truck to Tsangkou Air Base. The place looked like a scene out of a war movie— desolate, with landing strips, hangars, barracks, and Quonset huts, all dwarfed by jagged mountains from where the wind howled that winter of 1947, driving temperature to twenty degrees below zero.

Sibit was assigned to Love Company. When he checked into his barracks, two other Marines were packing to go home. A dog they'd named Lockerbox lay on the barracks floor. The departing Marines discussed taking him with them in a duffel bag, but they worried that he'd suffocate. Then a little boy who would play a major role in Sibit's life suddenly walked into the squad bay. He was dressed in tidy Marine greens, with a khaki shirt and tie. He spoke decent English and was returning from school in Tsingtao. Love Company was paying his tuition. Sibit was dumbfounded.

"This is Charlie, Roy," one of the Marines said. "You'll look after him, won't you?"

Sibit thought he meant the dog, until they made it clear they meant the boy. "Sure, I'll look after him," Roy said, not knowing what that entailed, nor how much Charlie meant to Love Company.

That afternoon, Charlie challenged Sibit to a game of cards.

"What kind?" Sibit asked.

"Poker."

Charlie won. Their friendship didn't spark immediately; Charlie continued to go into the city and watch movies at the compound with guys who'd come before Sibit—Don Sexton, William Bullard, Clayton Mattice, Tom Barclay, and Arthur Buckley. But when they all left for home, he and Sibit drew close.

Charlie called him Sippie, and when he had to go to the bathroom, he joked, "I got to take a Sippie." It was the closest he ever got to talking like a Marine.

Sibit and Ray Brewington, another boxer, took Charlie to the YMCA gym and taught him to box; Charlie loved it. On Sundays, Sibit and Charlie went to mass together at St. Michael's, then bargain hunting in the city. Sibit noted that the Chinese merchants didn't like Charlie; they would taunt him in Chinese and laugh at him. But Charlie didn't seem to mind—he just bargained harder. They became friends during the year and a half that Sibit was in China. When Roy left in the fall of 1948, he said he'd try to get him to America.

Sibit wrote to Charlie, and Charlie wrote back two or three times. But the letters stopped and there was only silence for thirty years—until 1980, when Bullard received his letter. Then the two set out on their campaign to bring Charlie to America. Three years later, on Tuesday, 10 May 1983, Sibit stood before a glass partition in San Francisco International Airport, awaiting Charlie's arrival.

On board the Pan Am jet, the captain announced over the intercom, as the plane taxied to its gate: "Would Charlie Two Shoes from the People's Republic of China please come up front."

The other passengers watched a Chinese man in peasant clothes, looking haggard and older than his forty-nine years, shuffle up the aisle. "Mr. Two Shoes," the captain said, "Your friend and a customs agent are waiting for you outside."

Charlie wasn't expecting anyone to meet him in San Francisco. The first to disembark, he stepped into a glare of television lights and camera flashes. The customs agent led him down a tunnel to the glass partition. On the other side was a man he recognized from his boyhood. Sippie. They were both thirty-five years older now, gaunt and with far less hair, but to each, the other looked like an older version of what they remembered. Charlie grinned and pointed to Sibit, who pressed his hand against the glass. Charlie did the same, and for a minute they stood and stared at each other, wiping away tears. Then the agent led Charlie to customs.

"I'm so excited," Charlie told waiting reporters. "I can hardly believe it. This was my dream, but now it's coming true."

Leaving customs, moving through the journalists, he and Sibit embraced like long-lost brothers.

"Charlie, you smell like garlic," Sibit joked. They laughed.

Threading through the crowd, they boarded a United Airlines flight for Cleveland, along with an NBC news crew that had taped the reunion. After a stopover in Denver, a stewardess told Charlie that a passenger in first class wanted to see him.

George McDonald, bearded and bald, who in the last chaotic days of the Marines' involvement in Tsingtao had asked anyone aboard the transport ship in the harbor if they knew what had happened to Charlie, had caught the flight to Cleveland to join the reunion. "Honey, I'll buy you the biggest steak in Texas if you can get me on that flight in Denver," McDonald promised the ticket agent in Albuquerque.

McDonald and Charlie hugged, then reenacted it for the TV camera. Night had fallen by the time the plane landed at Cleveland Hopkins International Airport. The three were met by a huge welcoming party and more reporters. Sibit and Charlie were desperately tired, but the crowd pumped their energy. Sibit's youngest son, twelve-year-old Shawn—Charlie's age when Sibit had first met him—rushed toward Charlie to embrace him. Then a burly Detroit police officer embraced him. "Remember me?" said Ray Brewington. "I used to carry you around on my shoulders. I taught you to box."

"I remember. I remember," Charlie said. Then he saw a man standing shyly at the fringe of the crowd. He went over to him with his arms open.

"Hi Charlie; God bless you, God bless you," William Bullard said, embracing him. Bullard had not talked to Sibit in two years, since he'd received the contract to split the proceeds over Charlie, but he'd come to welcome Charlie to America anyway. He'd only learned of Charlie's arrival the night before, from George McDonald. It was Bullard's fifty-eighth birthday, and the trip was a present from his family. His daughter, Susan Wilson, had flown with him.

"It's been a long time, Charlie," Bullard said, as they walked off holding hands to retrieve Charlie's baggage.

"It's been a terrible long time, Bullard," Charlie responded.

That night as Arrie Sexton readied for bed in Greensboro, North Carolina, CNN announced on television: "In just a moment, the remarkable story of Charlie Two Shoes."

"Don, the TV just said something about Charlie Two Shoes," Arrie called out to her husband.

Don shrugged and turned off the set. He didn't know a Charlie Two Shoes, he said. He'd only known Charlie TuShu.

When Sexton awoke the next morning, he opened the *Greensboro News and Record* to a front-page photo of a Chinese man embracing another man. It was paired with an Associated Press story, datelined San Francisco: "A Chinese farmer known as 'Charlie Two Shoes' to U.S. Marines who befriended him as a boy 34 years ago arrived in America on Tuesday and burst into tears of joy as he embraced one of his old Marine buddies."

Sexton skimmed the caption, didn't recognize Sibit, and hurriedly left for a nearby diner to meet friends for coffee. As he walked in, they were talking about Charlie. They'd all heard Sexton's stories about China and wanted to know if this was the same Charlie. The diner's TV was tuned to the *Today* show. A waitress, who'd heard the stories for years, said that earlier in the show, Bryant Gumbel had interviewed two men at NBC affiliate WKYC, Cleveland. One man was from China and dressed in peasant clothes, the other an American in a three-piece suit. The waitress said she'd been carrying breakfast orders from the kitchen when Gumbel, who called the Chinese man Charlie Two Shoes, asked him why it was so important to come to America to visit his friends.

She froze to listen, balancing plates of eggs and bacon, and heard Charlie say in a quiet voice: "I have been wishing and dreaming all these years to be with my buddies. During all these thirty-five years, I never gave up hope to see my old friends."

Then Sexton drove home for his photographs of Charlie and the morning paper. "That's the same man that was on TV! That's the same American, too!" the waitress said when he returned.

In Bridgeport, Connecticut, Ed Grady was walking down a corridor toward his office at Harvey Hubbell, an electrical-equipment company where he was a vice president, when he ran into a colleague. Grady's friends knew all about Charlie, too. He carried a photo of him in his wallet and told everyone the story. "Hey Ed, I thought about you last night," the friend said. "I saw a story on TV about a Chinese man named Charlie who'd just flown in from Beijing. Could it be that kid you knew?"

Grady shrugged. "Everybody was called Charlie in those days."

At home his wife, Mary, had watched the newscast on NBC the previous night. She had seen Sandy Gilmour's story from Tsingtao and Beijing, about a man named Charlie who had been befriended by U.S. Marines decades earlier and was on his way to America to visit them, sadly leaving his family behind.

The story rang familiar. On her second date with Ed, soon after he had graduated from Dartmouth in the late 1940s, he had told her about Charlie and showed her the photo he carried in his wallet. She was touched by his love for the boy and his sadness at having to leave him.

Mary hadn't told Ed about the newscast last night, but this morning after mass, she met friends for breakfast at the Country Diner, near their home in Redding. Skimming the New York *Daily News,* she saw a photo of Charlie on the front page. Examining the face carefully, Mary knew she'd seen it before. She ran to the pay phone and breathlessly dialed her husband at work.

"Ed! I'm looking at a picture of this Chinese man in the *Daily News* who just arrived in the U.S. and I think it's Charlie! It says he's staying with a Roy Sibit in Tallmadge, Ohio."

Grady didn't know Sibit; he'd left China before Sibit had arrived. But he called Tallmadge information for his number, and Jean Sibit answered. "Oh, Ed, we've been looking for you!" she said. "We're having an open house on Sunday, and a lot of you guys are coming. You must, too."

So Grady called Mary to say they were spending the weekend in Ohio. That night they—like the Sextons in North Carolina—sat down to watch the CBS Evening News with Dan Rather. At the end of the newscast, Rather read his lead-in to the evening's final story: "Once upon a time, two great powers were united in a war against a common enemy. This was so long ago that war was widely perceived as just, the good guys versus the bad guys. When the war ended, the warriors of one great power befriended a little boy from the other nation. The friendship survived the decades long after the warriors returned home. If all that sounds like a fairy tale, it isn't."

Rather introduced correspondent Charles Osgood, who aired his second story on Charlie in three years. He told about how Charlie and the Marines had met and then described his arrival and the upcoming reunion in Cleveland. The nation watched William Bullard hug Charlie and the two walk off hand in hand, old friends back together.

Grady and Sexton wiped away tears and planned their trips to Ohio. Love Company was coming back together.

The following Sunday, 15 May 1983, was "Charlie Two Shoes Day" in Tallmadge; 450 people showed up to celebrate at Roy Sibit's split-level house on Laurann Drive. A "Welcome Home Charlie" banner hung across the front of the house, and many people wore "Charlie's Home" T-shirts. Neighbors came, and strangers came from all over. Reporters came to cover the story. People filed through the house all day. A Western Union telegram arrived from President Reagan:

Dear Roy, I wanted you to know that I am grateful to you and your friends for showing our distinguished visitor, Charlie Two Shoes, a bit of American hospitality. Your devotion and attention to him during your service in China are most commendable and in keeping with the Marine Corps spirit. Please convey my greetings in appreciation to your fellow Marines and a hearty welcome from Nancy and me to Charlie.

Love Company was there in force, of course: George McDonald from New Mexico, Rocky Rasile from Georgia, William Marsh from

149

Chicago, Clayton Mattice from Michigan, Berwyn Bragg from Ohio, Ray Brewington, and Ed Grady.

"Ed, what happen your hair?" Charlie asked Grady as the two embraced and laughed.

When asked about his first impressions of America, Charlie said it was even more dramatically different than he had imagined. He couldn't believe that there were really two or three cars in every driveway, and microwave ovens, color TVs, and pet dogs in the houses. In China dogs were for protection or food. "I wouldn't believe Roy would have a dog in the house," he mused to the party, pointing to the Sibits' spaniel, Buffy. "He never told me he had a dog. The first time I saw it, I didn't ask. I just thought, 'Oh, Roy, well, maybe it was different.' But then I go over to other houses and every house has a dog as a pet."

He told reporters that in his village of four hundred families, there were only twenty television sets, none of them color. His house in Chukechuang only had two 20 watt lightbulbs, and he and Jin Mie slept with their three children on a pad over a bed of stone and brick, heated from the chimney by air circulating through the bed.

He said he wanted to see the famous sights in America, like the Statue of Liberty, but first he wanted to see all his Marine buddies.

Before returning home, the aging former Marines of Love Company vowed to work together to bring Jin Mie and the children to America. Already they had Ohio senators Howard Metzenbaum and John Glenn and North Carolina senator Jesse Helms on their side. Soon other politicians, including Congressmen John Seiberling and Bob McEwen from Ohio and Tip O'Neill, the House Speaker from Massachusetts, would get involved.

Don Sexton got involved, too. He'd decided not to go to Sibit's for the party, but to wait until he could spend time with Charlie alone. Shortly after the reunion in Tallmadge, Bullard called him. "Sexton, where you been all these years? You been asleep?"

Sexton knew nothing about the efforts to bring Charlie to America or the rift between Bullard and Sibit. "William, I don't know. I watch the news and read the papers, and I don't know how I missed the story about Charlie," Sexton replied.

Bullard filled him in, telling him about the letter he'd received from Charlie in 1980, how he'd called Sibit, and about their efforts to contact everyone they could think of to help Charlie. He also told him about his falling out with Sibit and the contract he wouldn't sign. He said he'd gone to see Charlie in Ohio, but because of the rift, he and his daughter returned to North Carolina the next day.

Bullard told Sexton about the newspaper and television stories about him fixing up his parents' house, about the Charlie Two Shoes Fund, and about his plans for the biggest "pig pickin'" eastern North Carolina had ever seen.

Disturbed by what he'd heard from Bullard, Sexton called Jack Hutchins in Kentucky to ask what he thought. Big Hutch said he had driven to Ohio to see Charlie, but had stayed only a couple of hours because it was too difficult to get to him. Sexton decided to put his plans to visit on hold.

The split between Sibit and Bullard became national news when Sibit complained to reporters about Bullard's preparations to bring Charlie to Autryville. He said that Bullard's efforts to restore his parents' house for Charlie would invalidate Charlie's visitor's visa and sink three years' work getting Charlie to America and keeping him here. Sibit, more savvy in these matters than Bullard, knew that if it appeared that Charlie was in America under false pretexts or that he was in any way misrepresenting his status, he would be deported. Bullard's efforts, no matter how well meaning, could cause legal complications.[1]

Though Sexton had heard only Bullard's side of the story, he got an idea of just how bad matters were when he read a newspaper story quoting Sibit as saying that Bullard had "absolutely no involvement in bringing Charlie to America. . . . Charlie Two Shoes is not going to North Carolina."[2] Sibit stated that he alone was responsible for bringing Charlie to America.[3]

Eight days after Charlie's arrival, Sibit cabled Bullard to reiterate what he had already stated publicly, and to tell him that Charlie would not be coming to North Carolina, even to visit. Bullard's hometown newspaper, the *Sampson Independent,* which had written the first story about Charlie and the Marines three years earlier, editorialized that Charlie must be getting a bad first impression of America because of

the dispute: "The Chinese man who is now visiting former Marine buddies in this country on a six-month visa has been taken over and is being
'managed' by a former Ohio Marine . . . It is a shame this visitor from
China should be the center of such a disagreement. No one knows why
things happened as they did, but . . . Sibit's wife mentioned the fact that
they had been besieged with offers for books, movies, and television
plays about Charlie."[4]

Now newspapers around the country ran stories about the conflict.
To keep Charlie out of the fray, Bullard backed off. In late July Sexton
told his wife that he had to see Charlie, but he wasn't sure how he
should proceed, because of this ongoing conflict. No-nonsense Arrie
Sexton picked up the phone and called Sibit. She asked if he remembered her husband.

"Sure I remember Don Sexton!" Sibit said enthusiastically. She
handed the phone to Sexton, who told Sibit that he wanted to see
Charlie.

"Don, you come on up," said Sibit. "And don't stay in a hotel; you'll
stay here."

Sibit's response surprised Sexton, but he said it would be three
weeks before he could come. Then he asked to speak to Charlie.

Charlie wasn't home, Sibit said, nor was he available each time Sex-
ton called thereafter. Charlie was napping or taking a walk every time.
But time was ticking away on Charlie's six-month visa, and in August
Sexton called Bullard to say he and Arrie were going to Ohio.

Bullard encouraged him to go, but also urged him to call other Love
Company members who had invited Charlie to visit them. The
response from Sibit had always been that Charlie had to stay in Ohio, in
case there were new visa developments or he had to be interviewed by
the media or rushed to Washington, or they were too busy because they
were working on getting his family to the United States. As well, they
were fighting Charlie's upcoming deportation.

Don and Arrie drove up one weekend and checked into a motel.
When they called the Sibits, Roy insisted that they check out and
stay with him instead. That night he invited them to a reception.
Finally, Sexton saw Charlie. He was dressed in a blue suit with white
shirt and tie, not much taller than he had been at age fourteen. He

still had the smile that Sexton would have recognized anywhere.

The Sextons stayed several days with the Sibits, who treated them like honored guests. Sexton didn't note anything strange, only that Roy and Jean did most of the talking. Charlie remained conspicuously uninvolved in all of the plans for him. Still, he appeared happy, and the Sextons left with good feelings about the visit.

In his second week in America, Charlie hit the lecture circuit. Sibit arranged interviews with local and national media, and Charlie appeared on television and radio talk shows across the country. Sibit acted as his agent for personal appearances before any group that would listen to Charlie's story: the man who fled Communism and found a new home in America, with his Marine buddies. He always appeared in his Chinese peasant outfit. His every move was chronicled in the *Akron Beacon Journal,* which championed his efforts to remain in the country. Nine days after his arrival, in the 19 May 1983 issue, the *Beacon Journal* editorialized against U.S. officials:

> Mrs. Tsui and her children were denied visitor visas because the State Department feared their visit here might be permanent, in violation of U.S. immigration rules and quotas. It is a strange turn of events American logic would have us expect otherwise. In the more familiar scenario, China would have denied passage to Mr. Tsui's family, fearing they would defect and remain in the West. In this case, however, the Chinese government doesn't seem to care whether or not they return.
>
> The U.S. government, on the other hand, doesn't want to run the risk that Mr. Tsui and his family will try to stay here illegally after their visas expire. It issued only one visa—to Mr. Tsui, on humanitarian grounds—concluding that he could not abandon his family back in China.

It was a remarkable lesson in democracy for Charlie. He hadn't known that a newspaper could be so critical of the government. Between interviews, he rode in parades and gave speeches about his life and travails. Vice President George Bush had been scheduled to be honorary grand marshal in Akron's International Soap Box Derby Parade;

when he was unable to attend, Charlie filled in and rode through the streets of Akron in an open convertible.

Three weeks after Charlie's arrival, Sibit took him to Washington to thank the Chinese embassy officials for arranging the passports. They also met with Congressman John Seiberling, the Democrat from Akron, and Conrad Bellamy, a State Department representative on the China desk. Seiberling had already pledged help in getting visas for Charlie's family, and he urged Bellamy to encourage the embassy in Beijing to reconsider its denial. (Bellamy did pass on this request, but it was denied nevertheless.) Charlie and Sibit also met with Ohio senators Metzenbaum and Glenn, and with Charles Percy, an influential Republican from Illinois. All three pledged their support.

As an honored guest at a reunion of the 6th Marine Division Association in New Jersey, Charlie told 350 former Marines of how he'd suffered because of his friendship with Love Company, and of how his dream to visit America and see his old buddies had come true at last. Many in the audience brushed away tears, and most promised to help get his family to the States too.

Charlie spoke to church congregations, senior citizens, schoolchildren, Rotarians, Civitans, Elks, Shriners, veterans' groups—audiences of a few and others of hundreds. He spoke to anyone who would listen, always dressed in the peasant suit he'd worn from China. Reporters and photographers followed everywhere he went.

Though journalists had easy access to Charlie, Marines did not. On the Fourth of July weekend two months after his arrival in America, Charlie was grand marshal of the holiday parade in Farmington, New Mexico. There he was the guest of George McDonald, president of an oil service company. But McDonald had picked up the tab for Sibit and his family to visit at the same time. When Charlie went away for a week to visit Ed and Mary Grady in Redding, Connecticut, Sibit showed up several days early to take Charlie back to Tallmadge.

Sibit told Charlie the only way to get his family over was to keep his story fresh in the minds of Americans, so each week Charlie gave speeches and interviews, made personal appearances, and went dutifully where he was told. But the circuit was growing tedious. He told the same story over and over again, answering the same questions: Do you miss your family? Why weren't they able to come? Was it hard to leave them?

Yet Charlie felt that Sibit knew best, and he was willing to do anything to bring his family to America. Jean Sibit drove Charlie to his engagements during the week, and Roy drove him on weekends. They'd tell each group of their efforts to reunite Charlie with his family, saying it was the U.S. government that denied their visit, not the Chinese. Then they asked for help—letters of support and money. Money came through the mail from strangers across America; letters flooded Congress, urging that Charlie be allowed to stay and his family permitted to join him.

Charlie never talked about his persecution in China, saying only that "our two great countries" needed to become better friends. To speak about his harsh treatment or the years in prison could imperil Jin Mie and the children and cut them off forever.

Three months after Charlie arrived, Sibit told him it was time to get his story on paper. They met with a lawyer, who prepared a contract for the split of all book and film proceeds from Charlie's life story. As Sibit recalls it, Charlie did not want anything, but Sibit insisted that he receive something. "Okay, Roy, how 'bout 10 percent," Sibit says Charlie responded, leaving Sibit with 90 percent.[5]

But Charlie's recollection differs. New to the country and knowing nothing of U.S. laws, never having even heard of a contract, Charlie says he trusted Sibit to make all the proper decisions for him. So when Sibit told him to sign, he signed.

Sibit hired JoAnn Blair, a freelance writer from Tallmadge, to interview Charlie and take notes. Day after day for two weeks, Charlie told about his life in painstaking detail. When he was finished, Blair gave her notes to Sibit. Charlie didn't learn until much later why Sibit wanted the notes.

As the expiration date of Charlie's visa approached, Sibit and a growing army of Charlie Two Shoes supporters intensified their efforts to get an extension. They called every influential person they knew to stop Charlie's deportation and bring his family over. Church groups took up petitions, students sent bags of mail, and in Milwaukee, Sister Blanda and the sisters of Marian Hall at St. Joseph's Convent prayed. Of course the nuns also wrote to their congressional representatives, and Sister Blanda followed Charlie's visit by keeping a scrapbook of newspaper clippings and photographs. The cause to stop Charlie's deportation had become a battle pitting a Chinese peasant and his supporters against the U.S. Immigration and Naturalization Service.

One night Charlie and the Sibits had dinner in Ann Arbor, Michigan, at the home of Leonard Woodcock, former president of the United Auto Workers and ambassador to China. Ex–Love Company member Ray Brewington, a Detroit cop, had arranged the invitation through his congressman, Representative David Bonior. After hearing Charlie's story and about the efforts to bring his family, Woodcock made calls to Washington.

In November 1983, Charlie's visa was extended six months, to May 1984. But no visas were released for his family, and although his affection for the United States grew stronger daily, Charlie knew he couldn't remain without his family.

For Charlie's first American Christmas, it seemed as if every tree in Tallmadge sheltered a gift for him. He and the Sibits spent Christmas Eve at the house of Jean's mother, Pauline Williams. All of Jean's family was there: Betty and Dick Sokol; Charlie and Dale Richards and their sons, Chuck and David; and Rosie Williams.

Jean's sisters had never heard of Charlie, never heard Roy mention him until the letter came to Bullard. Then, that was all he talked about: fulfilling a promise he'd made as a young Marine. They were proud of him.

Charlie could hardly contain his excitement as he made his way down a table piled high with food in Pauline's basement. He filled his plate, marveling that he was celebrating Christmas in America with a real American family, who treated him as one of their own.

Charlie knew about American Christmases, having spent four of them with the Marines. They'd decorated trees in the barracks and eaten special Christmas dinners in the mess hall. But this one was different. It was in a home.

The family sang, prayed, and commiserated the absence of his family. In toasts and prayers, they said they wished that Jin Mie and the children were with them, but maybe by next Christmas they would be. Charlie said he did indeed miss his own family, but he was grateful to be with his American one.

156

12 Months of speeches and interviews grew increasingly demanding for Charlie, always dressed as a Chinese peasant. He began to feel like a shill in a cheap sideshow. He wanted to live like an American and dress like one, but Sibit insisted on peasant garb; it was his costume in the show.

Granted another six-month reprieve, Charlie didn't know how much longer his dream would last, but he knew there was one person he had to see before he was banished back to China—his teacher, Sister Blanda. All these years, he'd thought she was dead.

It was Duke Bingham who found her. He had gone to Chinatown to play gin rummy with his friend Father Schmidt, at the Catholic church. The assistant pastor, Father Chun, quietly read a newspaper in the corner. As they played, Bingham talked about Charlie and how the Marines had pooled their money to send him to an American school in Tsingtao, where he had been taught by a nun named Sister Blanda. Suddenly Father Chun threw his newspaper in the air. "Sister Blanda! Tsingtao! I was in Tsingtao and knew Sister Blanda. She's alive. In a convent in Milwaukee."

Bingham rushed back to his office to call the convent, and soon she and Charlie were exchanging letters. One night in February 1984, Charlie called the convent and told her they must meet, either in Tallmadge or Milwaukee. They talked regularly from them on, often about religion.

Sister Blanda had always regretted that she hadn't been able to arrange the sacrament of confirmation for her "little Marines" before fleeing China. "You know, Charlie," she told him, "all these years you weren't really a Catholic, because you weren't confirmed. We must arrange that before you leave."

Charlie didn't understand. Life was full of uncertainties, but there were three things he had believed ever since he had lived with the Marines: that he was one of them, that in his heart he felt more American than Chinese, and that he was a devout Catholic. These beliefs had helped him to survive years of persecution. "Sister, you know me better than me. You led me to God, you arranged everything for me. Help me with this," Charlie replied.

She promised she would, and two weeks later she wrote to say that his confirmation would take place on 7 May at Our Lady of Victory Church in Tallmadge, with Bishop Sheldon of Akron performing the rite. Charlie would take preparatory classes with eighty-five ninth graders, and Sister Blanda, now eighty years old, would be his sponsor. Charlie wrote back excitedly:

Your letter reached my heart with joy. While reading it I was so much attracted by your vision and sweet voice. I felt like we were face to face. I can't help stop my mind from concentration of recalling my time of boyhood—everything came back just like a dream last night. Particularly the tragical tearful day of your departure can never be forgot. After you left me and us within three days we were almost spiritless sad. Then about not more than two months we all left the school and went under Communist control.

In closing, he thanked the sisters of Marian Hall for their prayers and wrote that he had called Jin Mie to tell her about all the work that had been done on their family's behalf. He also wrote that he hoped the politicians in Washington "would lift up their heart look more into the value of God's faith, hope and love, instead of making excuses not to issue visas" for them.

On Saturday, 5 May, five days before his first anniversary in America, with the expiration of his visa extension looming, Charlie was reunited with Sister Blanda. But when she entered the concourse at Cleveland Hopkins International Airport, Charlie didn't recognize her. He was expecting a nun in habit, but she had shed hers for lay clothes long ago and wore a dark blue suit. Then, looking into the elderly woman's kindly eyes and focusing on her smile, he recognized his teacher. He put his hands on her shoulders for a moment before hugging her.

At first neither of them spoke, but finally Sister Blanda said, "This is marvelous to be here after waiting so long. Can you believe it after all these years?"

"You still have the same voice," Charlie said. "It's just like a dream. I always expected to meet you in heaven. This seems like a miracle."

Two nights later they went to Our Lady of Victory Church, a five-minute drive from the Sibit home. Ray Brewington had come from Detroit, and Ed and Mary Grady had flown in from Connecticut. Charlie and Sister Blanda sat in front with the group of ninth graders, he not much bigger than they. He wanted to wear his Marine dyed black pants, but Roy preferred his gray peasant suit. Sister Blanda wore her dark blue suit. Charlie chose Matthew as his confirmation name, because Sister Blanda said it meant "gift for God."

After the ceremony, reporters gathered around Charlie and Sister Blanda. "I gave him his First Communion instructions," the nun said proudly. "Now I feel I have finished my job. Now he's on his own." She left for Milwaukee the next day.

A week later Charlie and Sibit drove to Cleveland to request another visa extension. After officials examined Charlie's hands to make sure he wasn't doing manual labor, they granted him until November 1984. Still, Sibit and Charlie knew the clock was running down. Their luck couldn't go on forever; sooner or later, he would be deported.

After Sister Blanda left, Charlie went back to making the same speeches, telling the same stories, answering the same questions. He began to wonder just how he was any better off than he had been in China, and how much longer he could bear the separation from his family. Those helping his cause looked for any strings to pull. Sibit told officials that he was willing to post a one-million-dollar departure bond to ensure that Charlie and his family returned to China, if they would grant four visitors' visas. In North Carolina, William Bullard and Don Sexton continued to work their senators and House members, and Sexton lobbied members of the 6th Marine Division Association. In Connecticut, Ed Grady did the same.

In July 1984, bombarded by correspondence from across the country, seven senators—including Edward Kennedy, Paul Tsongas, Howard Metzenbaum, Paul Laxalt, and Christopher Dodd—along with four U.S. House members, including Speaker Tip O'Neill and John Seiberling, sent a letter to Secretary of State George Schultz requesting assistance in securing visitors' visas for Charlie's family:

> The fact of the matter is that Mr. [Tsui] himself was unable to furnish sufficient proof of strong and binding ties to his country, yet the U.S. Embassy in Beijing used its discretionary authority and approved his non-immigrant visa request. While the [Tsui] family cannot provide the customary evidence to demonstrate that they do not intend to abandon their home country, we strongly feel that this is not a typical case and that recent developments require the Department of State and the U.S. Embassy to reconsider their position. Roy Sibit, Mr. [Tsui]'s sponsor and a former Marine who knew him in China, has agreed to post a sizable departure bond to ensure the family's return. For this reason, we urge the State Department to grant the [Tsui] family non-immigrant visas now.

Schultz forwarded the letter to the embassy in Beijing with his support, but the visas were denied. The denial dealt Charlie a severe blow. He had been so encouraged by Schultz's support; certainly with that much weight behind his cause, the embassy would relent and grant visas to his family. Certain that his time in the United States was coming to an end, Charlie began to prepare for the likelihood of returning home. He would leave voluntarily, sparing himself the humiliation of deportation.

He continued making speeches about his love for America and his grand hopes, as he was paraded around in his peasant costume, but it became more difficult now. Two weeks later Don and Arrie Sexton saw

Charlie's despondency, when they made their second visit to Ohio. At dinner, as Sibit and Sexton discussed the status of the visas, Charlie sat silent, lost in thought.

Not only was Charlie's joy gone, Sexton also noted tension between Charlie and Sibit. On his first visit a year earlier, Charlie had shared everything with Sibit—letters, phone calls, thoughts—but no longer. Now, it seemed to Sexton, they sniped at each other like an old married couple. Francis Wade, a former Marine from nearby Macedonia who was helping with the cause, saw it too, but he wasn't sure what had caused the rift. One evening during a walk around Sibit's neighborhood, Charlie told Sexton, "You know, Don, if my family comes over here, Roy will never let us leave his house."[1]

Sexton didn't respond; he didn't know what to say. He only hoped that things didn't worsen so that he would have to choose sides. He knew that Sibit had worked hard for Charlie, but he also saw that Sibit seemed to control Charlie's life.[2]

After all the publicity and hype, after thousands of letters from ordinary Americans had been sent to leaders in Washington, after the top-level support, the campaign to bring Charlie Two Shoes's family to America had stalled. But despite his growing despair, Charlie's spirits were lifted at moments, by events such as a flight to Florida in the fall of 1984 to see his other teacher, Miriam Matthews Haddad.

Reading the newspaper in Ormond Beach several days after Charlie arrived in America, Miriam saw a photograph of a classroom in China. One of the children was a small Chinese boy dressed in a Marine uniform. His name was Charlie Two Shoes, the caption said, and he and the other students were taught by a nun named Sister Blanda.

"Ernie!" she shouted to her husband, pastor of Ormond Beach Presbyterian Church. "That's Charlie!" That night she called the Sibits. "Charlie probably won't remember me," she said, "but he knew me as Miss Matthews. I taught him in the American School in Tsingtao."

Charlie ran to the phone, so excited that he stuttered out her name. He asked about her life and her family. "Miss Matthew when will I see you?" he asked. "All these years, I think I never see you again. We must meet."

They met in late September 1984, knowing this brief visit might be their last. They spent the days talking about their time together in China, and Miriam took Charlie to Disney World. And, like everywhere else, there were interviews. He told the Daytona Beach *News-Journal:* "I do not want to hurt American law. My greatest comfort is that I am a Christian. If it is God's will that I go back to China and serve Him there, I will go in peace."

When he left Florida, Charlie was prepared to return home. But then, just as his hopes for another reprieve dimmed, his story and plight captured the attention of a U.S. congressman willing to do more than lobby for visas. He would help Charlie become a permanent resident so that he could stay in America. That would clear the way for his family to come too.

Bob McEwen, a thirty-four-year-old former Ohio state representative and son of a chiropractor from tiny Hillsboro, was running for his third term in Congress, and many felt that he harbored aspirations for the governor's mansion in Columbus. First elected to Congress in the Reagan landslide of 1980, McEwen was a fiercely anticommunist, conservative Republican who had built a reputation as a loyal foot soldier for the "Reagan Revolution" and supply-side economics. He was also known to champion causes on which others had given up.

The McEwen way of getting difficult things done entailed, simply, overcoming the professionals whose job was to convince people that what they wanted could not be done. "You have to remind yourself what we do for a living," McEwen taught his new staff members, "we rewrite laws. So whenever a taxpayer comes to us and needs something done, and you come away empty-handed because somebody sitting in some office . . . has told you regulations prevent your request, then they've been successful. They have persuaded you that it cannot be done."

McEwen felt that such was the case of Charlie Two Shoes, brought to his attention by Ohio representative Tom Watkins, who asked his help in October 1984, after all available options had been exhausted. McEwen's first instinct was to tell Watkins that he couldn't do anything, because Charlie and Sibit were in another congressman's district. But when he listened more, he realized that Charlie had spent the past year traveling around the United States, appearing in newspapers and on television and delivering pro-America speeches. If he was deported, he would be met by a contentious Communist government, and his life would be endangered.

McEwen had never served in the military, but he knew of the indignities that civilians suffered in war, as well as the acts of kindness that typically rose out of such bleakness. He was touched by the selfless acts of Charlie's Marine buddies, especially Sibit, who told him he had been taking time off from work, using accumulated sick days to spearhead the cause.

After winning reelection in November, McEwen met Charlie for the first time at a reception in Tallmadge. The six-foot-three congressman stooped over five-foot-tall Charlie, patted his back, looked him in the eyes, and said, "Don't worry. Nobody's going to send you back."

McEwen put his press secretary, Don Sico, on the case. They asked immigration officials for another visa extension. The request was denied, and Charlie was served notice that he had to leave the country by 14 January 1985. McEwen then urged State Department officials to step in, but they refused: the bureaucracy had hunkered down. That left one option and almost no time to exercise it—legislative relief in the form of a private bill. For Charlie to remain in the country, they had to rewrite the law.

Though only a small percentage of private bills are passed each year, McEwen was optimistic. In December 1984, he crafted a bill that would declare Charlie a permanent resident of the United States. To him, Charlie's plight was the reason private bills were available: beyond regulations and bureaucracy, here was a man whose life was at stake. He planned to introduce the bill on Inauguration Day the following month, with Charlie and the Sibits in front-row seats, their trip paid for by NBC in exchange for an exclusive interview on the *Today* show.

Charlie spent his second Christmas in America much like he had his first—with his American family. But now he had renewed hope that a 125-word piece of legislation would deliver his ultimate dream. Five days before deportation proceedings began, McEwen announced his intent to sponsor legislation that would keep Charlie in the United States. He urged INS not to take action against Charlie until a House Judiciary subcommittee had had a chance to review the legislation.

But Donald Russell, district INS director in Cleveland, was adamant: Charlie had to leave. Russell told reporters, "He's had more than enough time for a visit. There's nothing available to him under the regular visa process." If Charlie did not leave when told, he would be brought before a deportation hearing. If he was deported, he had diminished chances of ever returning.

Escalating the battle, McEwen took the case to television. Days before the inauguration, ABC flew Charlie to New York for *Good Morning America*; McEwen was interviewed from Washington. "If I'm allowed to stay here," Charlie told cohost Joan Lunden, "I'd just like to have my family come and share my dream."

"Charlie really wants to stay here, Congressman," Lunden said. "What can be done for him?"

"Joan, the first thing we've done is contact the commissioner of the INS and ask that he personally become involved in this case, to understand the uniqueness of it and to act in a compassionate manner," McEwen responded. "If he's unable to prohibit deportation, then I have prepared legislation that would allow Charlie to stay as a citizen."

But at midnight on 4 January 1985, Charlie's visa expired. Russell said he would proceed with a deportation hearing. Sibit did not tell Charlie about this, knowing that he would immediately demand a flight back to China. So Charlie headed to Ronald Reagan's second inauguration as an illegal alien.

Monday, 21 January 1985, was one of the coldest Inauguration Days ever. Because of the cold, the public ceremony was canceled, so Charlie missed his brush with history. But later, on the House floor, Bob McEwen introduced H.R. 548, for the relief of Tsui Chi Hsii under the Immigration and Nationality Act.

With the public inauguration canceled, reporters needed stories to fill the gap. At a news conference, McEwen told them that Charlie's story was a poignant reminder of the true meaning of American ideals. "Our nation is a beacon of hope to the oppressed and tortured people of the world. America stands for freedom and opportunity." He explained that special legislation was necessary, since Charlie didn't fit into any of the categories for which permanent residency was normally granted: for the child, spouse, or parent of an American citizen.

164

McEwen said that President Reagan had pledged to sign H.R. 548 when it passed.

Charlie told the reporters that he hoped the legislation would enable him to bring his wife and children to a new life. "My most important concern is not whether I can stay or not. My concern is to have my family come here to join me in my American dream."

The bill was assigned to the House Judiciary Committee's Immigration, Refugees, and International Law subcommittee, chaired by Romano Mazzoli, a Democrat from Jack Hutchins's home state of Kentucky. Big Hutch wrote to Mazzoli: "Charlie is seeking permanent residency through the American process. In a forthright manner he is promoting the causes of his chosen land. He offers benefits to our country, not problems."

Ohio governor Richard Celeste offered help. Numerous cities, including Akron and Cleveland, passed resolutions supporting the bill. After Charlie addressed a joint session of the Ohio legislature, the Ohio House Federal Relations Committee passed its own resolution urging Congress to approve the bill. Congress was besieged with letters urging members to support the bill.

But one congressman was not willing to lend support: John Seiberling, the liberal Democrat from Akron, descendant of the founders of Goodyear. The bill caught him off guard. He hadn't been informed of the legislation and was angry. He vowed to oppose the bill because, he said, Sibit had assured him that Charlie would make no attempt to remain permanently in the United States.[3]

Yet Charlie's visa had expired and he was still here. And there was another congressman who was trying to keep him from leaving. Charlie received notice that his deportation hearing was set for March, in Cleveland, with Judge Gordon Sacks presiding.

The hearing escalated tensions between Charlie and Sibit. Troubles had been building for months, ever since the second visa extension. Sibit later said that he and his family had treated Charlie "like a king" and had no inkling that Charlie felt any resentment.[4]

But as Charlie remembered things, whenever he complained that he could no longer bear living apart from his family and wanted to go back to China, Sibit reminded him of all that had been done for him.[5]

"That's why I want to go back," Charlie said. "I don't want to cause all these people any more trouble."

Finally, Charlie called George McDonald in New Mexico. McDonald sent him a plane ticket and told Sibit to let him visit for two weeks: they needed some time away from each other. When Charlie left Sibit's house, he had no intention of returning. He was desperately worried about his family in China. They had survived nearly two years without financial help from him, and he could not bear to think of them suffering any longer.

Two weeks in New Mexico extended to three, then four, with Sibit calling regularly, asking when Charlie was returning. "I just want to visit with George a little more," Charlie would say.

In the third week, Charlie told McDonald that he was not going back to Sibit's. "I'm too worried about my family. Please find the number for the Chinese embassy in Washington. I am going to tell them it is not working out; I want to go home."

"I know what's happening," McDonald replied. "I've seen it coming for a long time." Still, he tried to reason with Charlie, telling him he was so close to getting his family to America. He offered him his home, but Sibit called and convinced Charlie that a Washington immigration lawyer had found a way for Jin Mie and his children to join him. He had to come back. Returning to Ohio, Charlie decided he had made the right decision.

The Washington immigration lawyer was former Navy pilot Samuel J. Levine, known by State Department officials to take on difficult cases. Ed Grady had found him. After working the phone from his home in Connecticut and being passed through the State Department's bureaucratic maze, an official finally had put him in touch with Levine. Grady had suggested to Sibit that they meet in Washington to see Levine and to lobby the State Department.

Levine was in his office one morning when his secretary buzzed him. "Mr. Levine, you know I normally turn away calls, but I think you should take this one."

It was Roy Sibit. He told Levine what the Marines were up against and asked if he and Grady could see him. Later, in Levine's office, after relating Charlie's saga, they asked for his help. Levine said he would help at no charge—except for a round-trip ticket to Cleveland.

During the Vietnam War, Levine had flown top-secret missions from Japan, and the Marines had helped him many times. He considered this a payback of sorts. He talked about the possibility of sending Charlie's family to Canada and bringing them into the United States from there, but Grady vetoed that. It sounded nefarious, and the Marines wanted to do it on the up-and-up. Levine explored other ideas, but ultimately he concluded that McEwen's private bill was the most likely chance for relief. The best he could do, he told Grady and Sibit, was to buy Charlie more time to let the legislative process run its course.[6]

In late February 1985, after being hospitalized for surgery, Levine got Judge Sacks to delay the March hearing until 22 May. On the morning of the hearing, Charlie and Sibit, in Cleveland, and McEwen, in Washington, went back on *Good Morning America* with Joan Lunden.

"Charlie," Lunden began, "under our law you came to our country for a visit, and now the immigration department says you've stayed long enough and must leave. What are you going to tell that judge at the deportation hearing as to why you want to stay longer?"

"Well, Joan, I would like to ask them for a biggest favor to give me enough time to wait for the bill Congressman McEwen has introduced for me," Charlie replied.

But McEwen was no longer optimistic about the bill's passage. A single dissenting vote would defeat it, and Congressman Seiberling had voiced strong opposition. McEwen told Lunden that the judge's options were limited: "When he reviews the case, if he finds Charlie has overstayed his visa, he can order him deported or he can give him voluntary deportation status. Charlie has agreed to leave voluntarily. We're asking the judge to extend the visa for sufficient time to get his affairs together so he can leave voluntarily."

Later that morning Levine, Charlie, and Sibit entered the Federal Office Building in Cleveland surrounded by a knot of reporters and photographers. Levine knew Sacks could be gruff and inflexible, but he felt the judge would not deport Charlie immediately. Before the hearing started, Sacks called Levine and Russell Ezolt, the INS lawyer, into his chambers to see if an agreement could be reached.

"I've seen these cases before," Sacks told Levine, as gruff as Levine had ever heard him. "I'll give the guy thirty days, unless you convince me I should give him longer."

Levine thought for a minute. Charlie had never spoken publicly about his prison term and subsequent house arrest, because his family was still in China. If he criticized the Chinese government now to get special treatment, Jin Mie and the children would be put at risk. Levine knew that he could not tell the judge the full story of Charlie's persecution, even if it would help his client.

"This is a special case, Judge," Levine said. "First of all, if I applied for asylum from Mainland China, I'd get a year. But very simply, Mr. Tsui won't let me do that. He's going to place a harder burden on you: he wants you to look at the facts and be fair."

Sacks mulled over Levine's remarks. "Would two months satisfy you?"

"Nothing is going to satisfy me; I can't agree to anything," Levine responded. "I just want to present Mr. Tsui as he is and who he is, and then you as an American immigration judge decide what's fair."

Sacks went into the courtroom and called Charlie to testify. As Charlie told his story, Levine saw Sacks melt. "All the Marines, they treat me like a brother," Charlie told the judge. "I would like to share my life with more people and carry on more goodwill."

Ezolt asked Sacks to grant an extension of no more than thirty days. Levine said that his client would not contest any decision. Charlie respected U.S. laws and understood that he was deportable, Levine said. He asked the judge to give Charlie enough time to leave the country on his own. Sacks gave Charlie four more months, until 22 September. Then he had to leave voluntarily, or immigration officials would throw him out.

A month later, Sibit had Charlie sign another contract, this time with a third party—Akron Coca-Cola executive William Williams. This all-inclusive contract for the rights to Charlie's story gave 40 percent of the profits to Williams and 60 percent to Sibit and Charlie, though Sibit retained 90 percent of this through a previous contract. Charlie was now entitled to 10 percent of 60 percent of any profits made on his life story.[7]

But it appeared that there wasn't going to be any life story about Charlie and his dream, for McEwen's bill sat idly in Mazzoli's subcommittee, with the chairman "not inclined" to hold a hearing. If the subcommittee would agree to consider the legislation, U.S. law required that Charlie's deportation proceedings be placed on hold. But hope received a terrible blow when Seiberling went public with his opposition to a hearing.

"Seiberling Opposes 'Charlie Two Shoes' Bill," was the headline in the local section of the Akron *Beacon Journal*. The story, by Washington reporter William Hershey, reported that Seiberling had voiced his opposition to Mazzoli. Seiberling, an influential member of the House and one of Ohio's most liberal congressmen, said that he felt duped by Sibit—that Sibit "had not been straight" with him, since he'd assured Seiberling that Charlie and his family would return to China.[8]

Giving Charlie special treatment, Seiberling argued, would not be fair to thousands of other foreigners who were equally or more deserving of becoming permanent U.S. residents through the normal process. "This subverts the system," Seiberling said. Many applicants for permanent residency had been separated from their families because of war or disaster, but Charlie had chosen to be apart from his family for two years.

The story led to a bitter public dispute between Seiberling and Sibit. After Seiberling voiced his opposition, Sibit wrote to the *Beacon Journal* "to clarify the untrue statements made by Congressman John Seiberling":

> I would like to reply to his statement "we were not straight" with him.
> It is true that we were seeking visitors' visas for Charlie Two Shoes'
> wife and three children. We eventually exhausted all avenues legally
> available to us. When we were about to accept the fact Charlie would
> have to leave the country, another alternative was made available
> through Representative Tom Watkins and U.S. Congressman Bob
> McEwen. Congressman McEwen offered to sponsor H.R. 548. . . .
> Therefore I was straight with Congressman Seiberling.

In response to Seiberling's contention that others were equally or more deserving than Charlie, Sibit wrote that because of his association with the Marines, Charlie had "suffered a great hardship." He had been branded a counterrevolutionary and a spy and had been ostracized. Sibit went on to criticize the U.S. government for entering foreign countries "as goodwill ambassadors and befriending those around them," then leaving without being "accountable for their fate. If Charlie hadn't been befriended by the Marines, attended an American school, taught English and converted to Catholicism, he wouldn't have suffered for 20 years."

He also accused Seiberling of making a "political football" out of Charlie, and he wondered if Seiberling opposed the bill because McEwen was a Republican. "Is it possible because of the media's constant focus on the situation that Seiberling was not getting all the applause and publicity?"[9]

Seiberling countered with his own letter, "to set the record straight." He explained that Charlie had come to America on a temporary visa and had been admitted only after he had "assured our Embassy in China that he wished to enter the U.S. only to visit." Based on Sibit's assurance that Charlie did not intend to stay, Seiberling had pledged his support and help to get visas for the family. When those efforts failed, he had met with a State Department official and declared that he would "go to the mat" for Charlie, as long as he didn't stay. Seiberling wrote that he had drafted the letter of support to Secretary of State Schultz, signed by a dozen senators and House members.

He also contacted the ambassador in Beijing in September 1984, to express his concern. He stated that "he'd repeatedly assured the State Department that Mr. Tsui had no intention of seeking permanent resident status." To support McEwen's bill now would impair his credibility. Moreover, what was blocking McEwen's bill were the rules of the House immigration subcommittee, requiring the sponsor of a bill to show that the case involved "extreme hardship" that could not be remedied through existing law.

"The law already allows individuals with a well-founded fear of political persecution to be admitted. I have heard nothing that would support such a claim that he will face 'extreme hardship' if he returns to China," Seiberling wrote. Of the hundreds of thousands of immigrants admitted each year, he wrote, priority was given to those with relatives in America or those who could document extreme hardships at home. McEwen's bill made an "end run around those laws and all the people around the world patiently waiting their turn for admission using the process."[10]

While Sibit and Seiberling duked it out in the newspaper, Charlie, with little time left, wanted to see as much of America as he could. He had spent most of the past two years in Ohio, and he was very happy when Sibit told him in July 1985 that he would be flying the next day to North Carolina to visit Don and Arrie Sexton. Sexton had promised Sibit that he would deliver Charlie back to Ohio in ten days and that he would not take him to visit William Bullard in Autryville.

When Charlie arrived in Greensboro, television and newspaper reporters covered the story. Bullard saw clips of Charlie's arrival on the news that night and waited for Sexton's call, but it never came.

At dinner that first night with the Sextons, there was a lot of laughter. For the first time in months, Charlie felt the stress of the last two years lift. The next morning Charlie, Arrie, Don, and their son, Scott, headed south. Their first stop was Parris Island, South Carolina—boot camp, about which Charlie had heard so many horror stories from Marine buddies. After a tour and interview, they drove much farther south, to Merritt Island, near Cape Canaveral, Florida. They visited Charles Robertson, Love Company's captain and now a retired brigadier general, who had allowed his men to keep Charlie forty years earlier.

Robertson swept Charlie up in a bear hug. Charlie and the Sextons stayed the night in a guest house on the banks of the Banana River. In the morning, they were awakened by Robertson's commanding voice over an intercom: "Rise up, on the double! We've got breakfast on the table!"

When they got to the kitchen, Robertson was frying eggs and bacon. As he placed plates in front of them, Charlie turned to Sexton and said in amazement, "I cannot believe it. A general is cooking breakfast for me."

On the return home, knowing that he would be going back to Ohio soon, Charlie said, "You know, Don, I would love to live in North Carolina. If my family gets to come over, will you help me?"

"I will help you anywhere you want to go," Sexton answered.

They got back to Greensboro at two in the morning. Three hours later, sensing something amiss, Arrie looked in on Charlie. His room was empty. "Don, wake up!" she shouted to her husband. "Charlie's gone."

"He's not gone," Don said groggily. "He's out jogging. He's done that for years, every morning at five o'clock."

Later, on the way back to Ohio, they stopped in Hazel Green, Kentucky, to visit with Jack and Eula Mae Hutchins. Hutch had stayed out of the fight to keep Charlie in America. He had been working on an alternative plan: to hide him in a cabin in the hills near his house if immigration tried to send him back.

Sexton called the Sibits from Hutch's house and told Jean they'd be arriving a couple of days late. She reported good news: Congressman Seiberling's staff had issued a report concluding that President Reagan had the authority to intervene and permit Charlie's family to visit. Seiberling had also asked the State Department to determine whether Charlie would be subject to persecution or extraordinary hardship if he was deported, and he had told Mazzoli that he hoped his subcommittee would consider McEwen's bill. McEwen had written Attorney General Edwin Meese of Seiberling's findings.

That night Sexton, Hutch, and Charlie stayed up until morning reliving old stories. Charlie played a toy harmonica that belonged to one of Hutch's grandchildren. He hadn't blown a harmonica since his mother had burned his in 1949, but he managed the Marine Corps Hymn. The next day Hutch's daughter brought Charlie a German-made harmonica like the one Poncho Groves had given him in China. Before they left, Hutch lined up an interview with a newspaper in nearby Compton, Kentucky. Kentucky was Mazzoli's state, and Hutch wanted to pressure him to give H.R. 548 a fair hearing.

On the way back to Tallmadge, Charlie played all the tunes that Groves had taught him, marveling at how easily they came back after all these years. After delivering Charlie to Sibit and returning home, Sexton called Bullard to apologize. "William, it was the only way I could make it work," he explained.

In Washington, H.R. 548 remained buried under a stack of legislation, never to surface for any subcommittee hearing. As the 22 September deportation date neared, Charlie was granted an additional eighteen days. But he had already accepted his fate and began to prepare for the trip home, bewildered by the slow pace of the U.S. government and excited about seeing his family at long last.

But McEwen wasn't finished. He had played every card—the State Department, INS, courts, and legislation—but they had all come up losers. There was only one left, the most unlikely and difficult of all: the President of the United States. Earlier, while flying back from Cincinnati with Reagan on Air Force One, McEwen had told him about Charlie. The president said that he already knew the story and suggested that McEwen contact Meese, himself a former Marine.

McEwen phoned Meese, but afterward felt he had not stressed how critical time was. Just days before Charlie's deportation, at a White House picnic that Reagan was hosting for members of Congress, McEwen saw his opportunity. He found himself approaching the buffet line with Meese and the president. McEwen was not going to let the moment pass.

With the Truman balcony as a backdrop, McEwen drew the president and Meese to a corner of the lawn and made his final pitch for Charlie. "Mr. President, we've tried everything. We've played the regulations as far as they can go. Now time is of the essence. We need an executive decision. Otherwise the regulations are going to guarantee an injustice is done."[11]

Reagan considered, then turned to his attorney general. "Ed, let's see what we can do. Let's do what's right."

As the president walked away off to join his guests, Meese clicked off all the things that needed to be done before he could take up the matter. McEwen stopped him: "All that's been done. It's down to you, Ed. If you don't parole him, INS is going to send him packing."[12]

The following day, 19 September, late on a Friday afternoon, the attorney general of the United States granted Chinese peasant farmer Charlie Two Shoes an indefinite stay of deportation, allowing him to stay in America as long as he desired and to apply for permanent resident status. Meese cited humanitarian grounds for his decision, saying that Charlie meant so much to the Marines he came to visit. "They feel strongly that he should be allowed to remain here, and he is anxious to stay."

The decision meant that Charlie's family could join him. The long ordeal was finally over.

Or was it?

13

The years during which Charlie pursued his dream half a world away were miserable ones for Jin Mie and their children. They wrote that they were fine and told him not to worry, but Charlie knew that without his guidance and income, they had to be suffering in an already dirt-poor existence. Even with him they'd barely scraped by, but now, because he couldn't work in America and wasn't able to send them money, he knew it was all that Jin Mie could do to put food on the table. Yet he felt deeply that everything would work out—his family's suffering would be vindicated, his prayers would be answered. As the months in America lengthened into years, Charlie realized how much he loved and admired Jin Mie, a woman who had suffered as much as he, all because of him. Still she had defended and stood by him at every misfortune.

With an infant when Charlie was sent to prison, she fought her in-laws for not helping him. When he was spurned by close friends during his years of persecution, she argued with them, too. She supported Charlie's plans to go to America, and she struggled to support her three children after he left.

One image of Jin Mie stood out in Charlie's mind and crystallized her character for him: Eight years into his house arrest, two years before his citizenship was restored, unable to bear any longer the small house, with her children in rags and eating worse food than other village children did, Jin Mie decided to build a bigger and better house.

She did most of the labor herself: After toiling all day in the hop fields, she had Charlie and Yin Whee go out with a cart and bring back the biggest boulders they could find. At night, while everyone slept, she chipped away at the boulders with a hammer until they were reduced to gravel. Then she sold the crushed rock to a cement company, earning enough money for materials to build a new house next to the old one.

With her husband in America, Jin Mie continued to work in the hop fields. Yin Whee took Charlie's place at the government-run farm, and Yin Tao and Yin Chao stayed in school. After her day in the fields, Jin Mie worked into the night clearing rocks from a vacant plot of land, tilling it with a hoe to grow broccoli, cabbage, radishes, corn, and sweet potatoes for her family. She never complained, and always told her children that their father would keep his promise and bring them to a better life in America. She never doubted him.

But along with day-to-day survival, Jin Mie and the children had to deal with the petty jealousies of many villagers. Ever since Charlie had been a boy and gone to live with the American Marines, he had been envied by his neighbors. Now that he was in the fabled promised land with wealthy Americans, they knew he would be sending money to his family. But no money came, just more hardship for Jin Mie.

On the day that Charlie went to Beijing to catch his flight to America, a rumor swept the village that he had been arrested by government agents at the airport. Unsure whether the rumors were true, Jin Mie grew frantic. Yin Tao returned from school to find his mother and sister crying. They told him the rumor, and he began to cry too. "My father never did anything wrong," he moaned.

They waited anxiously for Yin Whee to return from Beijing, where he had gone to see his father off. But it was a long train trip home, and he wasn't due for two days. Jin Mie couldn't sleep until he returned. If the rumor was true, if her husband had been arrested, her son could have been as well. Yin Tao would wake during the night and check on his mother, only to find her lying quietly with her eyes open, filled with tears.

Finally Yin Whee returned. Jin Mie rushed to him. "Did you see your father get on the plane? Did you see the plane fly away?" she asked frantically.

"Yes, I saw him get on the plane," Yin Whee said. "The TV camera crew was there too; they filmed him getting on. I saw the plane take off."

When Jin Mie told him about the rumor, he scoffed. "Don't listen to these people, Mother. They're just jealous our father is going to America."

But Jin Mie's relief was temporary. Six months later, another rumor swept Chukechuang, this one even more painful: stories had been written in the American press that Charlie had abandoned his family and wanted to divorce Jin Mie.

Yin Tao did not believe it. He remembered how his father had been forced to carry human manure to the fields, how, in the middle of thick, hot summer nights, he had awakened to find his father fanning him and his brother and sister, how his parents had always fed the children the best foods, especially meat, the rare times when they had it. Of course his father would never abandon his family. Yet nagging in his mind was the memory of the last day with his father: he had spoken in another language to the American reporter from NBC. What is this strange language? he had wondered in bewilderment.

A few days after this vicious rumor had started, a letter arrived from Ohio. It included newspaper stories of Charlie's first few months in the United States and photos of his Marine buddies and of the friends he'd made. Charlie wrote about life in America, about cars, dogs as pets, televisions, and electric stoves. He told them that he loved and missed them. There was nothing about divorce or abandonment. Instead, the letter contained the business card of NBC researcher Eric Baculinao, who had found Charlie for Sandy Gilmour to interview and who had helped him get his visa and plane ticket. Charlie instructed Jin Mie to call Baculinao when the time came for her to go to Beijing to get visas for the family. He would help her, too.

Other letters followed every two weeks, filled with the sights and sounds of America, and in each, he told his children to respect and look after their mother. "I am waiting for you here. I am sure that some day soon we will be together in this great country because of all the hard work being done by our American friends."

Charlie kept reassuring them as the time apart grew longer and longer. "You must keep your faith, and trust our friends."

177

Their hopes for a reunion were finally raised in June 1985, when one of the Marines about whom Charlie had written fondly, Ed Grady, came to Tsingtao with his wife, Mary, on a tour that had been set up by the 6th Marine Division Association. Ed and Mary spent three days in Tsingtao and met Jin Mie and the three children, brought to the city by her brother. Jin Mie had dressed Yin Chao in a pretty pink dress with a bow in her hair to match, and the boys in crisp new white shirts. Before leaving, the Gradys assured Jin Mie, through a translator, that every-thing possible was being done to bring them to America.

Then, one day in late September 1985, a messenger from the Party office ran to the house with news that her husband was on the phone. Something wonderful had happened, Charlie told her. The attorney general of the United States, a man with great powers, had given her and the children humanitarian paroles. Though Jin Mie didn't under-stand the terminology or know who Ed Meese was, she understood that she and her family were free to go to America. Charlie told her they had tickets on a 3 October flight to San Francisco.

Meese's decision to grant humanitarian paroles made them immune from immigration laws. Their four-thousand-dollar plane tickets had been paid for by Leon Toups, as promised. The State Department said that visas would be cleared through the embassy in Beijing. That after-noon, Jin Mie rushed to Yin Tao's and Yin Chao's school with the news that they must leave for Beijing in two days to take the same flight to America that their father had taken two and half years earlier.

As Yin Tao left, his teachers told him to study hard in America; per-haps one day he could return to help the village. One teacher, Bi Nei Fang, said, "American education is the best in the world. Take advantage of this opportunity. Accomplish something in America."

Though they had waited twenty-nine months for this moment, they were unprepared when it came: there was much to do in such little time. That night as Jin Mie readied them to travel, the children said good-bye to their friends, relatives, and teachers, knowing it was unlikely they would ever return. Yin Tao lay awake all night thinking about America and seeing his father. They left the following night, Thursday, packing schoolbooks, favorite clothes, and souvenirs from friends.

Jin Mie sold their two houses to a close friend, as prearranged, for the equivalent sum of one thousand dollars. Charlie had asked Jin Mie to bring gifts for friends in America and an *erhoo*—a two-string Chinese musical instrument. Jin Mie hadn't known that her husband played the *erhoo,* but she asked his friend, Lee FuYe, to get one.

They boarded a bus for Tsingtao, then took a train to Beijing. Arriving Friday morning, they went to the U.S. embassy to get their visas. They had to go through two checkpoints, Chinese and American, before entering the embassy. At the Chinese security point, they were required to fill out applications, just as Charlie had done two years earlier, and show proof that they were eligible for visas. But all Jin Mie had were the passports and a letter from Charlie. Still, the Chinese guard allowed them to pass, and Jin Mie felt that the hardest part was over.

She was wrong. At the American visa desk, a clerk examined her name and shook his head. "You have been denied visas before, why do you keep coming back?" he asked Jin Mie rudely.

She explained that she had received a call from her husband saying they had been cleared to go. But the clerk said he knew nothing about it. Jin Mie swept her two sons and daughter out of the embassy, past the Chinese checkpoint, ready to return to Chukechuang and forget about America, even if it meant humiliation and the fact they no longer had a home. Charlie's dream had cost her too much heartache.

Then she remembered the business card that Charlie had mailed her: Eric Baculinao, the NBC researcher who had told Charlie to contact him when the family was departing. She had Yin Whee, who had met Baculinao when he had accompanied his father to Beijing, call the bureau, but Baculinao was away on assignment, and no one knew when he would be back.

There was nothing to do but check into a cheap hotel and wait, though if they couldn't get their visas the next day, Saturday, their trip to America would be in jeopardy. The following Monday, 1 October, was the anniversary of the Communist Revolution. It was a national holiday and everything shut down. On Saturdays the embassy was open only until noon. Early that morning, Jin Mie had her son call the NBC bureau again. This time Baculinao answered. "Can you help us?" Yin Whee asked. "Our plane is leaving for America but we can't get visas."

179

Baculinao said he would pick them up at their hotel and take them to the embassy himself to help clear up the problem. The guard at the Chinese checkpoint stopped the family again, this time with an NBC camera filming the event. "Why do you keep bothering us? You were turned down yesterday. There is nothing that can be done."

Baculinao showed his press credentials, and the guard let the family pass. At the first of three visa windows, Jin Mie received the same greeting: "Why are you back again? There is nothing we can do for you."

Baculinao explained to the clerk that a mistake had been made: the U.S. State Department had cleared this family to fly to the United States. The clerk said he knew who Charlie Two Shoes was, but he had no authorization to issue his family visas. He needed supporting documents before he could stamp their passports.

Baculinao told Jin Mie and the children to stay put. He raced back to his office and rifled through files for an Associated Press story that he had seen a few days previously, disclosing Ed Meese's humanitarian paroles to the family of Charlie Two Shoes. He found the single page of four paragraphs and rushed back to the embassy, sliding the proof under the clerk's window as a clock on the wall ticked dangerously close to the noon hour.

The clerk left with the release, then returned. Fifteen minutes before closing time, he stamped the visas with four resounding thuds. To celebrate, Baculinao took the family on a taped tour around the city, then to the Great Wall.

Still, there was much to be done before leaving. There were two days left to shop for wall hangings, slippers, and porcelain statues to bring to American friends. Jin Mie had done none of it yet, unsure that she would be granted the visas. But on 3 October, Baculinao loaded their suitcases into his car and drove them to the airport himself. As his crew taped the departure, they boarded a jet and took off to reunite with Charlie—a mother and three children from a village of Chinese peasants entering a strange new world.

As morning dawned in America, Charlie, Roy Sibit, and Ohio State representative Tom Watkins—unaware of the problems Jin Mie and the children had endured—were also jetting to San Francisco. Charlie wore his peasant suit. With them were Dick Russ and his crew from a Cleveland television station. Back at the Sibit home in Tallmadge, preparations were under way for another celebration, with Ed and Mary Grady coming from Connecticut, Don and Arrie Sexton from North Carolina, and Ray and Millie Brewington from Detroit.

As the flight from Beijing pulled up to the gate, Charlie nervously awaited his first glimpse of his family in twenty-nine months. For the moment, all his troubles had vanished. He felt only joy. How had his children changed? Yin Tao had been only eleven and Yin Chao nine when he had left. What would they think of their new country? He noticed that Sibit seemed excited too: the moment he had worked so hard for was here.

Shortly before the plane arrived, four immigration officials, a director and three assistants, had showed up to welcome Charlie's family to the United States on behalf of INS. So Jin Mie and the children wouldn't have to wait in customs, the director sent one of his assistants to expedite the reunion. Charlie watched through a window as Jin Mie, Yin Whee, Yin Tao, and Yin Chao were escorted into a small room where they were officially welcomed to the country and told that he was waiting beyond the door. Smiling broadly, their long ordeal over, they left the room.

When Yin Chao saw her father, she broke into a run. Charlie caught her up, and they cried together. Charlie later said that at the moment he held his wife and children close to him, he felt his heart suddenly freed, as if he'd been locked in darkness for years and suddenly a window had been opened.

Yin Whee held the *erhoo* above his head, protecting the delicate instrument from the crush of the crowd. "Once the Marines were my family; now all America is," Charlie told reporters after immigration officials gave each family member an American flag. "I'm so thrilled I don't know what to say except thank you America."

At the Cleveland airport, the Tsuis were met by a huge cheering crowd. Ten-year-old Rebecca Bowers of Tallmadge ran to Yin Chao and presented her with a Cabbage Patch doll. It was the second one she'd received since arriving, and these were the first dolls she had ever owned. Jean Sibit ran to Jin Mie and Charlie and gave them both hugs.

181

Don Sexton stood in the background. Charlie had asked him not to come because he didn't want him to see how things in Tallmadge had deteriorated. But Sexton and Arrie had felt that they had to personally welcome the family. At least on this night at the airport, and later at the Sibits' open house, everything seemed to be as it should: good friends hugging and cheering that their labors had borne fruit.

On the late-night news, Russ asked Charlie if he had any regrets about leaving China. "I have no regret whatsoever," Charlie answered. "For my wife and children it is like coming to a magical world; it is almost like heaven. On the plane ride, my family and I talked about all the hardships we have gone through, and I told them that the U.S. is the best place for us."

At last they could start a new life.

The United States, even with its strange language and customs, may have been the best country for Charlie and his family, but it took no time for Jin Mie and the children to realize that the Sibits' house was not the best place for them to live. On their first day in America, the Marines and their relatives took the family to a shopping mall. As cameras and reporters followed, merchants gave them balloons and ice-cream cones, and the children stared in wonder at popcorn popping. When they loaded into cars to go back to the Sibits, Sexton asked Charlie to ride along with him and Ed Grady, but Roy said that Charlie should go with him. Sexton was surprised; he'd thought that once the Tsuis were all in the States, Roy would be more relaxed about Charlie's comings and goings.[1]

The children were given new names in their new country: Yin Whee became Jeff; Yin Tao, David; and Yin Chao, Susan. Charlie legally changed his own name, to Charlie Tsui. But their new American life was not as they had expected. Jin Mie and the two older children noticed that Charlie bowed his head and grew quiet whenever he was with Sibit, yet became cheerful and talkative when they visited Jean Sibit's sisters and mother.

And there were culture clashes. Jin Mie and the children didn't speak English and had trouble adjusting to American food; Jean Sibit served only American dishes and complained about the odors from the foods that Jin Mie cooked downstairs, where the family lived in a den crowded with cots. This was not the beautiful private house that Charlie had promised. They were cramped into a single room and Charlie was frequently gone, away making speeches or waiting tables and washing dishes at Philip Wong's House of Wong Chinese restaurant in Akron.

Yet Charlie assured them they would have their own home soon, reminding them that this was better than the hardships they had faced in China. But Jin Mie wasn't so sure.

Neither was Don Sexton. For months he'd known that Charlie was unhappy at the Sibits' and wanted his own home. He and Arrie had received a letter from Charlie in August 1985, shortly before his family's arrival, saying how lonely he was and hinting at his plans:

> There are much more strange things happening I didn't tell you because I don't want to hurt your feeling. You are so dear to me you are the first one who know a little about the truth. Everybody else only know what Roy and Jean want them to know. I love Roy as a fellow Marine. I appreciate what he has done for me. But . . . when the time come I'm going to settle in Greensboro with my family so I can always be close to you.

The two youngest children were enrolled in school, Susan in fifth grade and David in seventh. Jeff, by now twenty-two years old and with little education, went to work at a Chinese restaurant in Tallmadge. As Charlie and Jeff earned money, relations between the two families worsened.

The Sibits helped the Tsuis house-hunt, but Roy was never satisfied with anything they saw. Each day Jin Mie and the children, homesick for their own culture and relatives, grew more disenchanted. They began to tell Charlie that they were worse off here than in China and wanted to go back. But he insisted that things would improve when they got their own house.

Shortly after the Tsuis' reunion, Don Sexton began to get panicked phone calls from Charlie during his customary 5:00 A.M. jog. He would leave the Sibits' house, run to a convenience store two miles away, and call Greensboro collect.

Concerned about the worsening relations, in October Sexton confided in Francis Wade, a former China Marine who lived a few miles from the Sibits, in Macedonia. He told Wade that he and Charles Mon-nett, another China Marine and a survivor of the battle for Okinawa, were secretly arranging to bring the family to Greensboro, because Charlie had said that Jin Mie and the children did not feel comfortable in Ohio. But now Charlie was starting to talk about taking his family back to China. Sexton told Wade that they had to get them away from the Sibits' house. Wade and his wife, Phyllis, offered their help.

On 31 October, Charlie called Sexton, so upset that Sexton barely understood him. He said that he and Sibit were not getting along at all. Things were very bad between them, and there had been a physical fight. He told Sexton he would call the next morning and asked him to tape what he was going to tell him. But it rained so hard that morning that Charlie could not go on his daily jog and had to wait until the fol-lowing day. Then, on tape, Charlie told his story:

"All these two and a half years, Roy always said, 'You call Bullard, you call any of the Marines and ask them for a job and house.' So I took the challenge the other night and I called Bullard. I know Bullard was surprised. But I said, 'Bullard, I need a house and a job.' And he said he would check into it. . . . Roy got very mad.[2]

"All these years, I can't even write to anyone I want," Charlie told Sexton, "all the letters had to go through him before they were mailed out. If anybody called me, Roy would listen; and all the letters that come to me are censored."

Charlie said that Sibit had grabbed him during the argument and pushed him up against a door. He broke loose and ran out of the house, but Shawn Sibit followed asking "that there be no hard feelings." They went back into the house together.[3]

Roy Sibit tells a different story. He says when he returned from work on the afternoon in question, Jean ran up to him at the door. "Roy, they're leaving; they're going back to China!"

Sibit says he found Charlie and the family in their basement bed-room. He told Charlie that many people had gone to great trouble to make his dream come true, and if they went back to China, it would be a slap in the face to them all, even the President of the United States. Charlie sat and listened, but suddenly he lunged from his chair and grabbed Sibit by the throat. Both men fell back into a door with such force that the knob knocked a hole in the wall, and then Charlie ran out of the house. Sibit told his son Shawn to bring him back. When they returned, Charlie apologized, and Roy said all was forgotten.[4]

Whatever happened that day, it was clear to Sexton and to other Marines that events in Tallmadge were reeling out of control. Action was needed.

A week later Charlie called Sexton again, frantically asking how long it would take for the family to move to Greensboro. Sexton told him that arrangements were being made, but it would take time to find a house and raise the money for a deposit and first month's rent.

"Don, we don't need anything fancy," Charlie said. "Please, hurry, as fast as you can."

Three days later—ironically, on the Marine Corps birthday, 10 November—matters came to a head. As after the first confrontation, two different versions emerged from the ashes of a friendship that had begun thirty-eight years earlier in China and ended that day in Ohio.

Charlie's side: The day began early, with Charlie on his morning jog to the phone booth to dial Greensboro. He was due to work that morning at the House of Wong but hadn't told Sibit, because that afternoon he was supposed to go to an event at a Chinese-American church in nearby Kent, where the Tsuis and the Sibits were to be the guests of honor.

Charlie feared that the event was just another ploy by Roy to get someone to persuade him to remain at the Sibits. On the phone to Sexton he'd told Roy he wanted to move his family to another house, and that Jean Sibit's sisters, Betty Sokol and Rosie Williams, were helping house-hunt. Sibit was adamant against their leaving. Before hanging up, Charlie again urged Sexton to accelerate efforts to move his family south.

When he returned from his jog, he called Rosie and asked her for a ride to work. He had to be there at eight in the morning, and everyone was asleep. She, her sisters Betty and Charlie Richards, and their mother, Pauline, had become Charlie's confidantes. Even before his family came, Charlie had told them he'd thought of returning to China, but Rosie had assured him that she and her sisters wouldn't allow any harm to come to him.

One night, Rosie and her sister Charlie saw the problem firsthand. They sat in the parking lot at House of Wong and watched their brother-in-law pull Charlie out of the restaurant by the collar to take him to another speaking engagement.[5]

Rosie got Charlie to work on time, but mid-morning, Sibit called to tell him he would pick him up at noon to leave for the speaking engagement at the Chinese church in Kent. Charlie recalls that Sibit was visibly angry as they drove to Tallmadge to get their families. He says he jotted a note in Chinese to give to the congregation leaders: "Please ask my friend to let me go." Instead, he says, the note was translated and given to Sibit.

When they returned to Tallmadge, Sibit called Charlie into the kitchen. Jin Mie followed. Shawn and Darrin Sibit were in the kitchen with their father; Jeff and Susan were in the basement bedroom. David came into the kitchen and saw his father at the counter, with Roy lecturing him about keeping obligations: "Charlie, when you commit yourself to something and make a promise, you gotta keep it. We told these people we'd be there; we gave them our word. You have to keep your word." He asked Charlie where he had gone so early that morning.

"Mr. Wong wanted me to work the lunch," Charlie said.

Charlie says that Sibit called him a liar, and tempers flared. As the two argued, Darrin Sibit wrapped his arm around Charlie's neck in a headlock. Both Roy and Jean began to punch Charlie's head, and Jin Mie frantically tried to pull Roy off her husband.

Roy pushed Jin Mie into a wall with such force that it cracked the sheetrock and she fell to the kitchen floor, unconscious. Seeing his wife motionless, Charlie bit into Darrin's arm to release his hold, then ran to a neighbor to call Rosie.

"Come quick! Roy kill Jin Mie," Charlie shouted. A neighbor, hearing the commotion, called 911. By the time Charlie and others gathered in front of the Sibits' house, paramedics were inside working on Jin Mie.[6]

Rosie had arrived and was inside also. "Jean, what happened; what's going on?" she asked her sister. "Where's Charlie and Jin Mie?"

"Get out of my house! Nothing's wrong! Everything's okay!" Jean Sibit shouted.

As paramedics took Jin Mie to Akron City Hospital, Rosie followed with Charlie and the family. Shortly, Betty and Dick Sokol, along with Charlie and Dale Richards, arrived at the emergency room. Betty noticed the bruise on Charlie's neck and wanted to take photos of it, but Charlie said he didn't want to make matters worse. She and others also saw red marks on Jin Mie's face.

Roy's side: Roy had arranged with Phil Wong for Charlie to have the day off, so Jean was surprised when she looked out the bedroom window at dawn and saw Charlie get into Rosie's car.

"Where's he going?" Jean asked.

"Maybe Rosie is taking him to look at a house," Roy replied groggily from the bed.

Jean and he then drove around Tallmadge looking for Charlie. They stopped at houses they knew were for rent, but found no sign of him and Rosie. Roy was concerned. They'd been invited twice by the Chinese congregation in Kent but had had to cancel both times so Charlie could work. Roy felt that Charlie was trying to get out of going to the event again, and that this time, he was determined they would go.

Back home, he called Phil Wong at the restaurant, but Charlie was not there either. At noon Charlie reported for work, and Mr. Wong told him to call Sibit, who came immediately. Soon the Tsuis and the Sibits were on their way to Kent. Roy was angry but only said, "Charlie, this is three times now; they've gone to a lot of trouble. We need to go."

They returned about four o'clock. Roy called Charlie into the kitchen and lectured him about responsibility. As he spoke, he noticed that Jin Mie had come from downstairs. She went to Charlie, said something in Chinese, and smiled. Suddenly Charlie jumped from his stool and grabbed Roy by the throat with both hands. As Roy tried to free himself, he saw Jin Mie lie on the floor, her eyes fluttering.

At that moment, Shawn ran into the kitchen and tried to pull Charlie off his father. When Jean came from upstairs, Charlie hit her in the chest. Darrin tried to restrain him in a headlock, and the two fell back against the wall, breaking the sheetrock. Charlie ran out of the house to a neighbor's.

Jean rushed to Jin Mie, then called 911. Paramedics arrived within minutes, but Jin Mie didn't respond.[7]

Roy and Jean were stunned. They had no clue what had caused the incident. They said they hadn't known that Charlie resented his treatment and were dumbfounded when it came out in newspaper articles that he felt like a prisoner in their home.

"We treated Charlie like a king," Sibit said, denying he'd ever touched Charlie or Jin Mie. "I've never hit a woman in my life."[8] The day after the incident, Charlie called Sexton with his version of the story, and a day later, Sibit called with his.

The incident report filed by the Tallmadge Police Department did not clarify what or who had caused the fight, only that paramedics had been called to the Sibit home. They reported that Jin Mie had a "medical problem" and "what appeared to be a seizure" during a "domestic situation" between the two families. The report said that police had had to use physical force to separate the two families, and that the house had been damaged in the fracas.

Whatever happened that night, it divided the two families permanently. The Tsuis left the Sibits' house never to return, though to this day, Charlie remains grateful for all they did for him and his family.

After Jin Mie was released from the hospital that night, Betty and Dick Sokol took the Tsuis to their house. Dale Richards, another of Jean Sibit's brothers-in-law, called Sibit to tell him that Charlie and the family were at the Sokols and needed some of their belongings.

Francis Wade drove over to pick up the things. He found clothing piled on the sidewalk, but not Charlie's photos from China, nor his personal papers, including copies of all the contracts that Sibit had had him sign. Also missing was the flag that Bob McEwen had given him, the one that had flown over the Capitol on the day Ed Meese had said he could stay in America.

The Tsuis stayed with the Sokols for two weeks, until Mike Brannon, a construction-company owner and member of Betty and Dick's church, offered Charlie and his family a house in Ellet, if they made the mortgage payments. He also gave Charlie a job with his company. The congregation furnished the house with everything the Tsuis needed, and for the first time in months, a smile returned to Charlie's face. Jin Mie felt secure—for a while.

Five weeks after the fight, Charlie wrote to Sexton about why he had fled from Roy, ending with: "I got my own house and a job I like. Now my wife and children are as happy as can be, and don't want to go back to China anymore."

Don Sexton wondered if the family wanted to leave Ohio after all, but it soon became clear that Jin Mie was still afraid. Whenever she was alone in the house, she would lock herself in with the curtains drawn, and when they visited one of Jean's sisters, she would hide behind a couch if someone came to the door. In July 1986, Charlie repeated to Sexton his desire to move to North Carolina:

> I fully aware you are working hard in preparation for a better life for me and family. I certainly appreciate everybody's concern for us to be happier. Once again I want to confirm you I definitely will move to Greensboro as soon as possible.

In closing, he wrote that Jin Mie and Jeff were taking cooking classes: they wanted to open their own restaurant someday.

Sexton and Monnett were, indeed, working hard to get the Tsuis to Greensboro. They ran an advertisement in the Greensboro paper, with Charlie's photo and the headline: "Help Charlie Two Shoes Family to Come to Greensboro." The ad, paid for by the Charlie Tsui Fund, asked for a house to rent, money, and furniture. They collected $2,600.

Though they tried to keep their plans secret, rumors spread through Tallmadge that Charlie and the family were moving to North Carolina. Betty Sokol confronted Sexton by phone, concerned that people in her church would think Charlie ungrateful after all the help his family had received. Sexton apologized for the secrecy but said that Charlie wanted to get his family out quietly. Betty said she understood and pledged her help.

Others were not so understanding. In late May, Akron *Beacon Journal* columnist Stuart Warner skewered Charlie for his plans to move to North Carolina in a front-page column: "Tsui Chi Hsii's stay in the Akron area is almost over. The man we affectionately came to know as Charlie Two Shoes is leaving us, perhaps within the next week. No,

Charlie hasn't been deported to his native China. He apparently just found a better deal. With better weather. But he wasn't even going to say good-bye."[9]

Warner wrote how touched people in Akron had been when Charlie reunited with his Marine buddies. They had welcomed him, listened to his story about life behind the Bamboo Curtain, cheered him on as he battled bureaucracy to stay in America, hissed at Congressman Seiberling when they thought he wasn't supporting him, and rejoiced when Meese said he could stay.

"Never mind that thousands of foreign citizens were in the immigration line ahead of you—some as long as six years," Warner wrote. Finally, he went on, the townspeople had fought back tears when his family had joined him. Warner closed his scathing article by quoting Charlie:

"Someday, my second generation, they will repay all that I owe. I promise that. So many people have helped me here. It was a difficult situation to leave. I am very grateful. I just ask your sympathy."

Warner had an answer for him: "Sorry, Charlie."

A week later, Charlie and his family and friends loaded a rental trailer hitched to Francis Wade's van for the twelve-hour drive to Greensboro. David decided to stay with the Sokols until the school year ended, two weeks later. But Susan left with her parents; she'd already spent too much of her life without her father.

As they climbed into Betty and Dick Sokol's car, Wade following in his van, the Tsuis waved good-bye to Tallmadge, Ohio, and to the people who had become family—ironically, mostly Jean Sibit's family.

14

Saying good-bye was not easy for Charlie. His entire life had been a series of unhappy good-byes, little deaths, stabs at his heart, beginning with each Marine who had left Tsingtao when he was a boy. He'd been left weeping on the airstrip when William Bullard had flown off, and he'd stood at the window watching Sister Blanda leave in a taxi one rainy morning in 1949. There had been the good-byes to his wife and children, and the one he could not bring himself to make—to his father, whom he'd passed on the road the morning he'd left for America. He would die a year later. Now Charlie had to leave Ohio, and this time he wasn't even on speaking terms with his former best buddy, Roy Sibit.

Greensboro, a city of 180,000 built on textiles, where a famous Revolutionary War battle had been fought, seemed a world away from Ohio. In many ways, for the Tsui family at least, it was. Gone was the fear that Jin Mie felt whenever she was left alone, or whenever a knock came at the door.

Newspaper reporters and crews from three television stations were waiting in Don and Arrie Sexton's driveway on Boulevard Street, along with William Bullard, who'd driven over from Autryville. The only reason Charlie gave reporters for leaving Ohio was that Jin Mie couldn't get used to the harsh winters. "And if she doesn't like the humidity in Greensboro," Stuart Warner wrote in his column, "another of Charlie's Marine buddies lives in New Mexico."

They moved into a tidy three-bedroom home on Greenpoint Drive. Charlie and Jeff went to work at Monnett Carpet Company, in the warehouse, preparing orders for subcontractors. Jin Mie squirreled away the money they earned for a house they would buy someday.

As in Ohio, many people, mostly strangers, showed hospitality, bringing donations to the house—towels, clothing, curtains, pots, and pans. A friend of Sexton's donated a '74 Buick, and Sexton tuned it in his shop. It didn't run like the souped-up cars that Sexton was used to working on, but it was good enough to take Charlie and Jeff back and forth to work, Charlie sitting on extra cushions to see over the steering wheel.

To repay the kindness shown her family, Jin Mie insisted that the Sextons eat at least one meal a day at her house. Nothing pleased Charlie more than being able to return generosity to his Marine buddies, now free to visit. The family, able to go wherever they wanted, drove to Autryville to visit Bullard and see the house that he and his neighbors had fixed up, the house that had caused the well-publicized rift with Roy Sibit. (The house remained empty for two years, then Bullard rented it out, realizing that Charlie and his family would never live there.)

Bullard took them to Spivey's Corner, and the annual hog-calling Hollerin' Contest to give them a taste of country life. Charlie was on the program to speak, but Sibit found out about it and wired him at Bullard's house: "I have been advised by council that your media appearances may violate our contractual arrangements. Please advise organizers of media events to contact me before any appearances by you so that no breach of contract occurs."[1]

Charlie had already appeared at events in Greensboro—mostly at churches and civic groups—without consequences, so, after watching clogging and listening to the hog callers, he spoke anyway. "We feel we belong here. We love North Carolina, and love its people."

The rift between Charlie and Sibit not only ruined friendships and split Jean Sibit's family in two, it drove a wedge into the 6th Marine Division Association. After Charlie returned from Autryville, Charles Monnett wrote the association requesting money to finance a trip for Charlie and his family to Albany, New York, for the upcoming reunion in September 1986. The association declined; officials were getting clear messages that the breakup was causing problems between members. In the end, neither Charlie nor Sexton nor Monnett attended the reunion.

Jeff didn't mind working hard, long hours, but he wanted to do it in a Chinese restaurant—not in the carpet business. "I want to cook," he told his father. Charlie felt badly for his oldest child, who had suffered so much during his years of persecution. Something had to be done for Jeff. Charlie told Sexton and Monnett of his son's unhappiness, and both called all the Chinese restaurants in Greensboro but none had an opening.

Finally, a friend of Sexton's who owned a steak house hired Jeff to prep for the cooks. Jeff bought a scooter, and each morning he puttered off to work. The family worried about him all day, until he puttered home smelling of grease. Money was tight in Greensboro; it was a struggle to pay rent and buy food and clothes. Even the barest essentials were dear on what Charlie and Jeff brought home. Jin Mie took a job too, looking after the baby of a Chinese lawyer, Manlin Maureen Chee, who offered any legal help the family might need.

Arrie Sexton told Charlie that his children could eat breakfast and lunch in a school program subsidized by the government, but Charlie wouldn't do it: America had already given him so much. Instead, to make extra money, he persuaded a crew of carpet installers to take him along on weekends. David, though young and small, begged his father to take him too, so that he could help the family. They would go in Charlie's Buick, often coming home at midnight.

One night Jin Mie noticed that David's hands were cut and callused from working with the rough carpet. They hurt him so much that she could not hold them.

"Please don't tell father," David said. "If he knows my hands are blistered, he won't take me out again; I want to help him make money."

Jeff wasn't happy in his new job. David and Susan struggled with English in school. Charlie and Jin Mie worried constantly about how they would make ends meet. Charlie hid their troubles from Sexton and the other Marines—he didn't want to disappoint Don or have him worry. Jeff suggested that the family look for opportunities elsewhere. Charlie did not want to leave Greensboro—five months earlier, he'd been pilloried by the media in Ohio. How would it look leaving Greensboro so soon, after so many had helped them? "I don't want to leave Don," Charlie told Jeff. "I don't know that many people. There would be no one to protect us."

But he knew Jeff was right. Things weren't working as he'd hoped.

In October 1986, another angel dropped into Charlie's life: Francis Chan of Chapel Hill, who owned an electronics repair shop and a popular Chinese restaurant in neighboring Carrboro—the Jade Palace. Chan, a native of Hong Kong, and his Taiwanese wife, Jenny, had lived in Chapel Hill since 1975. They had read about the Tsuis in newspaper stories and seen interviews on television. As president of the local Chinese Association, Francis called to offer help. Charlie thanked him but said that he and his family were getting along well in Greensboro.

Two weeks later the Chans drove to Greensboro, to see them. "How is life treating you?" Chan asked Charlie as they sat around the table getting acquainted.

"Very well; we are happy," Charlie said, hesitant to discuss family problems. "The children are happy in school. We are making a good living."

"Well, if you need any help in any way, call," Chan said. "We will do all we can."

Charlie liked the Chans, and their visit made Jin Mie happy. It had been a long time since she had been able to socialize in Chinese. A week later the Chans and an associate knocked unexpectedly on Charlie's door, this time with an offer. The manager of their restaurant was leaving in two weeks. Did Charlie want the job? Charlie didn't understand why they were coming to him. Mr. Chan must know dozens of Chinese who could do the job.

He called Don Sexton and asked him and Arrie to come over. Chan explained his offer to Don, adding that he knew education was a priority for Charlie's children, and that Chapel Hill schools offered the best opportunity for students with language barriers. He promised to help Charlie move, set up the family in a house, and give Jeff a job in the kitchen.

Charlie didn't know what to do. He didn't want to leave Sexton and Greensboro. "What do you think?" Charlie asked Don and Arrie after the Chans left.

Sexton didn't know what to say, but Arrie spoke up. "Charlie, this is up to you; we want you to be happy, but we don't want anyone exploiting you anymore." The offer sounded so good, she explained, they couldn't help but feel suspicious.

That night, Don tossed and turned without sleep. He didn't know anything about Mr. Chan. What if things didn't work out for the family? They'd be stranded in a town where they knew no one. And how was he going to explain this to the other Marines who had sided with Charlie over Sibit?

Still, Sexton thought the offer could be a good opportunity—if Chan wasn't a con man. The next day Sexton suggested to Charlie that he wait before accepting the offer. But Charlie said the family had already taken a vote, and the consensus was to move.

Jeff left in December to start work at the Jade Palace, two weeks before Charlie began training as a manager. They kept their home in Greensboro, just in case. Jeff lived with other workers, and Charlie in a room in the Chans' house. Jenny Chan taught Charlie the basics of the business: bookkeeping, taking orders over the phone, tallying the night's revenue, and ordering supplies. Charlie did not catch on easily, but his English was exceptional, and he had a knack for charming customers.

Just before Christmas, Chan furnished a truck and moved the family the forty miles to Chapel Hill. Business at the Jade Palace picked up as Charlie's story became well known in town. Jin Mie laundered the restaurant's tablecloths and linens. David and Susan enrolled in Chapel Hill schools, and their English improved rapidly. On weekends, David waited tables. In the kitchen, Jeff became the number-one chef.

Don and Arrie were pleased at how quickly the Tsuis adapted to life in Chapel Hill. They were always welcome at the Palace, and Chan was keeping his word. He and Sexton spoke several times about getting the family a house. Chan said he was looking at an investment house near downtown Chapel Hill and would loan Charlie the down payment.

Within months after moving into their new home, Charlie paid Chan back. Several months later, Chan approached Charlie about a new venture, a statewide chain of fast-food Chinese restaurants. He wanted to use Charlie's famous name, calling the franchises Charlie Two Shoes. Chan would be the president and Charlie the vice president, just for the use of his name. He would not be required to do anything, and the money would pour in.

Charlie warily signed a contract, then Chan took him to a couple of McDonalds restaurants that were for sale in Cary, near Raleigh. "We're going to buy these and remodel them into Charlie Two Shoes Chinese restaurants," Chan envisioned.[2]

That night, Charlie told his family what he'd done. "Why did you do that?" David asked, visibly upset with his father. "We can't let anybody use your name for a business."

"Francis Chan said all I have to do is let him use my name, and there will be good money," Charlie explained.

"I don't think the business will work," David said. "And if it fails, it'll bring disgrace to your name." He called for a family vote. Charlie lost.

The next day, he told Chan's lawyer that his family had voted not to be part of the venture. Chan would have to come up with another name for his chain. When he told Chan, he was upset but said he understood. "If there is a family disagreement, there is no way we can proceed. I want you to be successful and your family happy, but if the family is unhappy, we can't do this."

Eighteen months after starting to work for Mr. Chan, Charlie and Jin Mie were buying groceries in Timberlyne shopping center, not far from their home, when they saw a For Sale sign at Thomas Tables. Always on the lookout for a place to start their own restaurant someday, they peeked through the window, saw tables everywhere, and thought it a table store.

It wasn't. It was a French restaurant that had gone out of business, and days later, when Jeff and David peeked in, they wondered if this could be the place they'd dreamed of—a place for their own Chinese restaurant. That night, they approached their father.

"We don't have the money or experience yet," Charlie said.

"Let's try," his sons pleaded.

So Charlie called, a deal was struck, and the next day, he gave the Chans two weeks' notice. In September 1988, the Tsuis opened their own restaurant with savings that Jin Mie had set aside. Jin Mie was the hostess and Charlie ran the business, using all he'd learned from Francis and Jenny Chan, now charming his own customers. David and Susan waited tables nights and weekends, and Jeff ran the kitchen. Charlie and Jin Mie called it Tsingtao Chinese Restaurant. It had sixty-five seats, white linen tablecloths, and a $1,700-a-month lease. They placed framed posters of Tsingtao on the wall—St. Michael's Cathedral and Pagoda Pier—and behind the bar, they hung old black-and-white prints of Charlie as a boy with his Marine buddies, along with a huge crest of the Marine Corps insignia. On the menu was a note: 10 percent discount to U.S. Marines, priests, nuns, and senior citizens.

Charlie was so proud of his new business, he wanted to show it off to his Marine buddies. He asked Sexton to help organize a reunion of Love Company. While preparing for the grand celebration, Charlie spoke with a customer one day about his family's ultimate dream: to be full-fledged American citizens.

Although Attorney General Meese had granted him and his family the right to stay in America, according to the intricate INS rules, they could work but not get green cards. Without green cards they could never apply for U.S. citizenship. They were in a state of limbo, their status indefinite.

The customer knew a good immigration lawyer in Raleigh and took Charlie to meet with him. Jack Pinnix told Charlie that he already knew his story. "How?" Charlie asked.

"Several years ago, two of your friends, William Bullard and Roy Sibit, came to see me. They were still trying to bring you over here, and wondered if I could help. I didn't think I could then, but I think I can help you now with your citizenship."

Charlie believes in angels; he attributes the good fortune that has befallen him to their intercession at key moments. Marines and a warden had been unlikely spirits indeed, but lawyers and politicians?

After Jack Pinnix talked to Charlie, he contacted Nick Galifianakis in Durham, because he saw that the only relief Charlie could get was from a private bill in Congress. But, as Charlie already knew, these were hard to come by. Galifianakis, the son of a Greek immigrant, was a former United States congressman who gave up a safe seat in 1972 to run for the U.S. Senate. He won the Democratic primary to face TV broadcaster Jesse Helms in the November election. Though leading the Democratic ticket, outpolling presidential candidate George McGovern, Galifianakis lost and returned to private law practice.

Galifianakis was moved by Charlie's story and plight. As the son of an immigrant who had come to America in 1912 and had been the first restaurant owner in Durham to serve blacks, decades before integration, Galifianakis empathized with Charlie's desire for citizenship. Being a former Marine and now a colonel in the reserves cinched his help.

Years before, private bills had been routinely introduced and passed; Galifianakis himself had done it in Congress, helping visiting faculty at Duke and the University of North Carolina. But since then there had been many abuses and much criticism, and now those bills were almost never allowed. A single objection by any member in the House or Senate sank them. Still, he signed on to help, with no idea what his commitment would cost in time and effort.

Versed in Congress's labyrinthine ways, Galifianakis figured that the best approach would be through the U.S. Senate. The White House was receptive to a bill—after all, Reagan and Ed Meese had already committed themselves to Charlie, and President George Bush would surely sign if Congress passed one. Yet Galifianakis also saw the Senate as the major stumbling block. If they approved the measure, he felt that the House would go along. Contacting old friend Senator Terry Sanford, former governor of North Carolina and president emeritus of Duke University, Galifianakis convinced him to introduce a bill granting citizenship.

Galifianakis's strategy was simple: Charlie had suffered because of his commitment to the U.S. Marines and the United States, and now former Marines, including the commandant, were going to bat for him. "Who is Congress to deny U.S. Marines who fought valiantly for their country when they want to help one of their own?"

It was a compelling argument, and Senator Sanford introduced Senate Bill 1338 on 20 June 1991.

In his elegantly deliberate North Carolina accent, Sanford spoke to the Senate: "Mr. President, I rise to introduce a bill to grant permanent residency to a very special person, Charlie Two Shoes, and his family. This is indeed an auspicious occasion because this bill would give permanent residency to a person who has a long-standing tie to the United States and the Marine Corps."

Many familiar with the story felt that the bill would pass. Earlier, Gen. Al Gray, Commandant of the Marine Corps, had written a congratulatory letter to Charlie:

> Indeed, your struggle to become what most of us take for granted—an American citizen—serves as an inspiration for all who cherish the ideals of freedom and democracy. When you formally swear your allegiance to this country, I know the prevailing sense in America will be that your affirmation began 45 years ago in Tsingtao, China. The unique friendship which developed between you and the United States Marines nearly a half century ago has evolved into an extraordinary symbol of courage, devotion and perseverance. For those seeking to define loyalty, they need only to look to Tsui Chi Hsii, "Charlie Two Shoes."

The day after Sanford introduced his bill, thirty aging members of Love Company and their wives and children gathered at Tsingtao Restaurant in Chapel Hill to toast the success of the boy they'd adopted after the great war that many of them had fought to end. Don Sexton had worked for months finding the Marines whom Charlie had known in China. Big Hutch came with Eula Mae; so did George McDonald, Ed Grady, William and Lorraine Bullard, Charles Robertson, and, of course, Don and Arrie Sexton. Only Francis Wade didn't make it; his wife, Phyllis, had died eight days earlier.

The Sextons arrived first, Arrie helping to decorate Charlie's restaurant with red, white, and blue streamers and favors. Galifianakis and Pinnix updated the gathering on the private bill, and at dinner that night, a cake was wheeled out. On top: the announcement about Sanford's bill. "I am so moved to see my buddies here today," Charlie told them. "There is still more work to be done, but with the help of Nick Galifianakis and Jack Pinnix and Senator Sanford, the dream I made when I first met you guys will come true."

The only thing left was to make their buddy "Citizen Charlie." They returned home to start another letter-writing campaign, but it would take more than letters.

Sanford's bill passed unanimously and was sent to the House. There, it died. More exactly, it was killed—not brutally, but insidiously, in a subcommittee of the Judiciary Committee. Subcommittee chairman Romano Mazzoli still did not like private bills, though he began to soften under the persistent prodding of Galifianakis, an old friend who made numerous trips to Washington to plead Charlie's case. Yet the bill still wasn't going anywhere. Congressman Lamar Smith had an objection: He'd heard that Charlie had stolen silk in China and been in prison. He asked the State Department to make inquiries.

Where did that suddenly come from? Galifianakis wondered. Then one day he and Pinnix were in Sanford's office discussing Charlie's case with legislative assistant Jennifer Hillman, when a call came from Roy Sibit. He asked Hillman to warn Sanford that Charlie had been convicted of stealing silk in China and had served a term in prison—not as a political prisoner.[3]

Galifianakis and Pinnix explained what had happened, and deflected the problem. The State Department investigation came back completely clearing Charlie: "As there was widespread interest in Mr. Tsui's case, the application for the visitor visa was scrutinized carefully for any event which would have made him ineligible to receive a visa. No grounds on ineligibility were identified. Although Tsui Chi Hsii spent several years in prison in China, it was determined that the imprisonment was clearly for political reasons and not for any crime which would make the applicant ineligible for a U.S. visa."[4]

It came too late—the 102d Congress adjourned, and Sanford's bill died sine die, meaning that the entire process had to be started over when the 103d Congress reconvened in January. But Sanford was defeated for reelection in November, as Bill Clinton was elected president. Congressman David Price, from Charlie's hometown of Chapel Hill, picked up Sanford's mantle and introduced a bill for Charlie at the beginning of the new Congress.

Letters poured into Washington from the well-oiled Marine letter-writing machine and from thousands of others after Charlie was pro-filed in *Parade* magazine and in *Reader's Digest*. If anyone deserved to become American citizens, they resoundingly said, it was the Tsuis: they had suffered so much because of Charlie's dream. Norman Vincent Peale wrote that Charlie's story was one of the most inspirational he had ever read. With Charlie exonerated by the State Department, Gali-fianakis felt that chances of getting citizenship were good.

But other events intervened—a seismic world event, yet another that touched Charlie. Earlier he had been involved with the Great Leap For-ward, the Cultural Revolution, the Gang of Four, and Nixon's visit to China that had opened relations between the two countries. Now he got caught up in the events and repercussions of Tiananmen Square in Beijing.

In 1989, a democratic wind blew across China. During the last decade, moving away from strict Maoist ideological orthodoxy, the leadership relaxed its tight control, initiating numerous reforms. Deng Xiaoping decentralized political and economic authority. However, this relaxation whetted the appetite for more. Pro-democracy fervor spread throughout the country, especially among intellectuals on uni-versity campuses, causing alarm within the old-guard Chinese leader-ship—especially as they watched Communism collapse in Eastern Europe and the Soviet Union.

The wall had come down in Berlin and the Soviet bloc had split apart. The Cold War had ended with democracy the winner, but Party hard-liners were determined that China would not suffer the fate of other Communist countries. There were no Gorbachevs in Beijing, and the pro-democracy movement was crushed swiftly and brutally at Tianan-men Square in 1989. News photos of a student in front of tanks crossing the square were flashed throughout the world, evoking outrage in many countries—the United States in particular—especially when it appeared that intellectuals and students were being persecuted.

Relations between China and the United States had been steadily improving, but now they suddenly froze; talk of granting "most favored nation" trading status to China ended abruptly, as concern grew for human rights. China became the focus of human-rights abuses, an emblem of a discredited, anachronistic form of government. In Congress, a bill was introduced that gave asylum to Chinese dissidents. It was an umbrella bill that covered all Chinese in America awaiting green cards—including Charlie.

Galifianakis and Pinnix had mixed feelings. If the bill passed, it would make Congressman Price's private bill moot, because such bills could be introduced only if there was no other relief. The Tiananmen Square bill offered relief. However, they knew that Charlie didn't want to slip into America by a "back door" administrative procedure. Charlie did not want to be classified a dissident. He wanted to improve Chinese-American relations, not be lumped in with those who had fled China for political reasons. Galifianakis and Pinnix had to prevail mightily on Charlie not to look this gift horse in the mouth. The bill would give him what he wanted—U.S. citizenship—even if it wasn't wrapped quite the way he liked.

The 6th Marine Division Association invited Charlie to their 1993 convention in Minneapolis, paying all expenses "while furnishing us the opportunity to express our admiration and affection."

Charlie wanted to go, but he was concerned that resentment might linger among some Marines because of his rift with Sibit. He asked Sexton to go with him. "I don't want to go without you, but I'd look ungrateful if I turned them down," Charlie said.

"You should go," said Sexton, who was unable to attend. "They want to make it up to you. Nothing's going to happen to you. They'll protect you."

So Charlie accepted. But as the event drew closer, he worried about Sibit. What if his supporters, or Roy himself showed up? He had cause to worry, for as he flew to Minnesota, Roy and Jean were driving there. Sibit wanted to clear his name.

Sibit waited all day to talk with the executive board, but was told they didn't want to hear him. He considered telling his side of the story to the general assembly, but former Marines said he would be shouted down. Charlie was the honored guest: now was not the time to explain his side. The next morning, Jean Sibit told her husband they should leave.

That day, Galifianakis wired him that Congress had passed the bill granting asylum to Tiananmen Square dissidents. He and his family could get their green cards; the five-year clock to become citizens had begun to tick. That night at the banquet, Charlie addressed the gathering. He spoke of his appreciation for what the 6th Marine Division had done for him and of his love for America and for the people who had helped him achieve his dream. When he finished, the convention host, Jim Chaisson, presented him with a certificate of appreciation, then announced, "I am pleased to tell you that today Congress approved Charlie and his family for green cards."

He turned to Charlie. "Now you are one of us."

Not quite. The dream of citizenship is still unrealized. Soon perhaps, but not yet.

Epilogue

The men who were once young Marines are now old, have children and grandchildren. The little boy they adopted has grown older too, with children and a grandchild of his own. The story that started at a barbed-wire fence on a remote airstrip in northern China after World War II has become a rich tapestry of life in America. Long ago, young men went off to fight a war in a faraway place and returned to a very changed world—one that has changed even more since then.

The little boy at the wire suffered immensely because of his friendship with these men, but now he is a part of their world. Each month, at least one of the Marines visits him at his restaurant. They sit and talk and marvel at all that has happened. They would not have found one another again without Charlie. They would not have regrouped as Love Company, as Marines, and fought a final battle for what they believed, against great odds, with no purpose for gain and no ulterior motive. The last battle is the highlight of their lives. Ending triumphantly, it completes a circle of love, dedication, determination, and loyalty.

The former Marines are mostly retired: Ed Grady, Jack Hutchins, Charles Robertson, William Bullard, George McDonald, Fred McGowan, J. C. Lacey, all live quiet lives. Don Sexton still works on cars in his garage in Greensboro, North Carolina.

Sister Blanda, now ninety-four, is at the same convent in Milwaukee that she first went to in 1918. Though confined to a wheelchair, she is in good health—and cheerful—spunkily complaining that "God is taking me one part at a time." Charlie's other teacher, Miriam Matthews Haddad, and her husband, Ernie, split their time between Florida and the mountains of North Carolina.

Roy Sibit still lives in Tallmadge, Ohio. He remains bitter about what happened. Concerned that no one knows his side of the story, in 1997 he self-published *No Good Deed Goes Unpunished,* about his efforts to bring the Tsuis to America and the fight that ended their friendship.

Charlie is still saddened by what came of his friendship with "Sippie," and he hopes that one day they can put their differences aside. Until then he's happy opening his Chapel Hill restaurant seven days a week, greeting patrons, and taking orders over the phone. Many of the children of his regular customers call him Mr. Charlie, a title he clearly enjoys, and the younger ones come not necessarily to eat the food, but to see him. Jin Mie is hostess, and Jeff runs the kitchen. David is in medical school, and Susan in pharmacy school. In early 1993, Jin Mie, concerned for her eldest son, took Jeff back to China to find a wife. She had made inquires with relatives in Chukechuang and lined up several prospects.

After interviewing them to arrange a marriage, she and Jeff returned that summer to China to formalize arrangements. Determined that Susan not lose her Chinese roots, Jin Mie brought her also, for a summer of immersion in her native culture. Jeff married Ai Ling Wong, from the tiny village of Chong Zi, a mile from Chukechuang, and at the summer's end he returned to America without his bride.

In 1994, Charlie closed his restaurant. David and Susan were in college, and Jeff wanted to go back to China to live with his wife. He stayed a year, returning alone several months after daughter Anna was born—Charlie's granddaughter. On the day Jeff came home, he began prodding his father to open a new restaurant. He had a family to support and needed a job. Charlie, spending his retirement in his garden and at the public library, was enjoying his life of leisure. But he relented, and in 1997, he and Jin Mie opened a new, larger restaurant—Charlie's.

Now the family is working to get Ai Ling and Anna to America. Nick Galifianakis and Jack Pinnix are helping. Meanwhile, Jin Mie searches for a wife for David and a husband for Susan. Charlie hopes they won't have to go to China to find them.

Fifty years ago Charlie Tsui was just learning about America, forming his dream to come here. He persevered against overwhelming odds, suffering travails and hardships that few Americans can imagine. The United States is indeed the land of dreams, but for many, the most difficult dream to realize is getting here. Charlie never gave up.

People throughout the world dream Charlie's dream to come to this country and raise a family. What is now the United States has been pursued for more than three hundred years, no less today than in 1698, and every generation of Americans is enriched by those from afar who join them. These people bring dedication, energy, and new ideas. The country is rejuvenated by these dreamers, who in turn inspire others to dream. They are the life blood of America, a transfusion that constantly refreshes and invigorates. In the process of being absorbed into the larger society, they shed the skins of their previous culture; they become Americanized, with each generation growing more distant from its roots.

It will be difficult for Jin Mie, who grew up in Chukechuang, to watch her children and grandchildren become absorbed in another culture. She arranged her son's marriage and wants to do the same for her other son and daughter. Will her daughter, Susan, do the same for her own child? Will her granddaughter, Anna, even consider doing it for her child?

Who could have foretold Charlie's future on the day the American planes landed at Tsangkou, a hundred yards from his village? Who can foretell the future now? The best one can do is plan for it. And so Charlie plans for the day when he will become a U.S. citizen. It should be soon. When it happens, the Marines of Love Company will be invited, and Miriam Matthews Haddad and Sister Blanda, too.

Charlie will wear his best suit jacket, a tie secured by a Marine Corps clip, and the wool pants that were once Marine green, the ones his mother dyed black. Jin Mie has patched them. And let out the waist.

Notes

CHAPTER 1

1. Sid Moody, "Desire for Glory," Associated Press. Appeared in the *Charlotte Observer*, 12 February 1995, as "On Tiny Iwo Jima, an Epic Collision."
2. Evan Thomas, "Invasion That Wasn't," *Newsweek*, 24 July 1995, 24–30.
3. Henry I. Shaw Jr., *The United States Marines in North China, 1945–1949*, 6.
4. Ibid.,7.
5. David Perlmutt, "Dixie Mission," interview with Herbert Hitch in the *Charlotte Observer*, 5 July 1992.

CHAPTER 2

1. Shaw, *Marines in North China*, 15.
2. Winston Churchill, "The Iron Curtain," *The Annals of America*, 367. See also Shaw, *Marines in North China*.
3. Barbara Tuchman, *Stilwell and the American Experience in China*, 527.
4. Ibid.

CHAPTER 3

1. Shaw, *Marines in North China*, 23.

CHAPTER 4

1. Han Suyin, *The Morning Deluge*, 478.
2. Ibid., 475.
3. Ibid., 457.
4. Ibid., 490.

5. Interview with Miriam Matthews Haddad, Fleetwood, N.C., May 1997.
6. Ibid.

CHAPTER 5

1. Suyin, *Morning Deluge,* 498.

CHAPTER 6

1. John Lukas, *A History of the Cold War,* 87–89.
2. William Manchester, *The Glory and the Dream,* 657–58.
3. "China: The People's Republic," *Random House Encyclopedia,* 1348–49.
4. Manchester, *Glory and the Dream,* 703.
5. Ibid., 663.
6. Ibid., 669.
7. Ibid., 670.
8. John Bryan Starr, *Understanding China,* 241.

CHAPTER 7

1. Howard Chan-Eoan and James Walsh, "The Last Emperor," *Time,* 3 March 1997, 61–68.
2. Ibid.

CHAPTER 9

1. "Ping Pong Diplomacy," Associated Press Biographical Service, sketch 4503, Richard Nixon, issued 1 February 1973.
2. Ibid.
3. Jimmy Carter, *Keeping Faith: Memoirs of a President,* 186.
4. Ibid., 188.
5. "The United States of America," 1978 *Congressional Quarterly,* 161-A.

CHAPTER 10

1. Telephone interview with Duke Bingham, August 1997.
2. Letter from Roy Sibit to Ji Chaozhu, Chinese embassy, Washington, D.C., 25 October 1982. (A copy of this letter is held by the authors.)
3. Interview with Roy Sibit, Tallmadge, Ohio, April 1997.

CHAPTER 11

1. Sibit interview.
2. Larry Cheek, "Charlie Two-Shoes Not Coming to N.C.," *Fayetteville Times,* 19 May 1983.
3. Sibit interview. Also Cheek, "Charlie Two Shoes Not Coming to N.C."
4. Editorial, *Sampson Independent* (Clinton, N.C.), 1983.
5. Interviews with Roy Sibit and Charlie Tsui. Sibit has invoked this contract on a number of occasions. Though many have asked to see it, including the authors and their attorney, Sibit declines to share it. During a five-hour interview with Sibit in Tallmadge, Ohio, the authors asked to see a copy, but Sibit said it was packed in a box in the attic and would take days to find. The authors' attorney wrote to a lawyer in Akron, who said he represented Sibit, and asked for a copy of the contract. Despite three attempts, he never heard back. In at least two interviews with the authors, Sibit has acknowledged the ninety-ten breakdown.

CHAPTER 12

1. Telephone interview with Don Sexton, September 1997.
2. Ibid.
3. William Hershey, "Seiberling Opposes 'Charlie Two Shoes' Bill," Akron *Beacon Journal,* 19 June 1985.
4. Sibit interview.
5. Telephone interview with Charlie Tsui, September 1997.
6. Interview with Samuel J. Levine, September 1997.
7. This contract between William Williams, Roy Sibit, and Charlie Tsui was eventually voided.
8. Hershey, "Seiberling Opposes 'Charlie Two Shoes' Bill."
9. Letter from Roy Sibit, 20 June 1985, addressed to the editor, *Beacon Journal.*
10. Letter from former U.S. representative John Seiberling, 26 June 1985, addressed to the editor, *Beacon Journal.*
11. Interview with former U.S. representative Bob McEwen, Charlotte, N.C., August 1997.
12. Ibid.

CHAPTER 13

1. Sexton interview.

2. Tape of Charlie Tsui speaking with Don Sexton by telephone.

3. Tsui tape. Also Sexton interview.

4. Sibit interview.

5. Interview with Rosie Williams and Charlie Richards, Tallmadge, Ohio, April 1997.

6. Tsui and Williams interviews. Also interview with David Tsui, 1997.

7. Sibit interview. Also interviews with Jean Sibit and Shawn Sibit.

8. Interview with Roy Sibit, Tallmadge, Ohio, April 1997.

9. Stuart Warner, "The Climate Isn't Right for Charlie: Media-Wise Immigrant Will Try Southern Exposure," Akron *Beacon Journal,* 22 May 1986, A1.

CHAPTER 14

1. Telegram from Roy Sibit to Charlie Tsui, c/o William Bullard, 21 June 1986.

2. Tsui interview.

3. Interview with Nick Galifianakis, Durham, N.C., October, 1997. Also William Canterbury, "A Noted Feud Finally Aired," Akron *Beacon Journal,* 24 January 1993.

4. Letter addressed to Romano Mazzoli, chairman of the House subcommittee on Immigration, Refugees, and International Law, from Steven K. Berry, acting assistant secretary for Legislative Affairs, U.S. State Department, 23 September 1992. The information in the report was provided by Arturo Macias, the consul-designate for the U.S. embassy in Beijing at that time. Berry wrote that Macias was "very knowledgeable about the case," because he was the chief consular officer who authorized Charlie's visitor's visa.

Bibliography

Carter, Jimmy. *Keeping Faith: Memoirs of a President.* New York: Bantam, 1982.

Chan-Eoan, Howard, and James Walsh. "The Last Emperor." *Time,* 3 March 1997, 61–68.

"China: The People's Republic." *Random House Encyclopedia.* New York: Random House, 1990.

Churchill, Winston. "The Iron Curtain." *The Annals of America,* vol. 16, *Encyclopaedia Britannica.* Chicago, 1976.

Gray, Jack, and Patrick Cavendish. *Chinese Communism in Crisis.* New York: Praeger, 1970.

Kissinger, Henry A. "The Philosopher and the Pragmatist." *Newsweek,* 3 March 1997, 42–47.

Lawliss, John. *The Marine Book.* New York: Thames and Hudson, 1988.

Lukas, John. *A History of the Cold War.* Garden City, N.J.: Doubleday, 1962.

Manchester, William. *The Glory and the Dream.* Boston: Little, Brown, 1974.

Moody, Sid. "Desire for Glory." Associated Press article on fiftieth anniversary of the battle of Iwo Jima. *Charlotte Observer,* 12 February 1995.

Mossman, Billy C. "Ebb and Flow, November 1950–July 1951." Washington D.C.: Center of Military History, U.S. Army, 1990.

Perlmutt, David. "Dixie Mission." Interview with Herbert Hitch in the *Charlotte Observer,* 5 July 1992.

Shaw, Henry I., Jr. *The United States Marines in North China, 1945–1949.* Washington, D.C.: Historical Branch, G-3, Headquarters, U.S. Marine Corps, 1968.

Snow, Edgar. *Red Star over China.* New York: Grove, 1968.

Starr, John Bryan. *Understanding China.* New York: Hill and Wang, 1997.

Suyin, Han. *The Morning Deluge.* Boston: Little, Brown, 1972.

Terrill, Ross. *800,000,000:The Real China.* Boston: Little, Brown, 1972.

This Fabulous Century. Alexandria, Va.: Time-Life Books, 1988.

Thomas, Evan. "Invasion That Wasn't," *Newsweek,* 24 July 1995, 24–30.

———. "Why We Did It." *Newsweek,* 24 July 1995, 22–30.

Topping, Seymour. *Journey between Two Chinas.* New York: Harper and Row, 1972.

Tuchman, Barbara. *Stilwell and the American Experience in China.* New York: MacMillan, 1971.

INTERVIEWS

Eric Baculinao, Duke Bingham, JoAnn Blair, Sister Blanda, William Bullard, Jenny Chan, Nick Galiafinakis, Sandy Gilmour, Ed Grady, Mary Grady, Miriam Matthews Haddad, Jerry Hanson, Jennifer Hillman, Jack Hutchins, John Randall Hutchins, J. C. Lacy, Samuel J. Levine, George McDonald, former congressman Bob McEwen, Fred McGowan, Charles Monnett, Jack Pinnix, Charlie Richards, Dale Richards, Charles Robertson, Dick Russ, former senator Terry Sanford, Arrie Sexton, Don Sexton, Jean Sibit, Roy Sibit, Shawn Sibit, Don Sico, Michael Sneed, Betty Sokol, Dick Sokol, Charlie Tsui, David Tsui, Jin Mie Tsui, Rosemary Williams.

ABOUT THE AUTHORS

Michael Peterson, a former Marine, was awarded Silver and Bronze Stars for his service in Vietnam. He has written three best-selling novels: *A Time of War, A Bitter Peace,* and *The Immortal Dragon.* He lives in Durham, North Carolina, with his wife and five children.

David Perlmutt has been a prize-winning journalist for twenty-one years, the last seventeen at the *Charlotte Observer.* Many of his articles have appeared in newspapers across the United States and in national magazines such as *Reader's Digest* and *Parade.* He lives in Charlotte with his wife, Christie Taylor, and his daughter, Ainslie.

THE NAVAL INSTITUTE PRESS is the book-publishing arm of the U.S. Naval Institute, a private, nonprofit, membership society for sea service professionals and others who share an interest in naval and maritime affairs. Established in 1873 at the U.S. Naval Academy in Annapolis, Maryland, where its offices remain today, the Naval Institute has members worldwide.

Members of the Naval Institute support the education programs of the society and receive the influential monthly magazine *Proceedings* and discounts on fine nautical prints and on ship and aircraft photos. They also have access to the transcripts of the Institute's Oral History Program and get discounted admission to any of the Institute-sponsored seminars offered around the country.

The Naval Institute also publishes *Naval History* magazine. This colorful bimonthly is filled with entertaining and thought-provoking articles, first-person reminiscences, and dramatic art and photography. Members receive a discount on *Naval History* subscriptions.

The Naval Institute's book-publishing program, begun in 1898 with basic guides to naval practices, has broadened its scope in recent years to include books of more general interest. Now the Naval Institute Press publishes about 100 titles each year, ranging from how-to books on boating and navigation to battle histories, biographies, ship and aircraft guides, and novels. Institute members receive discounts of 20 to 50 percent on the Press's nearly 600 books in print.

Full-time students are eligible for special half-price membership rates. Life memberships are also available.

For a free catalog describing Naval Institute Press books currently available, and for further information about subscribing to *Naval History* magazine or about joining the U.S. Naval Institute, please write to:

Membership Department
U.S. NAVAL INSTITUTE
118 Maryland Avenue
Annapolis, MD 21402-5035
Telephone: (800) 233-8764
Fax: (410) 269-7940
Web address: www.usni.org